ISLANDS
and ROCKS
in the
South China Sea

Post-Hague Ruling

ISLANDS
and ROCKS
in the
South China Sea

Post-Hague Ruling

JAMES BORTON

Rev. date: 04/17/2017

To order additional copies of this book, contact:
Xlibris
1-888-795-4274
www.Xlibris.com
Orders@Xlibris.com
754869

TABLE OF CONTENTS

ACKNOWLEDGEMENTS

This collection of timely and valuable papers would not have been possible if it were not for the generous support and direction from Dr. Trang Si Trung at Nha Trang University, and Dr. Pham Dang Phuoc of Pham Van Dong University in Vietnam. This project becomes another valuable installment in an examination of the international law of the sea, the United Nations Convention on the Law of the Sea (UNCLOS), and the recent arbitration ruling made in The Hague, Netherlands.

Academics, delegates and other scholars gathered at an international workshop held in Nha Trang, Vietnam on the "Legal Status of Islands and Rocks under International Law and Practice in the South China Sea" on August 16-18, 2016. There they reaffirmed the principle of resolving international disputes by peaceful means on the basis of international law, including the 1982 UNCLOS.

This book is also dedicated to the thousands of fishermen who daily cast their lines in the South China Sea. They remain caught up in the ocean's political fray and remain on the dangerous frontlines of one of Asia's ongoing maritime boundary disputes.

Preface

Islands and Rocks in the South China Sea: Post Hague Ruling
James Borton

Ocean governance remains a critical issue in the contested South China Sea, due to continued territorial disputes, fishing exploitation, and ASEAN's power shift alignment towards China.

The Hague's unanimous ruling in 2016 made it clear that under the United Nations Convention on the Law of the Sea, China had no legal basis to claim historic rights over most of the contested waterway. In the favorable sweeping ruling for the Philippines, the decision stated that China had breached several UNCLOS articles, governing safety, the marine environment, and navigation at sea.

UNCLOS was adopted in 1982 and by June 2011, 162 nations had accepted it. The convention succeeded in defining such terms as "territorial sea," "exclusive economic zone" (EEZ), and "continental shelf." It also plainly set the rules on the utilization, exploitation, and conservation of maritime resources. The law of the Sea Convention remains the most important international agreement on ocean policy, since it codifies accepted international law and spells out generally accepted rules of law of the sea, including the right of free passage, demarcation of the territorial sea, and freedom of the high seas.

The five-judge tribunal condemned China's behavior in its aggressive attempts to establish sovereignty by dumping tons of dirt and crushed coral to transform small reefs and rocks into artificial islands complete with airstrips and other military structures. Beijing has already established at least seven such bases, all of them equipped with access channels, helipads, radar facilities, gun and missile emplacements, piers, and other objects of strategic importance.

To all claimant nations and the world as a whole these actions are disturbing. However, the Philippines and other nations appear to be reluctant to challenge China, or even address the significance of The Hague's ruling. The Law of the Sea treaty sets rules for establishing zones of control over oceans based on distances to coastlines. In addition to China and the Philippines, Malaysia, Vietnam, Brunei, Indonesia and Taiwan all make territorial claims in the South China Sea. However, the tribunal's mandate is to address only maritime disputes, not the underlying land claims to the islands, reefs and rocks.

With no authority to enforce its ruling, and China, which has denounced the verdict and boycotted the legal process, the result is a test of international law. Over the past several months, China's continued policy of "might makes right", reflected in the number of coast guard ships patrolling the sea and often accompanied by their fishing trawlers, only serves to heighten rather than diffuse tensions.

Of course, Vietnam and other Southeast Asian nations, who were not party to the arbitration, find their own sovereign EEZ rights bolstered by the ruling. This includes Indonesia and Malaysia, since both have experienced encroachment into portions of their EEZ by Chinese fishing vessels in areas China claims as its traditional fishing grounds.

Philippine President Rodrigo Duterte's failure to pursue their nation's maritime claims against China in the post ruling, coupled with his stunning U-turn in foreign policy befriending Beijing and berating Washington, has led other ASEAN members to join ranks in not criticizing China's continued aggressive actions on maritime matters. Some analysts and SCS watchers speculate that Duterte is waiting patiently to assess how the new President-elect, Donald Trump, might handle the current South China Sea crucible.

It's worrisome for all to wait. With each passing week, China steadily expands its presence until its dominance of the sea is an incontestable fact.

With the exception of Vietnam, the Association of Southeast Asian Nations (ASEAN) has remained on the sidelines and has avoided any references to the tribunal's ruling at recent multilateral summits. However, if there is any potential for a unified response front from ASEAN membership to China it may come about due to the systematic and continued damage to the marine environment associated with reclamation and the continued damage done to coral reefs.

According to Professor John McManus, a marine biologist at the University of Miami, and who provided in depth analysis to the international tribunal, the South China Sea contains "highly productive fisheries and extensive coral reef ecosystems, which are among the most bio diverse in the world."

It has been established that the marine environment in the Scarborough Shoal and Spratlys includes, fish, corals, mangroves, and sea grasses as well as giant clams and sea turtles. Scientists, policy experts and governments may be better served listening to the voices of their own fishermen. There's a growing food security issue looming as a result of current overfishing practices and fishery collapses.

Garrett Hardin, author and ecologist whose views on the "tragedy of the commons," best reflects the dilemma of supporting sustainable development, interweaving economic growth and environmental protection. He writes,"The oceans of the world continue to suffer from the survival of the philosophy of the commons. Maritime nations still respond automatically to the shibboleth of the 'freedom of the seas.' Professing to believe the "inexhaustible resources of the oceans," they bring species after species of fish and whales closer to extinction."

The roiling sea has not enabled any of the claimants to bring together any resolution of sovereignty laws or complex maritime laws. Thus, in navigating through the rocks, atolls and artificial islands, territorial issues will ultimately be settled by political will and not by any arbitration ruling.

Bill Hayton, author of the South China Sea, The Struggle for Power in Asia, writes that the legal question about "ownership" of the South China Sea fails to correspond with any claimed historical context, where sovereignty remains overlapping, graduated, or patchy at best." So the thorny legal issues remain and provide a framework for more academic discussion and conferences like the one sponsored on August 17th-18th, 2016 by Nha Trang University in collaboration with Pham Van Dong University on "Legal status of islands and rocks in international law and practice in the South China Sea."

The conference attendees included leading international scholars who addressed a myriad of issues on the legal status of islands and rocks, the impact of the South China Sea Arbitration award, Vietnam-U.S.

cooperation and the urgent need for environmental cooperation, to name but a few of the subjects presented in this august anthology.

Vietnam's Professor Nguyen Chu Hoi argues in his paper that the environmental security issue is central to understanding how essential marine cooperation is for the future of the region. He writes, " the SCS is also one of the most important large marine ecosystems in the region and the world. About 300 million people in 9 countries (China, Vietnam, the Philippines, Brunei, Indonesia, Singapore, Malaysia, Thailand and Cambodia), and one territory (Taiwan) surrounding the SCS depends on the marine natural resources, especially the fishery resources (which) are daily livelihood sources for the coastal communities and islanders."

According to the U.S.-China Economic and Security Review Commission, although dredging, land reclamation, and the building of artificial islands are not activities unique to China, the scale and speed of China's activities in the South China Sea, the biodiversity of the area, and the significance of the Spratlys to the ecology of the region, make China's actions of particular concern. Even the international tribunal reaffirmed that the contested sea contains "highly productive fisheries and extensive coral reef ecosystems, which are among the most diverse in the world."

As an environmental policy journalist, I do not believe that maritime law alone will save the sea. After all, the tribunal ruling ignored by China, has no legal authority to resolve underlying and potentially explosive conflicts about sovereignty claims over land features; nor can it address the geopolitical issues at stake. Simply put; dangerous days lie ahead as more fisheries clash with Chinese authorities.

However, there's increasing evidence to suggest that science can provide confidence- building steps through diffusion and exchange of information on marine resources. What is known is that continued economic and population growth, often coupled with depletion of natural resources, intensifies conflicts like this one in the South China Sea. It's now time to engage the regional scientific community of maritime experts to initiate and to formulate policy choices in a series of marine workshops.

Policy shapers need to take a page or two from the region's fishermen since they understand the transnational and multilateral nature of South China Sea environmental issues.

An excellent case study is Vietnam's successful marine protected area on Cu Lao Cham, an island located about 20 kilometers from Hoi An's central coast. In this fishing community of 2,300, the islanders are harmoniously connected to the water. These fishers, some in their small wooden trawlers and many in the traditional round woven basket boats or "thuyen thung" cast their nets and lines for abalone, sea bass, grouper, lobster, squid and sea cucumber. Their home of more than 1,500 hectares of natural forest, houses a critical ecosystem that includes healthy coral reefs, seaweed and sea grass beds. During typhoons their protected harbor is a sanctuary for other fishermen, including those from China.

For now, ASEAN is the logical institution in the region to provide a framework and to champion environmental security in Southeast Asia. China's unilateral actions in their dangerous reclamations violate the terms of the ASEAN-China Declaration on the Conduct of Parties in the South China Sea (DOC-SCS). Unfortunately, China's attack on the ecological heart of Southeast Asia has not resulted in any censure or condemnation from ASEAN.

Of course, ocean governance does lend itself to specific cooperative measures found on islands like Cu Lao Cham and in other areas. ASEAN may rise to the occasion to broadly embrace these model ocean governance cooperative measures like establishing information exchange/ data mechanisms, enforcing fishing agreements, protection of endangered species, joint patrolling, and training of manpower on environment/ conservation management.

Marine scientists and the fishermen know that healthy coral reefs provide food, storm protection, and cultural identity to coastal communities and islanders. The challenge for all is to find a regional solution to protect these rain forests of the sea before it is too late.

James Borton is an independent journalist and senior fellow at the US-Asia Institute in Washington, DC. He previously edited *The South China Sea: Challenges and Promises.*

The Award of 12 July 2016 and Its Impact on the Clarification of Article 121 (3) LOSC

Erik Franckx

Abstract

A careful study of the genesis of Article 121, paragraph 3, of the 1982 United Nations Convention on the Law of the Sea indicates that the content of that provision was a compromise formula suggested by the Chairman of the respective Committee of the Third United Nations Conference on the Law of the Sea, when he needed to produce a single negotiating text in 1975. It is an amalgam of bits and pieces of the different main proposals that had been submitted up to that point. As a consequence, it lacks any internal logic. When proposed in 1975, it was certainly not meant to be a final text, but it nevertheless turned out to be one, as States, many of which wanted to further clarify this unclear provision, did not want to jeopardize the reached package deal when their "clarifications" proved unacceptable to certain other States.

International courts and tribunals, even though they had plenty of opportunities to tackle this specific issue, have steadfastly refused to do clarify this enigmatic paragraph 3. They rather preferred to hide behind the screen of maritime delimitation, where the rules applicable are much more flexible, instead of first tackling the preliminary question, namely whether a particular maritime feature constitutes an Article 121 paragraph 2, or rather a paragraph 3 feature.

The Arbitral Award of 12 July 2016, which could not rely on the rules of maritime delimitation to sidestep this issue in view of the declaration under Article 298 made by China in 2006, has now clarified this distinction. This thus constitutes a long awaited illumination of this perplexing provision of the Constitution for the Oceans.

The organization of an international workshop on the "Legal Status of Islands and Rocks in International Law and Practice in the South China Sea" could hardly have been held at a more appropriate timing, namely about a month after the rendering of the award by the arbitral tribunal established under Annex VII of the 1982 Convention on the Law of the Sea[1] between the Philippines and China.[2] The arbitral tribunal indeed devoted almost one fifth of its award to the very topic of today's conference, namely what it described as "The Status of Features as Rocks/Island".[3]

Moreover, it is a particular pleasure for me to have been invited once again to this conference series organized jointly by the Pham Van Dong University and the Nha Trang University and to have been asked to speak on the theme "The Award of 12 July 2016 and Its Impact on the Clarification of Article 121 (3) LOSC". The reason is that when I was asked to participate in the previous such workshop, entitled "Paracel and Spratly Archiplelagos: Historical Truth", on 19-21 June 2014, I presented a paper entitled "Rocks and Islands". I looked up the PowerPoint presentation that I used at that time and in my last slide, entitled "Conclusion", I

---

[1] United Nations Convention on the Law of the Sea. Multilateral convention, 10 December 1982, United Nations Treaty Series (UNTS), vol. 1833, 397-581. This convention entered into force on 16 November 1994 (available at <www. un.org/Depts/los/convention_agreements/texts/unclos/unclos_e.pdf> (all webpages were last visited 4 July 2016)). Hereinafter 1982 Convention.

[2] See The Republic of Philippines v. The People's Republic of China (available at https://pcacases.com/web/view/7), where amongst other documents related to this case, also the award on the merits rendered on 12 July 2016 can be found (available at http://www.pcacases.com/pcadocs/PH-CN%20 -%2020160712%20-%20Award.pdf). Hereinafter 2016 Award.

[3] 2016 Award, *supra* note 2, pp. 175-260 (paras. 385-648). It thus concerns 86 pages out of an award, which counts 477 pages in total.

listed under a first bullet point the many occasions on which international courts and tribunal had side-stepped the thorny issue of trying to clarify the distinction between paragraphs 2 and 3 of Article 121 of the 1982 Convention, often by relying on the rules of maritime delimitation.[4] And now I would like to quote in full the second, and last bullet point of my conclusion-slide made at that time, which read: "Will Philippines v China be first arbitral tribunal dealing with the issue?"

At that time it was a rather daring statement, for many scholars doubted whether the Arbitral Tribunal would come to the conclusion that it had jurisdiction in view of the Chinese declaration made about ten years after this country had ratified the 1982 Convention on 7 June 1996.[5] In this declaration of 2006, China excluded all the categories of disputes referred to in paragraph 1 (a) (b) and (c) of Article 298 of the 1982 Convention from compulsory dispute settlement, i.e. including consequently those "disputes concerning the interpretation or application of articles 15, 74 and 83 relating to sea boundary delimitations, or those involving historic bays or titles".[6] But after the arbitral tribunal had decided in its award on jurisdiction of 29 October 2015[7] that it did have jurisdiction to consider the Philippines' submissions numbers 3, 4, 6 and 7, which all related to this distinction, be it with some conditions for submissions numbers 4 and 6,[8] and that it reserved consideration of submission number 5, also related to the same issue, to the merits phase,[9] the chances that this tribunal would

---

[4] Instead of first tackling the issue whether a particular maritime feature fell under Art. 121 paragraph 2 or 3 of the 1982 Convention, the court rather decided that the feature would only generate a 12 nautical mile territorial sea for delimitation purposes, making a preliminary determination of the exact nature of the feature according to Art. 121 simply redundant.

[5] Information to be consulted at the website of the United Nations Division for Ocean Affairs and the Law of the Sea (available at http://www.un.org/depts/los/reference_files/status2010.pdf).

[6] Declaration of 25 August 2006 (available at http://www.un.org/depts/los/convention_agreements/convention_declarations.htm#China%20Upon%20ratification).

[7] The Republic of Philippines v. The People's Republic of China, award on jurisdiction (available at https://pcacases.com/web/sendAttach/1506). Hereinafter 2015 Award.

[8] 2015 Award, *supra* note 7, paras 400, 401, 403 and 404 respectively.

[9] *Ibid.*, para. 402.

have to make some comments on the issue increased substantially for the simple reason that this tribunal, unlike courts and tribunals that preceded it,[10] would clearly not be able to hide behind the screen of maritime delimitation in view of the Chinese 2016 Declaration.[11]

Since 12 July 2016 I have been fortunate to attend a number of conferences relating to the 2016 Award in Washington D.C., Hong Kong, Vietnam as well as to visit the Ministry of Foreign Affairs of Taiwan (the Republic of China), and it will probably not come as a surprise that the first reactions in these different quarters were quite different in substance.

Against this perspective, the present paper intends to have a closer look once again at Article 121 (3): Firstly, the situation will be briefly depicted as it was in the past (Part 2); secondly, an analysis will be undertaken of the contribution of 2016 Award; and thirdly, some conclusions as to the relevance of this 2016 Award on the further development of the situation in the South China Sea will be arrived at (Part 3). But before doing so, in view of the obvious confusion in the press, a few words deserve to be addressed on the exact role played by the Permanent Court of Arbitration with respect to this arbitration initiated by the Philippines against China on the basis of Annex VII of the 1982 Convention (Part 1).

1. The 2016 Award and the Permanent Court of Arbitration

Having travelled quite intensively since the rendering of the 2016 Award and having read many newspapers along the road commenting on this award, I was struck by the utmost confusion as to the body thought to be the drafter of this award. Since the proceedings had been held in the Peace Palace in The Hague, the home of the Permanent Court of Arbitration (created in 1899)[12] as well International Court of Justice

---

[10] See *supra* note 4 and accompanying text.

[11] See *supra* note 6 and accompanying text.

[12] Convention for the Pacific Settlement of International Disputes. Multilateral convention, 29 July 1899. This convention entered into force on 4 September 1900 (https://pca-cpa.org/wp-content/uploads/sites/175/2016/01/1899-Convention-for-the-Pacific-Settlement-of-International-Disputes.pdf). Hereinafter 1899 Convention.

(created in 1945),[13] both institutions have often been accredited as the drafters of this award. This confusion reached such a magnitude that the International Court of Justice posted a disclaimer at the front page of its website in the English and French languages, the two official working languages of that court, which states:

> "The International Court of Justice (ICJ) wishes to draw the attention of the media and the public to the fact that the Award in the South China Sea Arbitration, (The Republic of the Philippines v. The People's Republic of China), was issued by an Arbitral, acting with the secretarial assistance of the Permanent Court of Arbitration (PCA). The relevant information can be found on the PCA's website (www.pca-cpa.org). The ICJ, which is a totally distinct institution, has had no involvement in the above mentioned case and, for that reason, there is no information about it on the ICJ's website."[14]

But also the reference to the website of the Permanent Court of Arbitration in the disclaimer by the International Court of Justice should be read with caution. As a member of a legal panel of a conference to comment on the 2016 Award on the very day it was rendered, namely 12 July, in Washington D.C.,[15] I seized the occasion to stress the exact

---

[13]   Charter of the United Nations. Multilateral convention, 26 June 1945, Arts. 92-95. This charter entered into force on 24 October 1945 (available at http://www.un.org/en/sections/un-charter/chapter-xiv/index.html).

[14]   This disclaimer in the English and French languages is both times accompanied by a similar statement in the Chinese language (available at http://www.icj-cij.org/homepage/index.php?lang=en and http://www.icj-cij.org/homepage/index.php?lang=fr, respectively).

[15]   Center for Strategic & International Studies (CSIS), Sixth Annual CSIS South China Sea Conference, Tuesday, July 12, 2016, 9:00 am - 5:15 pm. This conference was held at CSIS Headquarters, Washington D.C., United States of America. That panel was entitled "Legal Issues and Next Steps".

relationship between the Permanent Court of Arbitration on the one hand, and the Annex VII arbitral tribunal that rendered the award on the other.[16]

There has been a steady growth in the establishment of Annex VII arbitral tribunals ever since the late 1990s, reaching a grand total of 17 such cases at present.[17] However, none of the awards have been rendered by the Permanent Court of International Justice, since legal basis was not found in either the 1899 Convention[18] or the later 1907 Convention for the Pacific Settlement of International Disputes,[19] which together, constitute the founding conventions of the Permanent Court of Arbitration. That legal basis has rather to be found in Annex VII of the 1982 Convention. It is only because all of the States involved in these 17 legal procedures were a party to the 1982 Convention, that these proceedings could be instituted unilaterally by the respective claimant states.

The question can then be raised why these cases are nevertheless to be found on the website of the Permanent Court of Arbitration, as indicated in the statement posted by the International Court of Justice.[20] The only explanation is that Annex VII arbitral tribunals *may* request the Permanent Court of Arbitration to act as registry, but this no obligation whatsoever. Once constituted, it is up to the tribunal itself, after consultation with the parties, to decide on how it will deal with the duties linked to the registry. If one discards four cases that were transferred to the International Tribunal on the Law of the Sea after originally having been instituted under Annex VII, and where tribunal in other words had not yet had the

---

[16] An audiovisual file of this panel has been posted on the webpages of the CSIS (available at https://www.csis.org/events/sixth-annual-csis-south-china-sea-conference). Hereinafter CSIS Audiovisual File. A written paper, where these particular comments have been developed in greater detail, will be published at a later date by CSIS. The present comments are based on that paper. Hereinafter CSIS Contribution.

[17] See Annex 1. This annex was first included in the CSIS Contribution (*supra* note 16) and displayed during that conference (*ibid*, CSIS Audiovisual File).

[18] See *supra* note 12.

[19] Convention for the Pacific Settlement of International Dispute. Multilateral convention, 18 October 1907. This convention entered into force on 26 January 1910 (available at https://pca-cpa.org/wp-content/uploads/sites/175/2016/01/1907-Convention-for-the-Pacific-Settlement-of-International-Disputes.pdf).

[20] See *supra* note 14 and accompanying text.

possibility to rule on this issue,[21] 12 out of the 13 remaining Annex VII arbitral tribunals have relied on the Permanent Court of Arbitration for registrar services. Only in the first such arbitration, namely the Southern Bluefin tuna arbitration, which was held in New York, did the parties solicit the services of the International Centre for Settlement of Investment Disputes in this respect.[22]

It can therefore not be denied that a clear tendency exists at present for Annex VII arbitral tribunals to rely on the Permanent Court of Arbitration to act as registry. This has been captured very well by the Permanent Court of Arbitration which posts on its website the following statement:

> Since the 1982 Convention came into force in 1994, the Permanent Court of Arbitration has acted as registry in all but one of the cases that have been arbitrated under Annex VII of UNCLOS.[23]

The Permanent Court of Arbitration moreover assigns a so-called "PCA Case No." to all these Annex VII arbitrations making use of that court to act as registry.

---

21 It concerns the following cases (see Annex 1): 1) The M/V "Saiga" (No. 2) Case (Saint Vincent and the Grenadines v. Guinea), 1999; 2) Dispute concerning delimitation of the maritime boundary between Bangladesh and Myanmar in the Bay of Bengal (Bangladesh/Myanmar), 2012; 3) The M/V "Louisa" Case (Saint Vincent and the Grenadines v. Kingdom of Spain), 2013; and 4) The M/V "Virginia G" Case (Panama/Guinea-Bissau), 2014.

22 See Annex 1. It should moreover be noted that there is no direct relationship either between holding the arbitration at the premises of the Peace Palace in The Hague on the one hand, and opting for the Permanent Court of Arbitration to act as registry on the other. For obvious reasons, it was thought improper to fix the *locus* of the "Arctic Sunrise" arbitration between the Netherlands and the Russian Federation in The Hague. But even though the arbitral tribunal opted for Vienna as its seat in this particular case, it nevertheless requested the Permanent Court of Arbitration to act as registry.

23 This statement (available at https://pca-cpa.org/en/services/arbitration-services/unclos/) is correct if one does not take into consideration those arbitrations, initially instituted under Annex VII of the 1982 Convention, that were later transferred to the ITLOS (see *supra* note 21 and accompanying text).

Despite all these formal links that exist at present between almost all Annex VII arbitral tribunals and the Permanent Court of Arbitration -- which the latter carefully seems to nurture it must be admitted -- the fact remains that these awards can simply not be assimilated with awards delivered by that institution. This point can hardly be overstated at present, not only because of the clear confusion that exists in the media as mentioned before, but also because it might easily give rise the wrong impression that States from now on can bring any type of international dispute before the Permanent Court of Arbitration in a unilateral manner. The essential point to be remembered here is that this only holds true relating to law of the sea disputes within the framework of the 1982 Convention, and subject to the automatic and optional limitations to be found in that document.[24]

2. Article 121 (3) before the 2016 Award

In this part, two elements will be highlighted:[25] First it will be argued that the genesis of Article 121 (3) and the way in which it became part of the 1982 Convention, indicates that the provision lacks internal logic and as a consequence can hardly be applied using the normal methods of interpretation.[26] Secondly, it will be noted that courts and tribunals, which in such circumstances are normally looked at to provide guidance, have steadfastly refused to do so notwithstanding the fact that many occasions presented themselves for them to do so.

A. Genesis of Article 121 (3)

The origins of Article 121 (3) are to be found in the Third United Nations Conference on the Law of the Sea (UNCLOS III), because at the

---

[24] 1982 Convention, *supra* note 1, Arts. 297 ad 298 respectively.

[25] This part is based on *Erik Franckx*, The Regime of Islands and Rocks, in: *David Joseph Attard, Malgosia Fitzmaurice and Norman A. Martinez Gutiérrez* (eds.), The IMLI Manual on International Maritime Law, Volume I, The Law of the Sea, Oxford, Oxford University Press, 2014, pp. 99-124.

[26] Convention on Law of Treaties. Multilateral convention, 22 May 1969, UNTS, vol. 1155, 331, 332-353, Arts. 31-33. This convention entered into force on 27 January 1980 (available at https://treaties.un.org/doc/Treaties/1980/01/19800127%2000-52%20AM/Ch_XXIII_01.pdf). Hereinafter VCLT.

time of the first codification attempt undertaken by the United Nations with respect to the law of the sea, the so-called 1958 conventional system,[27] States were still in agreement that all islands should, as a rule, generate the same maritime zones as land.[28] However, with the spatial extension of maritime zones agreed upon during UNCLOS III, reaching 200 nautical miles and sometimes well beyond that limit as far as the seabed and subsoil are concerned, States were of the opinion that certain small maritime features should no longer be equated with land in this respect.

After different proposals had been submitted in this respect within the framework of the Second Committee of UNCLOS III, which resulted in a main trends document containing many variations,[29] its Chairman was instructed by the President of UNCLOS III to present a single negotiating text in early 1975. He did so on 7 May 1975,[30] producing a single text borrowing parts from the different proposals that had been made so far, but

---

[27]   This 1958 conventional system is composed of four conventions: Convention on the Territorial Sea and the Contiguous Zone. Multilateral convention, 29 April 1958, UNTS, vol. 516, 205, 206-224. This convention entered into force on 10 September 1964 (available at https://treaties.un.org/doc/ Treaties/1964/11/19641122%2002-14%20AM/Ch_XXI_01_2_3_4_5p. pdf); Convention on the Continental Shelf. Multilateral convention, 29 April 1958, UNTS, vol. 499, 311, 312-320. This convention entered into force on 10 June 1964 (available at https://treaties.un.org/doc/ Treaties/1964/06/19640610%2002-10%20AM/Ch_XXI_01_2_3_4_5p. pdf); Convention on the High Seas. Multilateral convention, 29 April 1958, UNTS, vol. 450, 11, 82-102. This convention entered into force on 30 September 1962 (available at https://treaties.un.org/doc/ Treaties/1963/01/19630103%2002-00%20AM/Ch_XXI_01_2_3_4_5p. pdf); and Convention on Fishing and Conservation of the Living Resources of the High Seas. Multilateral convention, 29 April 1958, UNTS, vol. 559, 285, 286-300. This convention entered into force on 20 March 1966 (available at https://treaties.un.org/doc/Treaties/1966/03/19660320%20 02-16%20AM/Ch_XXI_01_2_3_4_5p.pdf).

[28]   Convention on the Territorial Sea and the Contiguous Zone, *supra* note 27, Art. 10; and Convention on the Continental Shelf, *ibid.*, Art. 1.

[29]   A/CONF.62/C.2/WP.1, Third United Nations Conference on the Law of the Sea, Official Documents, vol 3, 107. The provisions relating to islands concern the numbers 239-43. See *ibid.* 140-42.

[30]   A/CONF.62/WP.8/Part II, Third United Nations Conference on the Law of the Sea, Official Documents, vol 4, 152.

---

which often lacked any common basis. Even though this text was clearly intended by its creator to be a mere basis for further negotiations and was expressly stated not to prejudice the position of any delegation,[31] its content did not change anymore. Not that everybody agreed to it. On the contrary, as evidenced by the many proposals submitted during the remaining year of UNCLOS III to change it, delegations introduced proposals spanning the whole spectrum from outright deleting to further refinement. But as none of these proposals was able to muster anything coming even close to a consensus, States preferred to stick to the 1975 formulation of the Chairman in order not to jeopardize the rest of the package deal.

The consequence of this particular genesis is also that the wording of Article 121 (3) lacks any internal logic, as it borrowed bits and piece of totally unrelated proposals. It defies consequently the customary rules of interpretation to be found in the VCLT.[32] Probably exactly because of this enigmatic wording, most delegations were of the opinion that their particular views on the issue, which as stated above widely diverged, could well be read into it.

In the specialized legal literature, one could therefore find the most diverse interpretations to be given to the different elements contained in Article 121 (3). But there was one point on which almost all of them agreed, namely that this particular paragraph of Article 121, contrary to the two preceding paragraphs, did not form part of customary international law.

B. Courts and Tribunals and Article 121 (3)

Confronted with such a perplexing provision, where the ordinary meaning is impossible to be found, the *travaux préparatoires* only confirm that the provision lacks any internal logic, and State practice concerning maritime delimitation is of limited utility as States do not have to base themselves on law to reach such agreements, States are simply lost at sea when trying to apply it in practice. In such a situation, one is inclined to look to courts and tribunals for guidance.

A careful analysis of these decisions and awards, however, leads to the conclusion that, even though occasions were plenty, these bodies have

---

[31] Introduction by the Chairman of the Second Committee, Third United Nations Conference on the Law of the Sea, Official Documents, vol 4, 153.

[32] See *supra* note 26 and accompanying text.

persistently refused to bring any clarity.[33] In cases where the parties have argued *pro* and *contra* the application of Article 121 (3) to a particular maritime feature, a preferred method of the International Court of Justice has for instance been to apply the law of maritime delimitation first, subsequently deciding that under those rules the maritime feature in question only receives a 12 nautical mile territorial sea, and finally concluding that under such circumstances there is no need any more to classify it as a paragraph 2 or rather paragraph 3 feature.[34]

A major, but at the same time somewhat incongruous contribution made by the International Court of Justice in view of its position just described in the preceding paragraph, is that it declared in 2012 that paragraph 3 of Article 121 forms an indivisible part with the two other paragraphs of that article. By necessity, it thus also forms part of customary international law, a fact that both parties to the case recognized.[35] By thus emphasizing the importance of paragraph 3, but at the same time refusing to clarify its meaning, the International Court of Justice in other words only added to the complexity for States having to apply this provision in practice.

3. Article 121 (3) after the 2016 Award

It is undoubtedly the great merit of the 2016 Award to have tackled the interpretation of Article 121 (3) for the very first time head on. As indicated above, after the 2015 Award relating to the jurisdiction, this was somewhat to be expected, as this tribunal would clearly not have the luxury to apply the law of maritime delimitation.[36]

It is not the intention of this paper to analyse the reasoning of the arbitral tribunal in any detail. This has been done by the present author in a written contribution to a conference jointly organized by the Chinese Society of International Law and the Hong Kong International Arbitration

---

[33] Franckx, *supra* note 25, pp. 120-23

[34] See *Maritime Delimitation in the Black Sea (Romania v. Ukraine)* (Merits) [2009] ICJ Rep 123, para 187, and *Territorial and Maritime Dispute (Nicaragua v. Colombia)* (Merits) [2012] ICJ Rep 691-92, para 120. In both cases the exact same reasoning was followed.

[35] *Territorial and Maritime Dispute (Nicaragua v. Colombia)*, *supra* note 34, 674, para. 139.

[36] See *supra* notes 5 to 11 and accompanying text.

Centre immediately after the rendering of the 2016 Award.[37] Only the main steps in the reasoning of the arbitral tribunal will be highlighted here.

The arbitration starts out by describing the views of the parties. The Philippines argued that a rock is not necessarily a solid piece of stone, but that also sandy or coral features can be fitted under this notion. Under the term human habitation, a stable group of people has to be understood remaining for a significant period of time on a particular maritime feature. This would exclude a mere military occupation from fulfilling this requirement. As far as the notion economic life of its own is concerned, only the territorial sea could be added to the territory of the feature itself, in order to determine the area where these economic activities can be undertaken.

As far as the views of China are concerned, the arbitral tribunal can only rely on public statements as this country *ab initio* refused to participate in the proceedings initiated by the Philippines. This country argues that by necessity, the sovereignty aspects of the matter must be settled first, and only then can the maritime claims of the features in question be appreciated. The country also stressed that only nine maritime features occupied by the People's Republic of China form the subject of the legal case against it, whereas this country has a claim over the Spratly Islands as a unit. The tribunal cannot find an outspoken Chinese position on the interpretation and application of Article 121 (3), but certain indications can nevertheless be discerned. First of all, China has spoken out in favour of the protection of the common heritage of mankind against claims of States that had established extensive maritime zones from minor maritime features in the framework of a meeting of the International Seabed Authority as well as the meeting of the States parties to the 1982 Convention, both held in 2009. If with respect to Scarborough Shoal it can only be inferred by implication that China believes this maritime feature generates an exclusive economic zone, this country on the contrary has clearly claimed such a zone around Itu Aba. No public statements can be found on the other maritime features individually, but the People's Republic of China did clearly express the position that the Spratly Islands as a unit do generate a territorial sea, an exclusive economic zone and a continental shelf.

After having reviewed the positions of the parties, the arbitral tribunal subsequently advances its own analysis of the issue. It is thereby

---

[37] This conference was held on 15-16 July 2016 in Hong Kong, People's Republic of China. The papers submitted to this conference will be published at a later date. This part is based on that paper.

guided by the normal rules of interpretation to be found in the VCLT,[38] implying that the tribunal will first look at the ordinary meaning of the words in their context and in light of the object and purpose of the 1982 Convention. Secondly, it will also take into consideration the subsequent practice of States, establishing an agreement between the parties. Finally, as supplementary means, the *travaux préparatoires* might be relied upon.

Concerning the ordinary meaning, the tribunal first comes to the conclusion that the term "rock" in Article 121 (3) cannot be limited to maritime features made up of solid material because this would lead to the absurd result that sandbanks would for instance be able to generate an exclusive economic zone and a continental shelf, whereas a comparable features made out of solid material would not. The word "cannot" implies, according to the arbitral tribunal, that a theoretical capacity is envisaged, not whether the maritime feature actually does fulfil certain conditions. This in turn means that historical evidence may be considered relevant: If a particular maritime feature was never inhabited or able to sustain an economic life of its own, then it provides a strong indication that it is to be considered as falling under paragraph 3, whereas in the opposite case it would probably point at the fact that it constitutes rather a paragraph 2 feature. With respect to the term "human habitation" the arbitral tribunal follows the argumentation of the Philippines, but refuses to provide an exact threshold. As far as the "economic life" is concerned, the arbitral tribunal emphasizes that the economic activities must be local, thus excluding merely extractive economic activities not serving the stable community living there. These activities, moreover, cannot relate to the exclusive economic zone or continental shelf, for that would lead to a circular reasoning. The word "or" finally should be understood in the sense that the presence of one of the two elements listed in that paragraph is sufficient for the feature to fall under paragraph 2. Even though the arbitral tribunal recognizes the close link between both elements linked by the word "or", it wanted to keep the door open for certain settled communities to be able to rely not on one single maritime feature, but on a number of them in order to sustain their economic subsistence. In arriving at these different clarifications, the arbitral tribunal very much relied on the object and purpose of the 1982 Convention, as for instance the fact that the exclusive economic zone was established for the benefit of the coastal

---

[38]　See *supra* note 26.

State. It also explains why States cannot change the characterization of a particular maritime feature as a low-tide elevation or a rock falling under Article 121 (3), as its natural condition is key to that determination.

Having said all that, the arbitral tribunal is fully aware that it still only provides an imperfect guide as it refuses to establish universal criteria that can easily be applied in all situations. Instead, a case-by-case approach is recommended, with as secondary rule that if a particular maritime feature falls close to the borderline, the careful assessment of historical evidence becomes important.

After the arbitral tribunal concludes that no subsequent practice establishing an agreement between the parties exists *in casu*, it then applies these criteria to the six maritime features pinpointed by the Philippines and rules that none of them can be considered to fall under Article 121 (2). As to the other features of the Spratly Islands, and especially the bigger ones such as Itu Aba, the arbitral tribunal considers them to fall close to the borderline that it established itself. Consequently historical evidence becomes important and to that extent the arbitral tribunal conducts its own research as to the natural state of these features in the archives of France and the United Kingdom. After a careful evaluation, the conclusion is reached that also these larger features amongst the Spratly Islands are to be qualified as Article 121 (3) features, allowing the arbitral tribunal to conclude that all the other, and thus smaller features of this island group are to be categorized likewise.

4. Conclusions

It has been demonstrated that Article 121 (3) constitutes one of these provisions of the 1982 Convention that States are simply unable to apply in practice as its uncertain content leads to a wide variety of possible interpretations. In a convention that was adopted by way of consensus, such grey provisions are not really to be considered exceptional.[39] As this provision started to generate difficulties between State parties even before

---

[39] One can also think of the delimitation provisions of Arts. 74 and 83, which only state that the result should be equitable, without giving any concrete directions as to the methods to be used to arrive at that end result. Also Art. 59 concerning disputes over the attribution of competence in the exclusive economic zone not clearly mentioned in the 1982 Convention appears to be such a provision in view of the criteria to be taken into account to solve such disputes.

the 1982 Convention had entered into force, a good number of such case have been brought before courts and tribunals since then.

In other domains where courts and tribunals have been requested to provide guidance to the States, these bodies have been very forthcoming in providing a detailed set of methods and criteria that should guide States in their relations with each other. The law of maritime delimitation forms a perfect example. Even though judicial decisions are only considered to constitute a subsidiary source of international law,[40] it has been stated that the maritime delimitation law of the exclusive economic zone and the continental shelf has become a kind of judge-made common law.[41]

A similar development, however, did not materialize with respect to the interpretation of Article 121 (3), even though parties at several occasions argued this issue before courts and tribunals. The only contribution until the 2016 Award had been the declaration in 2012 that this particular provision did form part of customary international law. However, by enhancing its importance, without giving any clarification as to its interpretation, the International Court of Justice in a way further increased the difficulties for States confronted with this issue in practice.

It is undoubtedly the merit of the 2016 Award to have provided, for the first time, concrete guidance for States on how to interpret and apply Article 121 (3). However, as the arbitral tribunal did not provide any universal standards, but rather promoted a case-by-case approach, it is submitted that this will probably not have been the last decision or award to address this particular issue. Just like the law of maritime delimitation, which has also not been created by one single decision or award, it is believed that it will be the interplay between these different decisions and awards that will further refine and develop the interpretation and application of Article 121 (3) as to the future.

---

[40] Statute of International Court of Justice, Art. 38 (1)(d). This Statute forms an integral part of the Charter of the United Nations, *supra* note 13.

[41] Jonathan I Charney, 'Progress in International Maritime Boundary Delimitation Law' (1994) 88 American Journal of International Law 227, 228.

Annex 1

*List of Annex VII Arbitrations**

#	NAME	PARTIES	INSTITUTED	AWARD/ TERMINATED/ TRANSFERRED	REGISTRY
1	Saiga	Saint Vincent and the Grenadines v. Guinea	1997	1998 (transferred to ITLOS)	NA**
2	Southern bluefin tuna	Australia v. Japan and New Zealand v. Japan	1998	2000 (award on jurisdiction and admissibility)	ICSID***
3	MOX plant	Ireland v. United Kingdom	2001	2008 (terminated upon withdrawal by claimant)	PCA***
4	Land reclamation by Singapore in and around the straits of Johor	Malaysia v. Singapore	2003	2005 (award on agreed terms)	PCA
5	Delimitation of the exclusive economic zone and the continental shelf	Barbados v. Trinidad and Tobago	2004	2006 (award on the merits)	PCA

6	Delimitation of the maritime boundary	Guyana v. Suriname	2004	2007 (award on the merits)	PCA
7a	The Bay of Bengal maritime boundary	Bangladesh v. India	2009	2014 (award on the merits	PCA
7b	Delimitation of the maritime boundary in the Bay of Bengal	Bangladesh v. Myanmar	2009	2009 (transferred to ITLOS)	NA
9	Chagos marine protected area	Mauritius v. United Kingdom	2010	2015 (award on the merits)	PCA
10	M/V "Virginia G"	Panama v. Guinea Bissau	2011	2011 (transferred to ITLOS)	NA
11	"ARA Libertad"	Argentina v. Ghana	2012	2013 (terminated upon agreement of the parties)	PCA
12	/	Philippines v. China	2013	2016 (award on the merits)	PCA
13	Atlanto-Scandian herring	Denmark in respect of the Faroe Island v. European Union	2013	2014 (terminated upon agreement by the parties)	PCA
14	"Arctic Sunrise"	Netherlands v. Russian Federation	2013	Pending	PCA

15	"Duzgit Integrity"	Malta v. Sao Tome and Principe	2013	Pending	PCA
16	Delimitation of maritime boundary in the Atlantic Ocean	Ghana v. Côte d'Ivoire	2014	2014 (transferred to ITLOS)	NA
17	"Enrica Lexie" incident	Italy v. India	2015	Pending	PCA

* Listed chronologically according to date of institution of proceedings (if on the same day, alphabetically according to name of the parties)

** Not applicable

*** International Centre for Settlement of Investment Disputes

**** Permanent Court of Arbitration

THE JURIDICAL ISLAND: FROM THE ISLAND OF PALMAS TO THE SOUTH CHINA SEA

Alyosius Llamzon

Abstract

The importance of islands in the international law on territory extends back to at least the seminal *Island of Palmas* arbitration. But the extension of the UNCLOS' 'land dominates sea' concept to islands, and not only to large land masses, made the juridical concept of the "island" take on the status of a potential leviathan, allowing tiny patches of land to create 200 nautical mile Exclusive Economic Zones that were of an importance out of proportion with the islands themselves. All that seemed necessary under Article 121 of UNCLOS was that the island be capable of a bare minimum of human habitation or economic life for it to have an EEZ or continental shelf of its own. UNCLOS thus provided the legal impetus

---

[42] © Copyright Aloysius Llamzon. A.B., J.D., Ateneo de Manila University; LL.M., J.S.D., Yale Law School. Senior Associate, King & Spalding LLP, New York City. Former Senior Legal Counsel, Permanent Court of Arbitration, The Hague.

The author acknowledges the title's inspiration from Prof. Gayle Westerman's book "The Juridical Bay" (Oxford, 1987), an important work on coastal-bay type waters as a source of national and international conflict.

19

for states to make expansive claims to islands for economic, military, or political reasons, with only threadbare historic and cultural links.

The spiral of ever-escalating claims to islands after 1982 would have continued unabated and with increased geopolitical ramifications. However, this legal "ticking time bomb" was diffused in a highly significant way through the *South China Sea* arbitration. The Tribunal defined an island in a manner that bears little resemblance to its colloquial understanding (nor indeed to Article 121(1)): the regime of islands under international law is now much more tightly circumscribed, and the cause of world public order is much the better for it. This work discusses the law of the seas' evolving juridical concept of islands, using two seminal arbitrations as bookends: the *Island of Palmas* and *South China Sea* cases. It argues that overall, international law is well served by the regime of islands fashioned by the *South China Sea* Tribunal.

*   *   *

It is an interesting accident of history that the two most important international decisions on islands centered on Southeast Asia – and that both involved the Philippines. In the 1928 *Island of Palmas* arbitration, the key issue was who – as between two then-colonial powers over modern Indonesia and the Philippines – was sovereign over a very small island off the coast of Mindanao, the large island in the southern Philippines.

One would not instinctively think that *Island of Palmas* has anything to do with the *South China Sea* arbitration almost a century later. Yes, they are both arbitrations conducted under the auspices of the Permanent Court of Arbitration; but they are from completely different epochs in international law – the very content of international law had changed so much from then, not least with the advent of the UN Convention on the Law of the Sea. After all, in the *South China Sea* proceedings and in the Award itself, both the Philippines and the Tribunal took pains to emphasize, again and again, that the case would not adjudicate over questions of who is sovereign over the features of the Spratlys.

But the two have important links. *Island of Palmas* articulated enduring rules about the acquisition of territory, and that is the parent of the "land dominates sea" idea that animates the 1982 Law of the Sea Convention, because Max Huber did not consider the regime of sovereignty over islands to be – in any significant sense – any different from that of any other *terra firma.* He did not – or at least did not seem – to have taken full account of the implications of sovereignty over the islands for its surrounding waters. But the focus was on the island itself, even if it was and still remains a very inconsequential island – it is about two miles in length, 3/4 of a mile in width [totaling 1.2 square miles or 315 hectares – larger by about 1/3 than the largest islands in the Paracels], and at the time it was decided, the island had about 750 persons as its population. In the process of rendering his decision, the sole arbitrator Max Huber (one of the leading international lawyers of his day) rendered a classic articulation on rules on territorial acquisition that have endured to this day. His reasoning that it was not so-called 'discovery' by western explorers, or contiguity (that is, how close the island was to the landmass of one of the claimants), but rather that open and peaceful displays of sovereignty – of *effectivité* – that is decisive in questions of territory (which led to the Netherlands being recognized as sovereign over the island, a fact that carries on to this day with Indonesia), is a classic that lives on to this day.

It is quite remarkable to think about: think about so much of the strife and race to occupy the different features of the world's seas and oceans – including the South China sea – can be traced to this reasoning. For Max Huber, it was immaterial that the island was closer to the Philippines' main islands than to Indonesia. So the modern argument that the islands in the Paracels and the Spratlys may be that much closer to Vietnam or the Philippines than Malaysia or China were not controlling. Instead, *effectivité* meant that States had every incentive to go physically to these often barren rocks and islands, incorporate them into vast municipalities that had almost no real inhabitants, all in a bid to exercise the "continuous and peaceful displays of sovereignty" that the *Island of Palmas* case required for the exercise of sovereignty.

It is important to remember, however, that the impetus for this race to occupy the rocks and islands that our forbears did not consider worth the effort did not arise from *Island of Palmas* itself. It was the international law principle on acquisitive prescription coupled with developments in the law of the sea decades later that provided the real impetus. The real link with the *South China Sea* arbitration started in the 1970s, when the concept of the Exclusive Economic Zone had its genesis. The 1982 Law of the Sea Convention then codified the principle, which is now considered part of customary international law, adhered to by UNCLOS parties and non-parties alike (such as the U.S.). It was that Convention's vast expansion of sovereign rights that gave real incentives to allow for tiny rocks and islets to take on an importance far removed from the landmasses themselves.

Indeed, the modern regime of islands under international law really is not concerned about the island itself and its potential *qua* island – it is the surrounding sea (the territorial sea, the contiguous zone, and the post-1982 Exclusive Economic Zone) that is all-important. Land is important only insofar as it allows for dominion over the sea. The remote islands of the Spratlys were treated prior to the Law of the Sea Convention – as the Tribunal knew explained with great clarity – as either a temporary base of operations for fishing and turtle shells or (and this really harkens back to an earlier age), to mine phosphate deposits (bird guano). These purely extractive interests in the islands meant that there was little incentive for humans to stay in the island once they were done extracting, and the evidence shows that human beings and even Japanese and French corporate interests were only temporarily at the islands – there was simply no continuous, indigenous population in the Spratlys. Nor should there be, especially in our modern age, where there little use for little rocks and islands to act as shelters – contemporary commercial fishing vessels are far more mobile and comfortable, and capable of being out in the open sea for months on end. (Small artisan fishermen in the Philippines and Vietnam may well be the exceptions to these – features such as Scarborough shoal, some 90 nautical miles off the coast of the Philippine main island of Luzon, is just close enough for small commercial fishermen, having little more than motorized outrigger boats, as a source of fish and to use those rocks as a temporary reprieve from the open seas in a manner that still resembles their ancestors).

But in the post-UNCLOS world, *governments* became the primary actors in occupying islands. States actively supported the shrinking of the common areas of mankind, ostensibly because coastal States were the best stewards of the seas surrounding them. This is of course true in many cases. But it is decidedly *not true* of remote islands that are not tethered to particular littoral States and lie instead in the middle of seas and oceans. What happened instead was a kind of international law-sanctioned free-for-all where the principle of *effectivité* articulated in *Island of Palmas* was the cause for States to try to occupy these remote features, both for economic and military reasons. An expanded EEZ and continental shelf meant that vast areas of the sea would be under the effective, internationally sanctioned control of the State that exercised sovereignty over the island. This is "land dominates sea" in its leviathan form, and many States, large and small alike, operated under the premise that sovereignty over these remote rocks and islands would bear the full benefits provided to landmasses under UNCLOS, no matter how tiny that rock or island might be.

The vagueness of the Convention certainly contributed to this large-scale exercise in flag- planting. For all its importance, the regime of islands under the Convention is covered by only one provision – Article 121. The article has been criticized by scholars Churchill and Lowe, (among others), who have observed that the provision is not particularly well drafted. And incredibly, despite its importance, Article 121 had never been interpreted in a meaningful way by any previous international decision – as the Tribunal noted [in paragraph 474], "Article 121 has not previously been the subject of significant consideration by courts or arbitral tribunals and has been accorded a wide range of different interpretations in scholarly literature."

Because of its singular importance to the regime of islands and the *South China Sea* arbitration, Article 121 is quoted in full below:

Article 121 Regime of islands

1. An island is a naturally formed area of land, surrounded by water, which is above water at high tide.
2. Except as provided for in paragraph 3, the territorial sea, the contiguous zone, the exclusive economic zone and the continental shelf of an island are determined in accordance with the provisions of this Convention applicable to other land territory.
3. Rocks which cannot sustain human habitation, or economic life of their own, shall have no exclusive economic zone or continental shelf.

Article 121 raises many questions. While subparagraph 1 purports to define what an island is, and subparagraph 2 lays down the land-dominates-sea idea animating all of the Convention by stating that islands generate a territorial sea, contiguous zone, EEZ and continental shelf as would any other landmass, subparagraph 3 is the key provision. It provides the principal caveat to subparagraph 2 – in the words of the tribunal, subparagraph 3 is a rule of limitation. It introduces the concept of "rocks" as a type of island that does not generate an EEZ or continental shelf. The Tribunal [at para 280] differentiated between "high tide features", which encompass everything in Article 121; "rocks", which fall under

121(3); and high tide features that are not rocks – which they termed "fully entitled islands". Only "fully entitled islands" benefit from Article 121(2), enjoying the same entitlements as other land territories. For purposes of the Convention, these islands are no different than other land territories [see Award, para. 389]. What the Award calls the "fully entitled island" can also be called the 'juridical' island, as the fully entitled island is a juridical construct of Article 121. Every feature that is not a juridical island does not generate an EEZ or continental shelf, and is thus far less valuable to States.

So the key question is: what islands are in fact not "juridical islands", i.e., are rocks? Again, Article 121(3) states that **"[r]ocks which cannot sustain human habitation OR economic life of their own shall have no exclusive economic zone or continental shelf."** The Tribunal took pains to analyze *all* of the crucial words of the provision [at para. 478]: "rocks", "cannot" "sustain" "human habitation" "or" "economic life of their own". Time does not permit me to go into every aspect of the Tribunal's extensive analysis, but allow me to highlight a few points.

On "ROCKS"

The key question here is: did "rocks" intend to signify geological or geomorphological criteria? No. According to the Tribunal, a "rock" under Article 121 is "a category of island", which is defined by that article as a "naturally formed area of land". Thus, a juridical rock, in the UNCLOS sense of the word, is not a rock in the sense we colloquially might think – it must be naturally formed, and cannot be the product of artificial building. But it need not actually be a hard, stony, craggy outbreak, as a casual observer might think.

The more convincing reason why a rock is not a "rock" within the meaning of the Convention is because if coral, sand, mud were considered not rocks, but actually remained above water at high tide, that could only mean, by process of elimination, that these non-rocks are in fact *islands*, even if they were incapable of human habitation or economic life. Calling such a result "absurd", the Tribunal decided instead that rocks "will not necessarily be composed of rock." [para. 482] The juridical rock is different from actual rocks.

On "CANNOT SUSTAIN HUMAN HABITATION"

Unlike the Tribunal, instead of taking the words of the next phrase separately, I would take the next few words as one: "cannot sustain human habitation".

When one takes those words together with the benefit of the Tribunal's analysis, it becomes clear that for an island to be a *juridical* island in the sense of the Convention, that island must ideally already have shown that human beings have lived there *over an extended period of time* (and not just as fishermen temporarily seeking shelter, as the evidence from the 1800s and early 1900s suggests). That would be powerful evidence and especially when an island lies close to a populated land mass [para. 484]. But if the island did not, as with those in the Spratlys, the question then becomes one of *potential* – does this island, in its natural state, have the potential of sustaining human habitation?

"Sustaining" and "habitation" are key words here, and the answer might be trickier than one would think. Even if one agrees with the Tribunal that an island is not made capable of human habitation by the importation of food, building materials for shelter, etc., it would still be a fairly restrictive reading of Article 121(3) to say that an island should disqualified from being a juridical island because advantage was taken of modern technologies – such as desalinization for example – in order to enhance an island's capacity for sustained human habitation. Technology becomes even more important with the Tribunal's requirement that capacity for human habitation be for an "indefinite time" [para. 492] **And yet this is precisely what the Tribunal did: it rejected the idea that humans can make meaningful technological improvements to turn the uninhabitable to the inhabitable.** OR more precisely – you can do so if you wish, but that remains a rock under UNCLOS – it is not a judicial island.

Indeed, the Tribunal goes farther in limiting what "human habitation" is: [at para. 489]

> In the Tribunal's view, the use in Article 121(3) of the term "habitation" includes a qualitative element that is reflected particularly in the notions of settlement and residence that are inherent in that term. The mere presence of a small number of persons on a feature does not constitute

permanent or habitual residence there and does not equate to habitation. Rather, the term habitation implies a non-transient presence of persons who have chosen to stay and reside on the feature in a settled manner. **Human habitation would thus require all of the elements necessary to keep people alive on the feature, but would also require conditions sufficiently conducive to human life and livelihood for people to inhabit, rather than merely survive on, the feature.**

Thus, the fact humans can survive in an island is insufficient for the tribunal – they must be able to "inhabit" that feature – a larger spectrum of human existence than survival is at play. The word "livelihood" is used [para. 490]. The word "community" or "group" [para 491] is also used. One is almost tempted to use the old biblical phrase: "man does not live on bread alone…"

Indeed, at this point that we now head back full circle into *Island of Palmas* – it turns out that the old standard of *effectivité*, or rather a specific aspect of *effectivité* that would require the exercise of sovereign will upon a piece of territory in a manner that affects the human beings that live or may potentially live there, is key not only to sovereignty, but also to the definition of the island itself. So although Annex VII arbitral tribunals cannot decide issues of sovereignty *qua* sovereignty, especially if respondent State makes the appropriate reservation against maritime delimitation issues under the Convention, **a Tribunal can nonetheless, under its general interpretive powers, approach the issue of sovereignty through the question of whether that speck of land can sustain human life. If it cannot, a key aspect of *effectivité* is lost.**

On "OR"

That single word caused a lot of controversy. Does Article 121(3) mean that either "human habitation" OR "economic life" suffice, such that if the island is capable of sustaining economic life but not human habitation, that island is nonetheless an "island"? The literal meaning of OR suggests so.

Both the Philippines and the Tribunal discuss what "logic" demands when reading article the "or" in Article 121(3). The Philippines argued that because "cannot" is used before "or", you have a double negative sentence structure and because of this, the two criteria are cumulative [para. 493] and "or" is effectively an "and". But the Tribunal disagreed, and did so in a manner that I personally find difficult to understand.

In para 494, the tribunal seems to differentiate between "logic" and "*formal* logic", and argues in an almost syllogistic fashion that while the text does create a cumulative requirement (it agrees with the Philippines to this extent), "the negative overall structure of the sentence means that the cumulative criteria describe the circumstances in which a feature will be *denied* such maritime zones." With this, the Tribunal concluded that the "logical result" is that either human habitation OR economic life are necessary, not both, for the island to be the "juridical.

Importantly, however, for the rest of the Tribunal's analysis, it adopts the interpretation that requires both human habitation and economic life to be fulfilled anyway. Why? Because often "formal logic accords imperfectly with linguistic usage" [para 495]. Here, therefore, using the colloquial understanding is better than "formal logic", or, one might say, textualism. And yet in para 496, we have this odd logic yet again: despite noting that the second phrase of Art 121(3) – "shall have no exclusive economic zone or continental shelf" – should be taken to mean that the "or" is an "and" because it would be "manifestly absurd" [para. 495]. But then in the next paragraph, instead of reading the "or" in the first half of the sentence as an "and", as it effectively did in the second half, it instead maintains the disjunctive term and holds that if *either* human habitation *or* economic life of its own is present, that island is a juridical island.[43]

But would this not in itself be an absurd result? As the Tribunal itself recognizes in the very next paragraph, "economic activity is carried out by humans and [] humans will rarely inhabit areas where no economic activity or livelihood is possible. The two concepts are thus linked in practical terms, regardless of the grammatical construction of Article 121(3)."

---

[43] para. 496: "Accordingly, the Tribunal concludes that, properly interpreted, a rock would be disentitled from an exclusive economic zone and continental shelf only if it were to lack *both* the capacity to sustain human habitation *and* the capacity to sustain an economic life of its own. Or, expressed more straightforwardly and in positive terms, an island that is able to sustain either human habitation or an economic life of its own is entitled to *both* an exclusive economic zone *and* a continental shelf (in accordance with the provisions of the Convention applicable to other land territory)."

On "ECONOMIC LIFE OF ITS OWN"

Here, a real contribution was made. Because the Tribunal maintained that the disjunctive "or" is meaningful, it had to contend with the possibility of an island having no real capacity for sustaining human habitation, but nonetheless becoming a juridical island because of its ability to have an "economic life of its own". It is very easy to think of situations where an island would hold very nominal interest for human populations living long-term – recall the British Anthropologist Robin Dunbar's observation that a "mean group size" where meaningful human interactions exist is about 150 persons, whether in modern times or even during pre-history (where tribes generally had those numbers). But even if nobody did live in that island, one would think that the island could nonetheless have an "economic life of its own", in the ordinary sense of those words, because of certain attributes it had. In the case of Itu Aba, for example, the island was the source of mining operations for a number of years by Japanese companies mining the guano for phosphates it could sell, presumably in the Japanese or Taiwanese markets. But the Tribunal held that these kinds of extractive uses of an island would not qualify for a rock's ascension into a juridical island.

The key phrase the Tribunal focused on was "of its own" – for the Tribunal, this meant that the economic life of the island had to be tied within the island itself: it could not rely upon the outside world as its only market, without having a local population that could benefit from the economic activity and build a life within the island itself as a result of that activity. In so doing, "economic life" thus became inextricably linked to sustained human habitation.

Overall, there is very little to criticize in the Tribunal's interpretation of Article 121(3). To practitioners, The Tribunal's painstaking use of the Vienna Convention on the Law of Treaties' criteria of *text, context,* and *object and purpose* will be very familiar. I identified a few points that scholars no doubt will find fault in, but the substantive findings made are, I think, very sound and will withstand the scrutiny of even those who believe that the *South China Sea* tribunal had no jurisdiction to render such an award in the first place.

*　　*　　*

In conclusion, one key impact of the Tribunal's interpretation of Article 121(3), at least to me, is this: instead of allowing for modern States to determine what juridical islands are, the Tribunal effectively required the criteria of human habitation and economic life to be determined with reference to a non-State dominated past – indeed, the time of the *Island of Palmas* arbitration and earlier. For the Tribunal, it is the indigenous peoples of the world, who had by the early 1900s seen and occupied virtually every speck of land in the world – islands included – that were viable, and made their homes there, that determine which islands are the true juridical islands worthy of full maritime entitlements under UNCLOS. Why do I say so? Because the Tribunal discounts every modern technological means in which an island is enhanced to make it more attractive for human existence. When you disallow States from turning an island into a juridical island by building military facilities; or by relocating people there who rely principally on the sources not *in situ* for food, clothing, and shelter (not even the surrounding sea); you are effectively turning the clock back by decades and even centuries, bringing the juridical concept of an island to a time where modern considerations of oil and gas in the continental shelf, and modern geopolitical considerations borne by nuclear submarines, aircraft carriers, and combat jets and bombers, are irrelevant.

The telling passage to me is paragraph 549, where the Tribunal states: "Humans have shown no shortage of ingenuity in establishing communities in the far reaches of the world, often in extremely difficult conditions. If the historical record of a feature indicates that nothing resembling a stable community has ever developed there, the most reasonable conclusion would be that the natural conditions are simply too difficult for such a community to form and that the feature is not capable of sustaining such habitation."

What this all means for the South China Sea is self-evident. None of the Spratlys, and potentially few if any islands in the Paracels, will be capable of generating expansive EEZs and continental shelves, notwithstanding all the governmental actions of the past three decades in building up military installations and communities of persons to live in those islands. In turn, this means that the semi-enclosed sea that is the South China Sea still has quite a lot of common heritage after all.

But I must add – this decision has implications far beyond this small but vital part of the world. The disputing States of the South China Sea are not the only States that are making expansive claims to their common heritage in the oceans. This also has significant implications for other countries making excessive claims, including countries like Japan and the United States (for example, the EEZ claims around Howland and Bakers islands, 1,700 nautical miles away from Honolulu).

Thus, in a very real sense, the *South China Sea* Tribunal is directly responsible for de- escalating tensions around the seas of the world and promoting world public order. Why? Because while there were many reasons for thinking that the UNCLOS never meant to support expansive claims to islands was not proper, there was no single authoritative voice that could actually say what the law is, until the Annex VII mechanism triggered what would be the *South China Sea* award. The singular importance of the *South China Sea* tribunal's contribution to international law is not that it ingeniously invented a new definition for islands, but that, in the best traditions of judicial reasoning, it took note of what, within the scope of its mandate, the possible outcomes were in its interpretation of Article 121(3), and it chose the one that best met the objectives of international peace and cooperation.

The genius of the decision was that it did so *without touching upon the question of sovereignty*. Ironically, by not being allowed to decide issues of sovereignty because of China's reservation under Article 297/98 of the Convention, the Tribunal's judgment became even more transcendent, in my view. Without deciding who was sovereign over Itu Aba, Scarborough Shoal, and the other features of the Spratlys, the Tribunal nonetheless found a way to clarify the regime of islands in a way that went a very long way towards resolving the underlying problems of the regime of islands created by UNCLOS. In so doing, the *South China Sea* may have a practical importance that outstrips even the *Island of Palmas* arbitration. The world would be better for it.

Philippines vs China: Islands after the Arbitration

Jay L. Batongbacal and Bertrand Theodor L. Santos

The Philippines filed its application for arbitration, it consciously limited its previous claims for maritime entitlements when it noted that the features were either incapable of generating additional maritime zones beyond the territorial sea or that it is best that declaration of maritime zones/entitlements beyond the territorial sea be held in abeyance pending negotiations or agreements by the claimant countries.

Prior to the arbitration, the Philippines was taking steps to harmonize its statutory laws to be compliant with the provisions of the Law of the Sea Convention, with no small opposition from Constitutionalists and Nationalists who espouse the maximalist position of invoking the Treaty of Paris of 1898 Between the US and Spain as well as full generation of maritime zones for the features in its possession. In fact, prior to the arbitration the Philippines was the object of freedom of navigation operations from its treaty ally the United States in response to what the US deems as excessive maritime claims.

This legal victory for the Philippines was made possible because it took the initiative to self-limit its claims to only what is allowed by international law as well as what seems to be practicable given the reality of multiple claimants to what is essentially an aggrupation of features located in the South China Sea. Thus, the Philippines determined that the Spratly's should not be joined to the Philippine archipelagic baselines and instead form a separate regime.

Philippines vs. China Arbitral Ruling: Defining an Island and a Rock in International Law

The tribunal seems to have started a path towards the development of a principle of international law with respect to the determination of the status of a land feature whether it is an island or a rock.

The key provision in determining the status of a feature in the discussion is Article 121 as reproduced below:

Article 121
Regime of islands

1. An island is a naturally formed area of land, surrounded by water, which is above water at high tide.
2. Except as provided for in paragraph 3, the territorial sea, the contiguous zone, the exclusive economic zone and the continental shelf of an island are determined in accordance with the provisions of this Convention applicable to other land territory.
3. Rocks which cannot sustain human habitation or economic life of their own shall have no exclusive economic zone or continental shelf.

Paragraph 3, which is the product of compromise from various positions advanced by the negotiating States, provided a standard for determining the capability of a feature to generate an EEZ and a continental shelf. However, the provision does not establish a definitive standard and is susceptible to multiple interpretations. As E.D. Brown points out, "the text is also intolerably imprecise in the meaning of 'cannot sustain human habitation or economic life of their own'."[44]

---

[44]   E.D. Brown, *The International Law of the Sea:* Volume 1: Introductory Manual (Aldershot, England and Vermont, USA: Dartmouth Publishing Company, 1994), p. 150.

The Tribunal interpreted Article 121(3) in favor of the interpretation requiring a stable human community to be considered as an island capable of supporting human habitation:

> "621. The Tribunal sees no indication that anything fairly resembling a stable human community has ever formed on the Spratly Islands. Rather, the islands have been a temporary refuge and base of operations for fishermen and a transient residence for laborers engaged in mining and fishing. The introduction of the exclusive economic zone was not intended to grant extensive maritime entitlements to small features whose historical contribution to human settlement is as slight as that. Nor was the exclusive economic zone intended to encourage States to establish artificial populations in the hope of making expansive claims, precisely what has now occurred in the South China Sea. On the contrary, Article 121(3) was intended to prevent such development and to forestall a provocative and counterproductive effort to manufacture entitlements.
>
> 622. The Tribunal sees no evidence that would suggest that the historical absence of human habitation on the Spratly Islands is the product of intervening forces or otherwise does not reflect the limited capacity of the features themselves. Accordingly, the Tribunal concludes that Itu Aba, Thitu, West York, Spratly Island, South-West Cay, and North-East Cay are not capable of sustaining human habitation within the meaning of Article 121(3). The Tribunal has also considered, and reaches the same conclusion with respect to, the other, less significant high-tide features in the Spratly Islands, which are even less capable of sustaining human habitation, but does not consider it necessary to list them individually."

With reference to the standard of capability to generate an economic life of their own the Tribunal interpreted it "to constitute the economic life of the feature, economic activity must be oriented around the feature itself and not be focused solely on the surrounding territorial sea or entirely dependent on external resources. The Tribunal also considers that extractive economic activity, without the presence of a stable local community, necessarily falls short of constituting the economic life of the feature."

> "623. In the Tribunal's view, all of the economic activity in the Spratly Islands that appears in the historical record has been essentially extractive in nature (*i.e.* mining for guano, collecting shells, and fishing), aimed to a greater or lesser degree at utilizing the resources of the Spratlys for the benefit of the populations of Hainan, Formosa, Japan, the Philippines, Viet Nam, or elsewhere. As set out above at paragraph 543, the Tribunal considers that, to constitute the economic life of the feature, economic activity must be oriented around the feature itself and not be focused solely on the surrounding territorial sea or entirely dependent on external resources. The Tribunal also considers that extractive economic activity, without the presence of a stable local community, necessarily falls short of constituting the economic life of the feature.
>
> 624. Applying this standard, the history of extractive economic activity does not constitute, for the features of the Spratly Islands, evidence of an economic life of their own. In reaching this conclusion, however, the Tribunal takes pains to emphasize that the effect of Article 121(3) is not to deny States the benefit of the economic resources of small rocks and maritime features. Such features remain susceptible to a claim of territorial sovereignty and will generate a 12-nautical-mile territorial sea, provided they remain above water at high tide. Rather, the effect of Article 121(3) is to prevent such features— whose economic benefit, if any, to the State which controls them is for resources alone—from generating a further entitlement to a 200-nautical-mile exclusive economic zone and continental shelf that would infringe on the entitlements generated by inhabited territory or on the area reserved for the common heritage of mankind

625. The Tribunal concludes that Itu Aba, Thitu, West York, Spratly Island, South-West Cay, and North-East Cay are not capable of sustaining an economic life of their own within the meaning of Article 121(3). The Tribunal has also considered, and reaches the same conclusion with respect to, the other, less significant high-tide features in the Spratly Islands, which are even less capable of sustaining economic life, but does not consider it necessary to list them individually."

Prior to the PH-CN arbitral decision, in the determination of island status, there are multiple interpretations of 121(3) based on state practice. On one hand, the UK withdrew its claim that Rockall generates an EEZ and Continental Shelf. On the other hand, Japan claims Okinotorishima as an island but is itself objected to by China, Taiwan and Korea. As Y. Tanaka puts it, "the most debatable issue is whether the legal status of islands should be qualified by socio-economic elements."[45] The function of the article 121(3) is said to be preventive in nature[46].

Conclusion

The tribunal was probably looking at the case from the point of view of finding a practical solution in the long-term, vis-à-vis the short term tensions and ill feelings the Ruling will generate from a number of States adversely affected by the Ruling's pronouncements.

---

[45] Y. Tanaka. *The International Law of the Sea*. Cambridge University Press. 2012.location. 4332

[46] *Ibid.*

Legal Status of Islands, Rocks in International Law and Countries' Practice in the South China Sea

Nguyen Quy Binh

I. REGIME OF ISLANDS IN UNCLOS

PART VIII

Article 121 Regime of islands

1. An island is a naturally formed area of land, surrounded by water, which is above water at high tide.
2. Except as provided for in paragraph 3, the territorial sea, the contiguous zone, the exclusive economic zone and the continental shelf of an island are determined in accordance with the provisions of this Convention applicable to other land territory.
3. Rocks which cannot sustain human habitation or economic life of their own shall have no exclusive economic zone or continental shelf.

Before the Arbitration Tribunal Award of July 12, 2016, the unclear definition of rocks' under Article 121 (3) of the UNCLOS may lead to different interpretations regarding the legal status of Paracels and Spratlys (as commented by Nguyen Hong Thao in one of his articles)[47]: "Unresolved questions may include: (1) What size and height would be required in order to qualify an object as an island or rock? (2) When is a rock capable of sustaining human habitation? (3) In the case of uninhabited rocks, if people and governments supply construction works, water, and food, would it be possible to meet the requirements of Article 121 (3)? (4) In relation to a rock, what is the definition of "an economic life of its own"? (5) If a lighthouse, runway, meteorological, hydrological station, bird sanctuary, a marine park, gas and oil exploration station, or other economic projects are built on a rock, would this qualify as distinct economic life? (6) Do islands and rocks have the same regime as mainland regime? (7) Can they be treated as mainland to get full territorial water rights, the EEZ, or continental shelf? and, (8) What is the effect of islands and rocks in delimiting the maritime zones of the mainland?"

Despite the international legal standing (UNCLOS) that a submerged feature or low tide elevation cannot be turned into an island that warrants maritime zones, China still insists its various geographic features are islands and tries to create facts on the ground to make them islands, as is the case now for many of the new land outcrops and improvements in the Spratly Islands.

II. RULING OF THE ARBITRAL TRIBUNAL ON THE REGIME OF DISPUTED ISLANDS IN THE SOUTH CHINA SEA

1. SUMMARY OF THE TRIBUNAL'S DECISIONS, PRESS RELEASE, (excerpt):

The Award addresses the issues of jurisdiction not decided in the Award on Jurisdiction and Admissibility and the merits of the Philippines' claims over which the Tribunal has jurisdiction. The Award is final and binding, as set out in Article 296 of the Convention and Article 11 of Annex VII.

---

[47]   Hong Thao Nguyen, 'Vietnam's position on the Sovereignty over the Paracel & the Spratlys: Its Maritime Claims', V JEAIL (2012), page 197

Historic Rights and the 'Nine-Dash Line': The Tribunal found that it has jurisdiction to consider the Parties' dispute concerning historic rights and the source of maritime entitlements in the South China Sea. On the merits, the Tribunal concluded that the Convention comprehensively allocates rights to maritime areas and that protection for pre-existing rights to resources were considered, but not adopted in the Convention. Accordingly, the Tribunal concluded that, to the extent China had historic rights to resources in the waters of the South China Sea, such rights were extinguished to the extent they were incompatible with the exclusive economic zones provided for in the Convention. The Tribunal also noted that, although Chinese navigators and fishermen, as well as those of other States, had historically made use of the islands in the South China Sea, there was no evidence that China had historically exercised exclusive control over the waters or their resources. The Tribunal concluded that there was no legal basis for China to claim historic rights to resources within the sea areas falling within the 'nine-dash line'.

Status of Features: The Tribunal next considered entitlements to maritime areas and the status of features. The Tribunal first undertook an evaluation of whether certain reefs claimed by China are above water at high tide. Features that are above water at high tide generate an entitlement to at least a 12 nautical mile territorial sea, whereas features that are submerged at high tide do not. The Tribunal noted that the reefs have been heavily modified by land reclamation and construction, recalled that the Convention classifies features on their natural condition, and relied on historical materials in evaluating the features. The Tribunal then considered whether any of the features claimed by China could generate maritime zones beyond 12 nautical miles. Under the Convention, islands generate an exclusive economic zone of 200 nautical miles and a continental shelf, but "rocks which cannot sustain human habitation or economic life of their own shall have no exclusive economic zone or continental shelf." The Tribunal concluded that this provision depends upon the objective capacity of a feature, in its natural condition, to sustain either a stable community of people or economic activity that is not dependent on outside resources or purely extractive in nature. The Tribunal noted that the current presence of official personnel on many of the features is dependent on outside support and not reflective of the capacity of the features. The Tribunal found historical evidence to be more relevant and noted that the Spratly Islands were historically used by small groups of fishermen and that several Japanese fishing and guano mining enterprises were attempted. The Tribunal concluded that such transient use does not constitute inhabitation by a stable community and that all of the historical economic activity had been extractive. Accordingly, the Tribunal concluded that none of the Spratly Islands is capable of generating extended maritime zones. The Tribunal also held that the Spratly Islands can not generate maritime zones collectively as a unit. Having found that none of the features claimed by China was capable of generating an exclusive economic zone, the Tribunal found that it could—without delimiting a boundary—declare that certain sea areas are within the exclusive economic zone of the Philippines, because those areas are not overlapped by any possible entitlement of China.

Lawfulness of Chinese Actions: The Tribunal next considered the lawfulness of Chinese actions in the South China Sea. Having found that certain areas are within the exclusive economic zone of the Philippines, the Tribunal found that China had violated the Philippines' sovereign rights in its exclusive economic zone by (a) interfering with Philippine fishing and petroleum exploration, (b) constructing artificial islands and (c) failing to prevent Chinese fishermen from fishing in the zone. The Tribunal also held that fishermen from the Philippines (like those from China) had traditional fishing rights at Scarborough Shoal and that China had interfered with these rights in restricting access. The Tribunal further held that Chinese law enforcement vessels had unlawfully created a serious risk of collision when they physically obstructed Philippine vessels.

Harm to Marine Environment: The Tribunal considered the effect on the marine environment of China's recent large-scale land reclamation and construction of artificial islands at seven features in the Spratly Islands and found that China had caused severe harm to the coral reef environment and violated its obligation to preserve and protect fragile ecosystems and the habitat of depleted, threatened, or endangered species. The Tribunal also found that Chinese authorities were aware that Chinese fishermen have harvested endangered sea turtles, coral, and giant clams on a substantial scale in the South China Sea (using methods that inflict severe damage on the coral reef environment) and had not fulfilled their obligations to stop such activities.

Aggravation of Dispute: Finally, the Tribunal considered whether China's actions since the commencement of the arbitration had aggravated the dispute between the Parties. The Tribunal found that it lacked jurisdiction to consider the implications of a standoff between Philippine marines and Chinese naval and law enforcement vessels at Second Thomas Shoal, holding that this dispute involved military activities and was therefore excluded from compulsory settlement. The Tribunal found, however, that China's recent large-scale land reclamation and construction of artificial islands was incompatible with the obligations on a State during dispute resolution proceedings, insofar as China has inflicted irreparable harm to the marine environment, built a large artificial island in the Philippines' exclusive economic zone, and destroyed evidence of the natural condition of features in the South China Sea that formed part of the Parties' dispute.

2. AN EXTENDED SUMMARY OF THE TRIBUNAL'S DECISIONS (excerpt):

The Status of Features in the South China Sea:

In its Award of 12 July 2016, the Tribunal considered the status of features in the South China Sea and the entitlements to maritime areas that China could potentially claim pursuant to the Convention.

The Tribunal first undertook a technical evaluation as to whether certain coral reefs claimed by China are or are not above water at high tide. Under Articles 13 and 121 of the Convention, features that are above water at high tide generate an entitlement to at least a 12 nautical mile territorial sea, whereas features that are submerged at high tide generate no entitlement to maritime zones. The Tribunal noted that many of the reefs in the South China Sea have been heavily modified by recent land reclamation and construction and recalled that the Convention classifies features on the basis of their natural condition. The Tribunal appointed an expert hydrographer to assist it in evaluating the Philippines' technical evidence and relied heavily on archival materials and historical hydrographic surveys in evaluating the features. The Tribunal agreed with the Philippines that Scarborough Shoal, Johnson Reef, Cuarteron Reef, and Fiery Cross Reef are high-tide features and that Subi Reef, Hughes Reef, Mischief Reef, and Second Thomas Shoal were submerged at high tide in their natural condition. However, the Tribunal disagreed with the Philippines regarding the status of Gaven Reef (North) and McKennan Reef and concluded that both are high tide features.

The Tribunal then considered whether any of the features claimed by China could generate an entitlement to maritime zones beyond 12 nautical miles. Under Article 121 of the Convention, islands generate an entitlement to an exclusive economic zone of 200 nautical miles and to a continental shelf, but "[r]ocks which cannot sustain human habitation or economic life of their own shall have no exclusive economic zone or continental shelf." The Tribunal noted that this provision was closely linked to the expansion of coastal State jurisdiction with the creation of the exclusive economic zone and was intended to prevent insignificant features from generating large entitlements to maritime zones that would infringe on the entitlements of inhabited territory or on the high seas and the area of the seabed reserved for the common heritage of mankind. The Tribunal interpreted Article 121 and concluded that the entitlements of a feature depend on (a) the objective capacity of a feature, (b) in its natural condition, to sustain either (c) a stable community of people or (d) economic activity that is neither dependent on outside resources nor purely extractive in nature.

The Tribunal noted that many features in the Spratly Islands are currently controlled by one or other of the littoral states which have constructed installations and maintain personnel there. The Tribunal considered these modern presences to be dependent on outside resources and support and noted that many of the features have been modified to improve their habitability, including through land reclamation and the construction of infrastructure such as desalination plants. The Tribunal concluded that the current presence of official personnel on many of the features does not establish their capacity, in their natural condition, to sustain a stable community of people and considered that historical evidence of habitation or economic life was more relevant to the objective capacity of the features. Examining the historical record, the Tribunal noted that the Spratly Islands were historically used by small groups of fishermen from China, as well as other States, and that several Japanese fishing and guano mining enterprises were attempted in the 1920s and 1930s. The Tribunal concluded that temporary use of the features by fishermen did not amount to inhabitation by a stable community and that all of the historical economic activity had been extractive in nature. Accordingly, the Tribunal concluded that all of the high-tide features in the Spratly Islands (including, for example, Itu Aba, Thitu, West York Island, Spratly Island, North-East Cay, South-West Cay) are legally "rocks" that do not generate an exclusive economic zone or continental shelf.

The Tribunal also held that the Convention does not provide for a group of islands such as the Spratly Islands to generate maritime zones collectively as a unit.

III. SOUTH CHINA SEA TERRITORIAL-SEA DISPUTES AND LEGAL POSITION OF THE CLAIMANTS.

China's claim:

China's claims to sovereign rights jurisdiction, and to "historic rights", with respect to the maritime areas of the South China Sea encompassed by the so-called "nine-dash line". China also claims unwarranted maritime zones through excessive strait/archipelagic baselines for occupied islands in the Paracels (Chinese law of June 15, 1996 providing straight baseline for the Paracels) and for the Spratly with vague rights based on "historic waters". China has promulgated related laws on the sea: Law 25-2-1992 on the Chinese territorial sea and contiguous zones, Law 15-6-1996 on the baseline system; Law 26-6-1998 on the Chinese exclusive economic zone and continental shelf. On May 7, 2009 China officially submitted its "nine-dash line" claim to the Commission on the Limits of the Continental Shelf (CLCS).

Chinese dredging activities: During 2013–2014 China began a substantial program of dredging and land reclamation at three sites in the Spratlys. The strategic effect of China's dredging and land reclamation makes it the most significant change to the South China Sea dispute since the 1988 Battle o f Johnson South Reef (Đá Gạc Ma). In September 2015, new satellite imagery revealed that China had completed an airfield and a 3,125-metre runway at Fiery Cross Reef (Bãi Chữ Thập). The main difference in China's activities is that they are constructing islands out of reefs that for the most part were under water at high tide. China and Taiwan have contended that Itu Aba meets the requirements for an island (versus a rock) under the articles of UNCLOS and consequently entitled to a 200 nautical mile Exclusive Economic Zone (EEZ).

Regarding the arbitration tribunal, China contends that the arbitration case is not about interpreting the United Nations Convention on the Law of the Sea (UNCLOS) with respect to maritime claims, but about the territorial sovereignty of those claims, which UNCLOS has no authority to determine. Moreover, the Tribunal itself does not have jurisdiction to determine sovereignty over geographic features in the region because its jurisdiction is limited to matters concerning the interpretation and application of UNCLOS, and again UNCLOS does not contemplate sovereignty. Lastly, Beijing asserts that Manila violated prior bilateral agreements and the 2002 ASEAN Declaration on the Conduct (DoC) of Parties in the SCS to settle maritime disputes with China through bilateral negotiation and not international arbitration.

The claim by Philippines:

The Philippines' current claim is said to be based on the Republic Act 9522 (10 March 2009) that signifies new Philippine archipelagic baselines + Republic Act 3046 (1961) as amended by Republic Act 5446 or the Philippine Baselines Law established Philippine baselines and basepoints and the Republic Act 7160 (Local Government Code of 1991) + the 1982 United Nations Convention on the Law of the Sea (Article 47 on archipelagic state and Article 121 with respect to the claimed islands in the South China sea). The Philippines recognizes that Philippine sovereignty over the waters within the baselines is subject to the rights of innocent passage and archipelagic sea lane passage, as provided for under international law.

According to Filipino legal experts, prior to Republic Act 9522, Philippine baselines law was not compliant with UNCLOS. The new archipelagic baseline system of the Philippines is composed of 101 line segments, ranging in length from 0.08 nm to 122.88 nm, with a total length of 2,808 nm. The archipelagic baseline system includes all of the Philippines' main islands and does not include Scarborough Reef or the Kalayaan Island Group.

The Philippines sent troops to the Spratly group for the first time in 1968. In April 1972, the Philippine government incorporated the Kalayaan group into Palawan Province as a municipality, and claimed in 1974 "its location rendered it strategically important to Philippine national security". On 11 June 1978, to further the claim of the Philippines on the island group, the late President Ferdinand Marcos, by virtue of Presidential Decree No.1599, formally annexed the Kalayaan Islands into the Philippines' 200-mile exclusive economic zone (EEZ). The Philippine claim extends over an area of 70,150 sq. nm. By the end of the 1970s, the Philippines had occupied a total of eight islands and two reefs. These features, such as Pagasa (Thị Tứ island), Kota (Loai Tá island), Likas (West York island),

Parola (Northeast Cay), Pugad (Southwest Cay), Lawak (Nanshan island), and two small islands, Patag (Flat island) and Panata (Lankiam Cay), excluding Southwest Cay, are still occupied by the Philippines today.

On April 8, 2009, the Philippines made a submission to the Commission on the Limits of the Continental Shelf (CLCS) concerning the continental shelf beyond 200 nm in the Benham Rise (Benham Plateau) region, east of the Philippines in the Philippine Sea. On April 12, 2012, the CLCS gave supportive recommendations concerning this submission, and on July 2, 2012, the Philippines delineated the outer limits of its continental shelf in the Benham Rise region on the basis of those recommendations. The map above depicts these outer limits of the Philippines' continental shelf claim in the south China Sea.

Malaysia's claim

Malaysia claims a small number of islands in the Spratly and contended that the islands are within its 200-miles exclusive economic zone and continental shelf, as defined by UNCLOS. Malaysia has defined the limits of its EEZ in 1979 with clear coordinates. Malaysia's argument of the islands of the South China Sea is based on *res nullius* and is said to be satisfied as when Japan renounced their sovereignty over the islands according to the San Francisco Treaty and there was a relinquishment of the right to the islands without any special beneficiary. Therefore, the islands became *res nullius* and available for annexation.

Malaysia has militarily occupied three islands that it claims. The Swallow Reef was under control in 1983 and has been turned into an island through land reclamation, which now also hosts a dive resort. The Malaysian military also occupies Ardasier Reef (*Terumbu Ubi*), and Mariveles Reef (*Terumbu Mantanani*). In 1999, Malaysia occupied Gabriela Silang Reef (Erica Reef) and Pawikan Reef (Investigator Shoal), causing the Philippines to protest. The Philippines decided to occupy Ayungin Reef (Second Thomas Reef) in 1999 due to this pressure. Together with Rizal Reef (Commodore Reef), Ayungin Reef can give the Philippines a sentry advantage in stopping other countries' occupation of features nearest to the Philippines.

Brunei claims

Brunei also claims part of the South China Sea considered as belonging to it its continental shelf and exclusive economic zone. In 1984, Brunei declared an EEZ encompassing the above-water islets it claims in Louisa Reef. Brunei states that the southern part of the Spratly Islands chain is actually a part of its continental shelf, and therefore a part of its territory and resources. Brunei does not practice military control in the area.

Vietnam's claim

Vietnam claims that it has occupied the Spratly and the Paracel islands at least since the 17th century, when they were not under the sovereignty of any state, and that they exercised sovereignty over the two archipelagos continuously and peacefully until they were invaded by Chinese armed forces and disputed by other claimants.

BD 55. Đại Nam Nhất thống toàn đồ (đời Minh mạng 1820-1841)

Vietnam has made public numerous historical evidences: "Miscellaneous Records of Pacification in the Border Area" composed by the dynasty's scholar Le Quý Đôn which defined Hoàng Sa (Paracel islands) and Trường Sa (Spratly Islands) as belonging to Quảng Ngãi District. In an atlas of Vietnam (Đại Nam nhất thống Toàn đồ － 大南一統全圖) completed in 1838 the Paracel and Spratly were shown as Vietnamese territory. Vietnam had conducted many geographical and resource surveys of the islands. The results of these surveys have been recorded in Vietnamese literature and history published since the 17th century. After the treaty signed with the Nguyễn dynasty, France represented Vietnam in international affairs and exercised sovereignty over these islands.

As regards continuous exercise of sovereignty, Vietnam's response to China's claim that the Cairo Declaration somehow recognized the latter's sovereignty over the Spratlys and that at the San Francisco Conference on the peace treaty with Japan, the Soviet Union proposed that the Paracels and Spratlys be recognized as belonging to China, but this proposal was rejected by an overwhelming majority of the delegates. On 7 July 1951, Tran Van Huu, head of the Bảo Đại Government's delegation of Vietnam to the conference declared that the Paracels and Spratlys were part of Vietnamese territory. This declaration met with no challenge from the 51 representatives at the conference. After the 1954 Geneva Accord when the French Indochina was split into three countries (Laos, Cambodia, Vietnam) and Vietnam was temporarily divided along the 17th Parallel; the Republic of Vietnam (RVN) exercised sovereignty over the Paracels and Spratly islands, placed border markers on the archipelagos and held military control over the majority of the Spratly Islands until 1975. After the Vietnam War, the unified Vietnam continued to claim the Paracels and Spratly islands as an integral part of its territory.

With regard to legislation, on 21 July 2012, the National Assembly of Vietnam passed the law on maritime zones of Vietnam, in which the status of islands has been provided along the line of Article 121 of UNCLOS: "Islands must be above water at high tide" (Article 19); "Islands which can sustain human habitation or economic life of their own have internal waters, territorial seas, contiguous zones, exclusive economic zones and continental shelves" (Article 20.1); "Rocks which cannot sustain human habitation or economic life of their own have no exclusive economic zone or continental shelf" (Article 20.2). This indicates that Vietnam has somehow redefined its legal position away from its previous position but still considers some offshore islands may entitle to have exclusive economic zones and continental shelves of themselves. Dated back to the legal position stated in the 12/5/1977 Government Statement regarding the maritime zones, Vietnam generally considers that the off-shore islands of Vietnam are entitled to have the territorial sea, contiguous zone, EEZ and continental shelf of their own (Point 5). Meanwhile, Point 4 of the Government Statement on 12/11/1982 also mentions that the territorial baselines for Hoang Sa (Paracel) and Truong Sa (Spratly) archipelagos shall be provided in a separate document, in accordance with Point 5 of the May 12, 1977 Government Statement. This, however, has not been realized. In light of the final award of the Arbitration Tribunal and given the contended maximum positions of different related claimants in the South China Sea, it is interesting to see how Vietnam might articulate its official legal position on "the ruling contents of the Arbitration Tribunal" as said/stated by the Foreign Ministry spokesman on July 12, 2016.

On 6 May 2009, Vietnam made a joint submission with Malaysia to the UN's Commission on the Limits of the Continental Shelf (CLCS) under UNCLOS, on the outer limit of their continental shelf claim beyond 200 miles. The joint submission by Malaysia and Vietnam lays mutual claim on continental shelf in the southern part of the South China Sea. The two countries declared that the joint submission involved only a portion of the outer limits of their continental margin, and contended that they reserve the right to make later submissions, either jointly or individually.

Malaysia and Vietnam acknowledged that there are unresolved disputes in the area under the submission, and emphasized that the submission does not "prejudice matters relating to the delimitation of boundaries between States with opposite or adjacent coasts." Vietnam also unilaterally submitted its continental shelf claim with respect to the northern part in South China Sea. Vietnam describes this "Northern boundary" limit as the equidistance line between the territorial sea baselines of Vietnam and the territorial sea baselines of the People's Republic of China. During the presentation before the CLCS, Vietnam declared that Vietnam's claim does not overlap with those of other coastal states. Vietnam further stated that the submission is "without prejudice to the maritime delimitation between Vietnam and other relevant coastal states."

IV. VIETNAM'S PRACTICE IN NEGOTIATING THE LEGAL STATUS OF OFF- SHORE ISLANDS IN THE SOUTH CHINA SEA

1. Sea boundary agreement with Thailand

There existed (before the conclusion of the sea boundary delimitation agreement in August 1997) an overlapping area between *Vietnam and Thailand* totaling 6074 km2 in the Gulf of Thailand resulted from maximum overlapping claims of two sides. Thailand claimed in May 1973 a median line between the two opposite coasts, and intentionally ignored the Vietnamese Tho Chu archipelago and Poulo Wai Island of Cambodia. In contrast the claim of (South) Vietnam in 1971 constituted a median line between offshore islands of Tho Chu and Poulo Wai and the opposite coast of Thailand without taking into account Ko Kra and Ko Losin rocks of Thailand. On 19 August 1992, Thailand added the rocks Ko Kra and Ko Losin to their baseline announced previously on 11 June 1970. These are uninhabitable formations of 1.5m above water at high tide, without appreciable economic life of their own.

Figure 1
Claims to Maritime Jurisdiction in the Gulf of Thailand

Source: Andi Arsana.

The two countries entered into official and substantive negotiations in 1992, first to determine the overlapping area and then discussed the effect of offshore islands of both sides for delineating the sea boundary. Negotiations on the effect of offshore islands were indeed the nutshell for an agreed delineation solution. Throughout the process, Thailand was indicating that Tho Chu archipelago should carry a weight of not more than a one-quarter effect, while accepted Ko Kra and Ko Losin of Thailand as rocks. Agreement was finally reached after 9 rounds held in 7 years, which grants Vietnam with 32.5% of the overlapping area (indicating a similar effect of Tho Chu islands). The two sides also agreed that the delineated line constitutes a single boundary for both the continental shelf and EEZ between Thailand and Vietnam. In the meantime, fishery issue, joint navy patrol, and agreement to treat any single oil field or gas structure that extends across the boundary line are also settled. The agreement was officially signed on 9 August 1997 and came into force on 27 February 1998. This maritime boundary agreement was the first agreement Vietnam concluded with neighboring countries. It also constitutes the first pact in South East Asia since the coming into force of 1982 UNCLOS. The result of the Thai- Vietnamese negotiations reflects the goodwill and determination of both countries to implement UNCLOS 1982, of which both Thailand and Vietnam are signatories

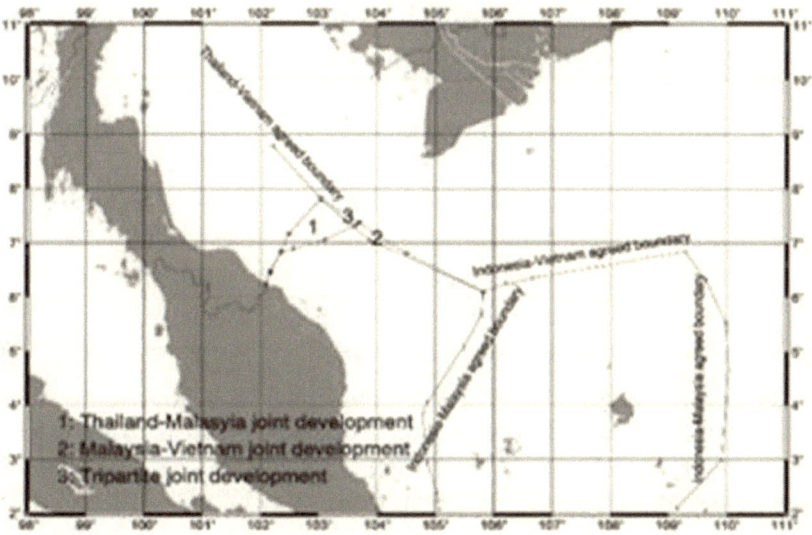

2. Vietnam - Cambodia agreement on historic waters:

Vietnam and its neighbor Cambodia have adjacent sea areas. Two countries used to have historic disputes regarding their sovereignty over some coastal islands; and their overlapping claims relating to the territorial sea, exclusive economic zone and continental shelf, are yet to be resolved.

On July 7, 1982, Cambodia and Vietnam signed an agreement claiming part of the Gulf of Thailand as historic waters. This agreement covers the area of 8000 square kilometers extending from the mainland to Tho Chu and Poulo Wai Islands, within their territorial baselines. The United States has made an objection to the agreement and views the historic claim to the waters in question as without foundation and reserves its rights and those of its nationals in this regard.

Also under this agreement, the two countries have agreed to use "the Brévie Line", which was an administrative line adopted by Governor Brévie in 1939, to become the dividing line for the coastal islands belonging to each country. By this agreement, the long-standing dispute between the two sides over the islands near the coast has been settled.

It was also agreed in the above said agreement that the two countries would continue to negotiate to settle their maritime overlapping claims in other area at a suitable time.

The Cambodian side has also shown, on several occasions, its intended claim on the territorial delineation line, linking it with the "Brévie Line" running around the Phu Quoc island of Vietnam.

3. Joint exploitation arrangement between Vietnam and Malaysia

There is an overlap of 2800 square kilometers in the Gulf of Thailand created by the claims of Vietnam in 1971 and Malaysia in 1979, respectively. The overlapping area is quite small since there exist no significant offshore islands on both sides' coasts. The Vietnamese continental shelf limit was proclaimed in 1971 by the then South Vietnamese government and was the equidistant line between the mainlands of Malaysia and Vietnam without taking into account offshore islands. Malaysia's claim is made through a territorial sea and continental shelf map published by its Mapping and Survey Department in 1979 showing the boundary, drawn as the equidistant line between Malaysia's Redang Island and the Vietnamese shore, ignoring islands off its coast.

Vietnam and Malaysia began negotiations in 1992. Since there appeared no possibility for early agreement on delimitation and in view of Malaysia' s already action to contract its national petroleum company to develop commercial exploitation of this oil-rich area, Vietnam and Malaysia then agreed to proceed with petroleum joint development.

Figure 1
Claims to Maritime Jurisdiction in the Gulf of Thailand

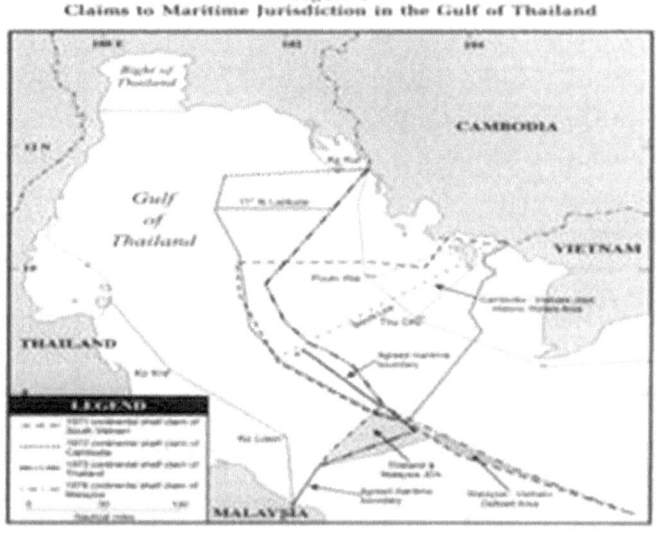

Source: Andi Arsana.

According to the 5 June 1992 agreement, the two sides nominated their national petroleum company, namely PetroVietnam and Petronas respectively, to discuss commercial arrangement on the principle of equality in rights and obligations. On 29 July 1997 the first barrel of oil was extracted from the area out of Joint development activity, contributing to the enhancement of bilateral economic and political relations.

In addition to the bilaterally overlapping area, there also exists a tripartite overlapping area between Vietnam, Malaysia, and Thailand (875 square kilometers, see the map below). Negotiations began in 1997 to re-define the overlapping area and agreement was reached on the principle of joint development of the "Defined Area". They have now come to technical discussion regarding a detailed joint development framework.

4. Determination of Vietnam-Indonesia continental shelf

The overlapping continental shelf was created by South Vietnam's 1971 claim based on the theory of natural prolongation of the landmass, and Indonesia's 1968 claim based on the concept of archipelagic state (Indonesia promulgated its archipelagic baseline in 1960, 22 years before UNCLOS). In drawing the outer limit with Vietnam, Indonesia uses the equidistant point between its furthest Northern off-shore island called "Small Natuna" and the Conson islands of Vietnam as a base (lavishly allowing the Conson islands 100% effect). Vietnam claimed its outer limit using the equidistant line between the Vietnamese and Borneo coasts. The overlapping area totals almost 37,000 square kilometers to the South-East of South China Sea.

The first round of negotiation were initiated in 1972 with South Vietnam, without substantive result. Negotiation with unified Vietnam started after 1975.

During the 1990s there was no progress made in negotiating the maritime disputes between Indonesia and Vietnam, but stability was maintained. This state of affairs continued into the early 2000s until a breakthrough was made leading to the agreement of June 2003 settling the maritime dispute relating to overlapping continental shelf claims between the two countries. After around 25 years of negotiation, the two countries eventually concluded their continental shelf boundary in the South China Sea. However, the EEZ boundary in the same area needs to be settled. Different with the case with Thailand, in Vietnam-Indonesia bilateral talks, the continental shelf and EEZ have been treated as separate issues. After the completion of the ratification process the Agreement entered into force on 29 May 2007. Negotiation on the exclusive economic zone has yet to begin. It is noted that Indonesian marine patrols have sometimes arrested Vietnamese fishermen alleged to be illegally fishing in Indonesian waters.

5. The Tonkin Gulf Agreement with China

The Tonkin Gulf is a large gulf with total area of 126,250 square kilometers (36,000 square nautical miles). Its width, at the maximum, is about 310 kilometers (176 nautical miles) and the narrowest breadth is around 207.4 kilometers (112 nautical miles). The Gulf consists of two mouths, one on the Northwest, namely "Qiong Zhou" strait, and the other on the South extending 207.4 kilometers in width from Cồn Cỏ island (of Viet Nam) to Hainan island (off China).

The Gulf contains, on the Vietnamese side, about 2300 small coastal islands and rocks (with Halong Bay as world heritage site). Notably, there exists in the middle of the gulf the "Bach Long Vi" island (White Dragon Tail), 110 km (50 nautical miles) from Vietnam's mainland and 130 kilometers from Hainan Island in China. On the Chinese side, it possesses a few small islands in the Northeast of the Gulf including "Wei Zhou" and "Xie Yang".

The negotiations on delimitation of the Tonkin Gulf between Vietnam and China started as early as 1974, but failed to reach the substantive stage until 1992, a year after normalization of bilateral relations in 1991. The negotiations lasted for 27 years, with 18 rounds of technical level plus 10 meetings at governmental level and many of Joint Working-Mapping Team (totally 49 meetings in all, and about 5 meetings on average each year).

On December 25th, 2000, the Agreement on Delimitation of the Tonkin Gulf was signed by the foreign ministers of Viet Nam and China in Beijing, marking the successful conclusion of lengthy negotiations. The delineated line contains 21 points, based on a equidistant line but then adjusted for equity, consisting of territorial waters boundary (point 1 to 9) and the rest for EEZ and continental shelves (point 10 to 21). According to the Agreement, Viet Nam is entitled to 53.23% of the Gulf's total area and China 46.77%; but outside observers note that the maritime boundary is closer to the Vietnamese than the Chinese coast.

During negotiations in the 1990s, Vietnam abandoned its initial claims of historic waters in the Gulf of Tonkin, and China also abandoned its proposal of a neutral zone in the shape of a rectangle in the middle of the gulf within which no exploration or exploitation should take place. Vietnam agreed not to give full effect to one of its islands, Bach Long Vi, which is 2.5 sq km, 62 meters above the sea level and approximately 50 nm from Vietnam. Bach Long Vi was given a 25% effect on the delimitation line. It is estimated that the difference between an equidistance line using Bach Long Vi as a base point and one ignoring the island completely is approximately 1,700 sq km. The Vietnamese islet of Con Co was given half effect in the southern areas of the Gulf of Tonkin. Other Vietnamese

Islands such as Co To and Quan Lan were given some but not full effect in the inner reaches of the Gulf. Further, both Vietnam and China agreed upon a common fishing zone, which made it easier for China to agree to a boundary line in the middle of the Gulf.

Sovereignty Assertion in the South China Sea: Militarization and the Construction of Artificial Islands

Carlyle A. Thayer[48]

Introduction

The South China Sea is a semi-enclosed sea that links the Indian Ocean with the Western Pacific. The security of sea lanes passing through it are vital for global commerce. It is estimated that more than US$5.3 trillion in commerce passes through the South China Sea annually. In addition, secure passage through and over flight are vital for the world's major maritime

[48] This paper draws on Carlyle A. Thayer, 'The Militarisation of the South China Sea,' in *Asia-Pacific Regional Security Assessment 2016: Key Developments and Trends* (London and Singapore: International Institute of Security Studies, 2016), 55-72; and Carlyle A. Thayer, 'The Militarisation of the South China Sea,' Presentation to International Conference on The Challenges to Peace and Security in the South China Sea,' co-organised by the Malaysian International Affairs Forum and HELP University, The Westin, Kuala Lumpur, July 28, 2016.

powers. The security of the sea-lanes, as well as the freedom of navigation and over flight by civilian and military ships and aircraft, are threatened by sovereignty and maritime disputes by the construction of artificial islands on rocks and low tide elevations in the Spratly Islands and their militarization. Any outbreak of conflict that disrupts the security of the sea-lanes would have an immediate and serious impact on the world's economy.

This paper provides an analytic overview of militarization and the construction of artificial islands in the South China Sea by five claimants: China, Taiwan, Malaysia, the Philippines, and Vietnam. The paper is divided into four parts. Part one provides an introduction. Part two considers what is meant by the term militarization. The paper argues that militarization constitutes a spectrum of activities from deploying military forces on a particular feature to making preparations for war. Along this spectrum there is a grey area where activity such as constructing airfields, piers and ports can serve both civilian and military roles. The paper argues that the placement of fighter aircraft, bombers, anti-ship missiles, amphibious landing ships and naval warships constitutes militarization at the high end of the scale and threatens regional peace and security. Part three discusses what military forces, weapons, and equipment have been placed on the features (rocks and low tide elevations) in the Spratly islands by the five claimants. Part four, the conclusion, discusses the implications for regional security following the award by the Arbitral Tribunal that heard the claims of The Philippines v China.

What Constitutes Militarization?

This section examines four sets of issues: (1) sovereignty assertion, (2) military activities in the South China Sea by the United States and China, (3) the war of words between the United States and China over who was responsible for the militarization of the South China Sea and (4) how to define militarization.

Sovereignty Assertion. The concept of sovereignty is generally associated in western literature on international relations with Jean Bodin's *Six Books of a Commonwealth* (1576), and more particularly the Treaty of Westphalia in 1648.[49] Sovereignty in this context refers to internal political

---

[49] Richard Falk, 'Sovereignty,' in Joel Krieger et al. eds, *The Oxford Companion to Politics of the World*, 2nd Edition (Oxford: Oxford University Press, 2001), 789-791.

arrangements in a state within a defined territory and with sovereign states as equal actors in the international system. In customary international law sovereignty is associated with the occupation and continuous administration over land territories including islands and rocks in the maritime domain.

For purposes of this paper 'sovereignty assertion' refers to actions by claimant states to physically occupy and build on features in the South China Sea to demonstrate continuous administration and thus claim sovereignty over these features. Sovereignty assertion also refers to the actions by states to assert sovereign jurisdiction over maritime zones adjacent to the features that they occupy.

The 1982 United Nations Convention on the Law of the Sea (UNCLOS), Article 121, provided a legal definition distinguishing between islands and rocks:

1. An island is a naturally formed area of land, surrounded by water, which is above water at high tide.
2. Except as provided for in paragraph 3, the territorial sea, the contiguous zone, the exclusive economic zone and the continental shelf of an island are determined in accordance with the provisions of this Convention applicable to other land territory.
3. Rocks which cannot sustain human habitation or economic life of their own shall have no exclusive economic zone or continental shelf.[50]

The Arbitral Tribunal that heard the claims of the Philippines against China ruled on the status of some of the features in the South China Sea (see discussion below). This award determined the maritime entitlements of islands and rocks that were the subject of dispute. States can only claim sovereignty over islands and rocks but not over low-tide elevations. Low-tide elevations are not subject to appropriation and their legal status cannot be changed by subsequent construction such as building artificial islands.

Because China refuses to accept the award of the Arbitral Tribunal and has pledged to defend its 'sovereignty' in the South China Sea the scene is

---

[50] United Nations Convention on the Law of the Sea, Part VIII, 66, UNCLOS came into force in 1994; http://www.un.org/depts/los/convention_agreements/texts/unclos/unclos_e.pdf.

now set for further assertions of sovereignty by China and confrontations with littoral states.

Military Activities in The South China Sea. In recent years the People's Liberation Army Navy (PLAN) has stepped up its annual military exercises in the South China Sea. According to a study by the Center for the Study of Chinese Military Affairs, the PLAN's North Sea Fleet conducted two operations between 2007 and 2009, the PLAN's North and South Sea Fleets conducted one operation each between 2010 and 2012 and eight operations between 2013 and 2014.[51] In late 2015, China conducted large-scale naval exercises that included war games that simulated long-distance assaults and landing operations. Other war games included live fire drills by surface ships simulating attacks on submarines.[52]

According to one security analyst, the PLA Navy Air Force 'is pretty active in the area with a regiment each of H-6 bombers and JH-7 fighter bombers and no fewer than three regiments of J-11 interceptors covering the South China Sea.' The long range J-11s and availability of aerial refueling aircraft 'implies that much of the SCS [South China Sea] is now de-facto Chinse airspace.'[53]

While China claims it does not interfere with freedom of navigation and over flight, its actions indicate otherwise. While China does not interfere with international commercial shipping that passes through the

---

[51]   Christopher H. Sharman, 'China Moves Out: Stepping Stones Toward a New Maritime Strategy,' *China Strategic Perspectives*, Washington, D.C.: Center for the Study of Chinese Military Affairs, Institute for National Strategic Studies, National Defense University, 2015. http://inss.ndu.edu/Portals/68/Documents/stratperspective/china/ChinaPerspectives-9.pdf.

[52]   'Disagreements over the South China Sea worsen as China digs in,' *The Economist*, 26 November 2015. http://www.economist.com/news/asia/21679265-chinas-hard-line-disputed-waters-shows-no-sign-softening-disagreements-over-south and Bill Geertz. 'War of words over South China Sea militarization heats up,' *Asia Times*, 30 November 2015. http://atimes.com/2015/11/war-of-words-over-south-china-sea-militarization-heats-up/.

[53]   Andreas Rupprecht, author of *Flashpoint China: Chinese Air Power and Regional Security* (Harpia Publishers, 2016) quoted in David Cenciotti, 'The U.S. Build-Up in the Disputed Waters of South China Sea Continues with Bombers, Carriers and Electronic Attack Planes,' *The Aviationist*, 19 June 2016. https://theaviationist.com/2016/06/19/things-heat-up-near-south-china-sea-two-u-s-aircraft-carriers-b-52s-and-ea-18g-growler-detachment/.

South China Sea, China does interfere with freedom of navigation of foreign military ships and aircraft by warning them they are entering a military security zone and threatening the safety of Chinese forces.

According to Admiral Scott Swift, Commander of the U.S. Pacific Fleet, routine commercial shipping that had previously sailed freely through international sea lanes in the South China Sea were being diverted from areas close to China's artificial islands. In addition, military operations in the South China Sea also had become subject to warnings to such an extent that China's 'unilateral assertiveness' was becoming 'unacceptable.'[54]

Further, according to Admiral Swift, fishermen from the region were 'intimidated by the manner in which some navies, coast guards and maritime military enforce claims in contested waters, fishermen who trawled the seas freely for generations are facing threats to their livelihoods imposed by nations with unresolved and often unrecognized claims.'[55] Although China was not mentioned by name, his reference to 'some navies' obviously referred to China.

Under the Obama Administration's policy of rebalancing towards the Asia-Pacific, the United States has increased its military presence in the South China Sea. IN September 2012, for example, two Carrier Strike Groups led by the USS *George Washington* (CVN 73) and USS *Carl Vinson* (CVN 70) combined to conduct dual carrier operations in the South China Sea. The U.S. also deployed four Littoral Combat Ships to Singapore, staged Poseidon P-8A reconnaissance flights out the Philippines, Malaysia and Singapore and over flights of the South China Sea by B-52 bombers. According to Admiral Harris '(e)verything that is new and cool is going to the Pacific' such as F-35s, DD-1000s, a Ford-class nuclear aircraft carrier, V-22 Ospreys and P-8A Poseidons.[56]

---

54 'U.S. Pacific Fleet commander says militarization in South China Sea is "unacceptable",' *Honolulu Star Advertiser*, 15 December 2015, http://www.staradvertiser.com/breaking-news/u-s-pacific-fleet-commander-says-militarization-in-south-china-sea-is-unacceptable/.

55 Ibid.

56 John Grady, 'PACOM CO Harris: More U.S. South China Sea Freedom of Navigation Missions Are Coming,' *USNI News*, January 27, 2016. http://news.usni.org/2016/01/27/pacom-co-harris-more-u-s-south-china-sea-freedom-of-navigation-missions-are-coming. The DD-1000 is a *Zumwalt*-class guided missile stealth destroyer designed as a multi-mission platform with a focus on land attack.

There is a crucial difference between Chinese and U.S. military activities in the South China Sea. China continually deploys Coast Guard vessels and PLAN warships in and around the Spratly islands on a permanent basis to assert its sovereignty. China's presence at Second Thomas Shoal, for example, was deemed to be a 'military activity' by the Arbitral Tribunal and therefore outside its jurisdiction. U.S. freedom of navigation operational patrols specifically challenge excessive claims to maritime zones and are not assertions of U.S. sovereignty. U.S. freedom of navigation operational and other patrols are transient in nature.

All other U.S. military activities are at the consent of regional states. When U.S. military ships and aircraft make port visits, carry out exercises or rotate through ports and airfields then come under the sovereign jurisdiction of the host country. The United States operates from Singapore, Indonesia, and Malaysia at the consent of their governments. U.S. forces in the Philippines come under the authority of a bilateral Visiting Forces Agreement signed on 9 October 1998.[57] The U.S. has been granted access to military ports and airfields in the Philippines on a rotational basis under the terms of the bilateral Enhanced Defence Cooperation Agreement signed in 2015. In recent years, small-scale amphibious drills have been carried out by armed forces from the U.S. and Philippines.

Long-standing U.S. military exercises with regional states under the Cooperation Afloat and Readiness and Training (CARAT) program are bilateral and are focused on capacity-building and cooperation in humanitarian assistance and disaster relief and are conducted with the agreement of the participating country.

Scarborough Shoal and Arbitral Tribunal Award. In March–April 2016 the United States reported unusual Chinese survey activities near Scarborough Shoal.[58] Classified reports from Australia's intelligence and analytic agencies leaked to the media stated that Beijing was poised to take 'decisive and provocative action,' suggesting that China was about

---

[57] The text may be found at
http://www.state.gov/documents/organization/107852.pdf.

[58] David Brunnstrom and Andrea Shalal, 'Exclusive: US sees new Chinese activity around South China Sea shoal,' Reuters, 18 March 2016, http://www.reuters.com/article/us-southchinasea-china-scarborough-exclu-idUSKCN0WK01B.

to commence the construction of a seventh artificial island on the rocks comprising Scarborough Shoal.[59]

The United States successfully deterred China by signaling it would oppose this course of action. In late April, the United States deployed a temporary detachment of five U.S. Air Force A-10C Warthog ground attack aircraft, three HH-60G Pave Hawk helicopters and four U.S. Navy electronic warfare EA-18G Growler aircraft to the Philippines.[60] The Warthogs flew air patrols near Scarborough Shoal.[61] The Growlers are equipped to detect, jam and destroy enemy radar emissions and communications systems.[62] Finally, also in June, the United States dispatched two carrier strike groups, CSG 3 and CSG 5, to conduct dual carrier flight operations and to 'practice war-fighting techniques that are required in modern naval operations' in the waters off the eastern coast of the Philippines.'[63]

CSG 3 included the Nimitiz-class USS *John C. Stennis* (CVN 74), Carrier Wing 9, the guided missile cruiser USS *Mobile Bay* and Destroyer Squadron 2 comprising the guided missile destroyers USS

---

[59] Carl Thayer, 'Australian Intelligence: China Poised to Take 'Decisive and Provocative' Action in the South China Sea,' *The Diplomat*, 15 April 2016. http://thediplomat.com/2016/04/australian-intelligence-china-poised-to-take-decisive-and-provocative-action-in-the-south-china-sea/.

[60] Michael Mazza, 'The odd couple: Warthogs & Growlers in the South China Sea,' American Enterprise Institute, 17 June 2016. https://www.aei.org/publication/the-odd-couple-warthogs-growlers-in-the-south-china-sea/.

[61] Jesse Johnson, 'U.S. sails carriers near South China Sea in bid to reassure Asian allies,' *The Japan Times*, 19 June 2016. http://www.japantimes.co.jp/news/2016/06/19/asia-pacific/u-s-sails-carriers-near-south-china-sea-bid-reassure-asian-allies/#.V6e0tsLr3IU.

[62] Kathlene Faith Manalo, 'South China Sea War: US Sends Four Attack Aircraft, Troop to Bolster Philippine Defenses?,' *Morning Ledger*, 17 June 2016. http://www.morningledger.com/south-china-sea-war-us-sends-four-attack-aircrafts-troops-to-bolster-philippine-defenses/1379485/.

[63] Jane Perlez, 'U.S. Carriers Sail in Western Pacific, Hoping China Takes Notice,' *The New York Times*, 18 June 2016, http://www.nytimes.com/2016/06/19/world/asia/us-carriers-sail-in-western-pacific-hoping-china-takes-notice.html?_r=0, and Nikko Dizon, 'US superforce patrolling PH Sea,' *Philippine Daily Enquirer*, 19 June 2016, http://globalnation.inquirer.net/140282/us-superforce-patrolling-ph-sea.

Stockdale, USS *Chung-Hoon* and USS *William P. Lawrence*. CSG 5 included the USS *Ronald Reagan* (CVN 76) super carrier, Carrier Air Wing 5, the guided missile cruisers USS *Shiloh* and USS *Chancellorsville* and Destroyer Squadron 15 comprising the guided missile destroyers USS *Curtis Wilbur*, USS *McCampbell* and USS *Benford*. According to Rear Admiral Marcus Hitchcock, commander of CSG 3, 'no other Navy can concentrate this much combat power on one sea or synchronize the activities of over 12,000 sailors, 140 aircraft, six combatants and two carriers.'[64]

In addition, prior to the award by the Arbitral Tribunal, the United States deployed three destroyers, the USS *Stethem*, USS *Spruance* and the USS *Momsen*, to demonstrate 'routine presence' in the South China Sea by sailing regularly within fourteen to twenty nautical miles of China's artificial features.[65] According to Bonnie Glaser, U.S. Navy ships spent more than seven hundred days in the South China Sea in 2015 and were likely to log up one thousand days in 2016. Glaser observed '9o0n any given day you are seeing two or more ships operating in the South China Sea.'[66]

Immediately prior to the 12 July deadline, China declared a 38,000 square mile 'no sail zone' in the waters between southern Hainan Island and the Paracels and conducted naval exercised from 5-11 July. Further military exercises were carried out in the same area after the Arbitral Tribunal rendered its award. China also announced on 18 July that it was conducting combat air patrols over the South China Sea including Scarborough Shoal by maritime reconnaissance planes, early warning aircraft, refueling planes,

---

64   Quoted in Dizon, 'US superforce patrolling PH Sea.'
65   David Larter, 'U.S. Navy destroyers stalk China's claims in South China Sea,' *Navy Times*, 6 July 2016, http://www.navytimes.com/story/military/2016/07/06/us-navy-destroyers-stalk-chinas-claims-south-china-sea/86777268/. One Virginia-class attack submarine, the USS *Mississippi*, (SSN 782), visited South Korea on its first deployment to the Indo-Pacific.
66   Quoted in Larter, 'U.S. Navy destroyers stalk China's claims in South China Sea.'

Su-30 jet fighters and H-6K long-range bombers.[67] Most recently, China announced that the PLAN would hold combined naval exercises –Joint-Sea 2016 – with Russia in the South China Seas in September.[68]

The above developments highlight that rivalry between China and the United States has intensified and forms the strategic overlay covering bilateral maritime disputes in the South China Sea.

The War of Words Over Militarization. In 2014 China began to implement a master plan to expand and consolidate its presence in the South China Sea. China transformed seven rocks and low tide elevations that it occupied into artificial islands. In the space of eighteen months China dredged and pumped sand from the seabed and coral ripped out of nearby reefs on its tiny features until they encompassed an area twelve square kilometres in size. [69] This contrasts with the efforts by other claimants – Taiwan, Vietnam, Malaysia and the Philippines – who expanded their land area by 0.4 square kilometres over four and a half decades.[70]

In 2015, the pace and scope of China's construction activities picked up markedly. China began to build infrastructure including airstrips and

---

[67] Jesse Johnson, 'Chinese Air Force flies "combat patrols" over Spratlys, Scarborough Shoal in South China Sea,' *The Japan Times*, 6 August 2016, http://www.japantimes.co.jp/news/2016/08/06/asia-pacific/chinese-air-force-flies-combat-patrols-over-spratlys-scarborough-shoal-in-south-china-sea/, and Levi Winchester, 'China sends fighter jets and bombers as bitter row over South China Sea intensifies,' *Sunday Express*, 7 August 2016, http://www.express.co.uk/news/world/697332/South-China-Sea-row-fighter-jets-bombers-Japan.

[68] Chris Buckley, 'Russia to Join China in Naval Exercise in Disputed South China Sea,' *The New York Times*, 29 July 2016, http://www.nytimes.com/2016/07/29/world/asia/russia-china-south-china-sea-naval-exercise.html? r=0, and Jeremy Page, 'China, Russia set up for naval war games,' *The Wall Street Journal* reprinted in *The Weekend Australian*, 30-31 July 2016, http://www.theaustralian.com.au/business/wall-street-journal/china-russia-set-up-for-naval-war-games-in-south-china-sea/news-story/fd17160956a793719199e3b9cd10124d.

[69] Admiral Harry Harris, Commander of the U.S. Pacific Command, quoted in 'China Accuses US of Militarizing South China Sea,' Voice of America News, 30 July 2015, http://www.voanews.com/content/china-accuses-us-of-militarizing-south-china-sea/2886799.html.

[70] Ibid.

---

multistory buildings. On 30 May, U.S. Secretary of Defense Ashton Carter addressed the Shangri-La Dialogue in Singapore and stated:

> The United States is deeply concerned about the pace and scope of land reclamation in the South China Sea, the prospect of further militarization, as well as the potential for these activities to increase the risk of miscalculation or conflict among claimant states. As a Pacific nation, a trading nation and a member of the international community, the United States has every right to be involved and concerned.[71]

Secretary Carter's remarks at the Shangri-La Dialogue set off a war of words over the militarization of the South China Sea between Chinese and United States that continues to the present. Two separate issues became entangled in this exchange: the purpose of the infrastructure being built on China's artificial islands, and U.S. freedom of navigation operational patrols (FONOP). In late July, for example, Yang Yujun, a spokesperson for China's Ministry of National Defence, stated, 'The Chinese side expresses its serious concern over U.S. activities to militarize the South China Sea region.'[72] Yang singled out U.S. naval patrols and joint military exercises for raising regional tensions. His remarks were a reference to the 20 May flight of a U.S. Navy P-8A Poseidon aircraft near Fiery Cross, Subi and Mischief reefs and the 18 July flight of another Poseidon over the area carrying Admiral Swift.[73]

In August 2015, at a private meeting between U.S. Secretary of State John Kerry and China's Foreign Minister Wang Yi on the sidelines of the

[71] Dr. Ashton Carter, United States Secretary of Defense, 'The United States and Challenges to Asia-Pacific Security,' IISS-Shangri-La Dialogue First Plenary Section, 14th Asia Security Summit, Singapore, 30 May 2015, https://www.iiss.org/en/events/shangri%20la%20dialogue/archive/shangri-la-dialogue-2015-862b/plenary1-976e/carter-7fa0.

[72] Associated Press, 'China Accuses US of Militarizing South China Sea,' Voice of America News, 30 July 2015, http://www.voanews.com/content/ap-china-accuses-us-of-militarizing-south-china-sea/3197818.html.

[73] Jim Sciutto, 'Behind the scenes: A secret Navy flight over China's military buildup,' 26 May 2015, http://edition.cnn.com/2015/05/26/politics/south-china-sea-navy-surveillance-plane-jim-sciutto/.

Association of Southeast Asian Nations (ASEAN) Regional Forum in Kuala Lumpur, Secretary Kerry raised concerns about 'China's large-scale reclamation, construction, and militarization of features' and called for all claimants 'to halt problematic actions.'[74] Wang Yi counter-charged the U.S. with militarizing the South China Sea by staging joint patrols and military drills with its regional allies and stepping up its use of military bases in the Philippines.[75] Wang further stated the U.S. and the Philippines should 'count how many runways there are in the South China Sea and who built them first.'[76]

On 25 September, President Xi Jinping made an official visit to Washington, D.C. At a joint press conference after his meeting with President Barack Obama, Xi stated, 'Relevant construction activities that China is undertaking in the Nansha [Spratly] islands do not target or impact any country and China does not intend to pursue militarization'.[77]

On 4 November, after the conclusion of the 3rd ASEAN Defence Ministers' Meeting-Plus (ADMM-Plus), Secretary Carter urged 'all claimants to permanently halt land reclamation, stop the construction of

---

[74]   Lindsay Murdoch, 'Beijing says building has stopped in South China Sea, but tensions remain at ASEAN,' *The Sydney Morning Herald*, 6 August 2015, http://www.smh.com.au/world/beijing-says-building-has-stopped-in-south-china-sea-but-tensions-remain-at-asean-20150805-gisjyq.html.

[75]   David Brunnstrom and Trinna Leong, 'Kerry raises South China Sea concerns with China's Wang,' Reuters, 5 August 2015, http://www.reuters.com/article/asean-malaysia-idusKCN0QA06C20150805.

[76]   Lindsay Murdoch, 'South China Sea island-building tensions rise at ASEAN talks,' *The Sydney Morning Herald*, 5 August 2015, http://www.smh.com.au/world/south-china-sea-islandbuilding-tensions-rise-at-asean-talks-20150804-girriu.html and Matthew Lee and Eileen Ng, Associated Press, 'US, China bicker over territorial claims in South China Sea,' *The Courier*, 5 August 2015, http://www.northjersey.com/news/u-s-china-bicker-over-territorial-claims-in-south-china-sea-1.1386751.

[77]   Jeremy Page, Carol E. Lee and Gordon Lubold, 'China's President Pledges No Militarization in Disputed Islands,' *The Wall Street Journal*, 25 September 2015. http://www.wsj.com/articles/china-completes-runway-on-artificial-island-in-south-china-sea-1443184818.

new facilities and cease further militarization of disputed features.'[78] Hua Chunying, spokesperson for China's Ministry of Foreign Affairs, retorted, 'What we are against is the attempt to militarize the South China Sea and even to challenge and threaten other countries' sovereignty and security interests under the name of freedom of navigation'.[79] Hua was referring to the FONOP by the U.S.S *Lassen* (DDG-82), a guided missile destroyer that passed within twelve nautical miles (nm) of Subi reef on 26 October.[80]

On 21 November Admiral Harris addressed a foreign policy forum in Canada where he called China's construction of artificial islands 'provocative'. He then reported that China had started 'building runways and support facilities to support possible militarization of an area vital to the global economy.'[81] Admiral Harris also revealed that Chinese military units were now warning ships and planes legally operating in the South China Sea that they were not permitted to enter China's claimed security zone.

A day later China's Vice Foreign Minister Liu Zhenmin asserted that 'to build necessary defence facilities on islands far away from our mainland is required by the need both of national defense and of safeguarding our islands and reefs. They should not be mistaken for actions to militarize

[78] Quoted in Lisa Ferdinando, 'Carter Reiterates Call for Peaceful Resolution in South China Sea,' US Department of Defense News, 4 November 2015, http://www.defense.gov/News-Article-View/Article/627673/carter-reiterates-call-for-peaceful-resolution-in-south-china-sea; and Thompson, 'Asean summit: Ends up without statement amid South China Sea row.' Secretary Carter later flew out to the U.S.S *Theodore Roosevelt* (CVN-71) aircraft carrier operating in the southern waters of the South China Sea accompanied by Malaysia's Defence Minister Hishammuddin Hussein.

[79] Quoted in Li Ruohan, 'FM slams Carter carrier visit in South China Sea,' *Global Times*, 6 November 2015, http://www.globaltimes.cn/content/951154.shtml.

[80] Andrea Shalal and David Brunnstrom, 'U.S. Navy destroyer nears islands built by China in South China Sea,' Reuters, 26 October 2015. http://www.reuters.com/article/us-southchinasea-usa-idUSKCN0SK2AC20151026.

[81] Bill Geertz. 'War of words over South China Sea militarization heats up,' *Asia Times*, 30 November 2015. http://atimes.com/2015/11/war-of-words-over-south-china-sea-militarization-heats-up/. The following quotations in this paragraph are taken from this source.

the South China Sea.'[82] Liu also claimed that 'major countries' outside the region 'are exercising their so-called freedom of navigation by sending airplanes and warships while strengthening military cooperation with countries in the region. Isn't that a trend of militarization? We should stay on high alert against it. Don't make troubles on purpose.'[83]

On 24 November Hong Lei, a Foreign Ministry spokesperson, stated that China had completed 'land reclamation' in June but 'some civilian facilities' were being built including two lighthouses'.[84] He then asserted, '(we) will also build necessary defense facilities on some islands and reefs. The relevant construction will be moderate, which has nothing to do with militarization, targets no countries, and [does] not obstruct various countries' enjoyment of freedom of navigation and over flight in the South China Sea in accordance with international law.'[85]

Tensions were raised in December when two U.S. Air Force B-52 bombers flew over the South China Sea within two nm of China's artificial islands. U.S. officials claimed the B-52 over-flight was 'unintentional' and not a freedom of navigation patrol.[86] On 20 January 2016 China's Navy Chief Wu Shengli told his U.S. counterpart, Admiral John Richardson, in a teleconference that '(o)ur necessary defensive step of building on islands and reefs in the Nansha (Spratly) Islands is not militarization... We will certainly not seek the militarization of the islands and reefs, but we won't set up defenses. How many defenses completely depends on the level of threat we face'.[87]

In late January 2016 the U.S.S *Curtis Wilbur* (DDG-54) conducted a second freedom of navigation operational patrol in the South China

[82]   Xinhua, 'China's construction on South China Sea islands should not be mistaken for militarization: Vice FM,' Xinhuanet.com, 22 November 2015, http://news.xinhuanet.com/english/2015-11/22/c_134842603.htm.

[83]   Ibid.

[84]   Geertz. 'War of words over South China Sea militarization heats up.' The following quotation is taken from this source.

[85]   Ibid.

[86]   Jeremy Page and Gordon Lubold, 'U.S. Bomber Flies Over Waters Claimed by China,' *The Wall Street Journal*, 18 December 2015, http://www.wsj.com/articles/u-s-jet-flies-over-waters-claimed-by-china-1450466358.

[87]   Reuters, 'China Says South China Sea Militarization Depends on Threat,' *Jakarta Globe*, 4 February 2016, http://media.thejakartaglobe.com/international/china-says-south-china-sea-militarization-depends-threat/.

Sea.[88] This time the operation was carried out near Triton Island in the Paracels. In what appeared to be a tit-for-tat response, two weeks later China deployed two batteries of the HQ-9 surface-to-air missiles and radar system on Woody Island.[89] Shortly after, Beijing deployed several Shenyang J-11 and Xian JH-7 combat aircraft to the islands.[90]In March, China conducted military exercises on and around the Paracel Islands, reportedly including the YJ-62 anti-ship missile system.[91] On 7 April, further satellite imagery revealed that China deployed two more J-11s to Woody Island and at the same time installed a fire-control radar system.[92]

China's action kept alive the war of words between the United States and China. Secretary Kerry told reporters, '(t)here is every evidence, every day that there has been an increase of militarization on one kind or

---

[88] Shannon Tiezzi, 'China Rejects Latest US FONOP in the South China Sea,' *The Diplomat*, 2 February 2016, http://thediplomat.com/2016/02/china-rejects-latest-us-fonop-in-the-south-china-sea/.

[89] Lucas Tomlinson and Yonat Friling, 'Exclusive: China sends surface-to-air missiles to contested island in provocative move,' Fox News, 17 February 2016, http://www.foxnews.com/world/2016/02/16/exclusive-china-sends-suface-to-air-missiles-to-contested-island-in-provocative-move.html; Editorial, 'HQ-9 missile prompted by US threat,' *Global Times*, 19 February 2016, http://www.globaltimes.cn/content/969330.shtml; and Zhang Yunbi, 'US warships incursion "aims to renew tension,' *China Daily USA*, 1 February 2016, http://usa.chinadaily.com.cn/epaper/2016-02/01/content_23340753.htm.

[90] Vasudevan Sridharan, 'Beijing deploys several fighter jets on South China Sea's Woody Island,' *International Business Times*, 24 February 2016, http://www.ibtimes.co.uk/beijing-deploys-several-fighter-jets-south-china-seas-woody-island-1545616.

[91] Bill Geertz, 'Pentagon Concerned by Chinese Anti-Ship Missile Firing,' *Washington Free Beacon*, 30 March 2016, http://freebeacon.com/national-security/pentagon-concerned-chinese-anti-ship-missile-firing/.

[92] Lucas Tomlinson and Yonat Friling, 'Chinese fighter jets seen on contested South China Sea island, evidence of Beijing's latest bold move,' Fox News, 12 April 2016, http://www.foxnews.com/world/2016/04/12/chinese-fighter-jets-seen-on-contested-south-china-sea-island-evidence-another-bold-move.html.

another It's of serious concern…'.[93] China's Foreign Ministry spokesperson Hong Lei invoked China's right to self-defence and 'international duties and obligations' to justify the deployment of the HQ-9 system. Hong asserted, '(w)e will deploy necessary national defence facilities on the islands. It's an exercise of self-preservation and defence, a right granted to [sic] international law to sovereign states'.[94]

Defining Militarization. Throughout the war of words between the United States and China neither side has defined what they mean by militarization. In everyday usage the term militarization means 'to put weapons and military forces in (an area)', 'to give a military quality or character to (something)', 'to give a military character to', 'to equip with military forces and defences', and 'to adapt for military use'.[95] Militarization can also be defined as equipping forces with weapons 'in preparation for war'.[96]

Mark Valencia, an Adjunct Research Fellow at the China National Institute for South China Sea Studies on Hainan island, notes that using the broadest definition of militarization the South China Sea has been militarized by all claimants long ago. According to Valencia, 'All have stationed military personnel there and built airstrips and harbors that have accommodated military aircraft and vessels.'[97] The same point was made by M. Taylor Fravel, who observed that many of the features in the South

---

93   Quoted in Simon Denyer, 'U.S. to have "very serious conversation" with China over suspected South China Sea missile deployment,' *The Washington Post*, 17 February 2016. https://www.washingtonpost.com/world/china-deploys-missiles-in-south-china-sea-as-obama-meets-rivals/2016/02/17/83363326-3e1b-4461-b97f-13406f6d104c_story.html.

94   Scott Murdoch, 'China rejects island missile claims,' *The Australian*, 18 February 2016, http://www.theaustralian.com.au/news/world/china-rejects-claim-of-antiaircraft-missiles-in-south-china-sea/news-story/7b8c14a6873b306b0411712fa0cb75f0.

95   *Merriam-Webster Dictionary*, http://www.merriam-webster.com/dictionary/militarize quoted in Mark Valencia, 'Who Is Militarizing the South China Sea?,' *The Diplomat*, 20 December 2015. http://thediplomat.com/2015/12/who-is-militarizing-the-south-china-sea/.

96   *The Free Dictionary*, http://www.thefreedictionary.com/militarization.

97   Valencia, 'Who Is Militarizing the South China Sea?'

China Sea occupied by China and other claimants, were garrisoned with troops and some minimum level of defensive weaponry long ago.[98]

Valencia also raises several pertinent rhetorical questions about the use of the term militarization. Does occasional military use qualify as militarization? Who determines what is meant by occasional? Does intent matter? What about cases where the military is used for humanitarian purposes such as search and rescue and disaster response? What about for defensive purposes only?

Mira Rapp-Hooper and Patrick Cronin concur with Fravel in arguing that militarization should not be broadly defined. They argue that U.S. policy-makers should be specific about what Chinese behavior and actions they find objectionable. They note that radar, communications equipment, and support facilities such as helipads, ports, and airfields are dual use in nature.[99] They offer six examples of what they consider militarization of China's artificial islands: rotating or basing armed Coast Guard and maritime law enforcement vessels, the regular rotation of military aircraft, the rotation or regular stationing of PLAN warships at port facilities, the deployment of advanced missiles, the stationing of amphibious forces capable of seizing disputed features, or aircraft, and prepositioning ammunition and other war-fighting material. They conclude '(r)otational fighter or medium-range missile deployments constitute militarization in the third degree.'[100]

In other worlds, militarization constitutes a spectrum of activities from deploying military forces on a particular feature to give that feature a military character to making preparations for war be pre-positioning military supplies and offensive weapons and platforms. Along this spectrum there is a grey area where activity such as constructing airfields, piers and harbors and deploying certain classes of warships and types of aircraft can serve both civilian and military purposes.

---

[98] Quoted in Jeremy Page, Carol E. Lee and Gordon Lubold, 'China's President Pledges No Militarization in Disputed Islands,' *The Wall Street Journal*, 25 September 2015, http://www.wsj.com/articles/china-completes-runway-on-artificial-island-in-south-china-sea-1443184818.

[99] Mira Rapp-Hooper and Patrick Cronin, 'American Strategy in the South China Sea: Time to Define "Militarization" and "Coercion",' *The National Interest*, 23 September 2015 http://nationalinterest.org/feature/american-strategy-the-south-china-sea-time-define-13914?page=2.

[100] Ibid.

Construction Activities by the Claimant States

In November 2002 ASEAN and China adopted the Declaration on Conduct of Parties in the South China Sea (DOC). The DOC should serve as the baseline in judging whether construction and other activities carried out by claimant states after November 2002 breached their pledge in point 5 to 'exercise self-restraint in the conduct of activities that would complicate or escalate disputes and affect peace and stability including, among others, refraining from action of inhabiting on the presently uninhabited islands, reefs, shoals, cays, and other features and to handle their differences in a constructive manner.'[101]

In 2014-15, the Spratly islands became the focus of attention due to China's rapid construction of artificial islands on submerged features (low tide elevations) and rocks in close proximity to other features occupies by the Philippines and Vietnam. China alone occupies the Paracel Islands and has gradually built up military facilities there since the 1950s. China argues that its 'land reclamation' is no different from what the other claimants have undertaken and defensive measures should not be confused with militarization. This section examines the extent to which China and other claimant states have militarized the features that they currently occupy in the Spratly islands.

China. China currently occupies eight rocks and low tide elevations in the Spratlys – Fiery Cross Reef, Subi Reef, Mischief Reef, South Johnston Reef, Gaven Reef, Hughes Reef, Cuarteron Reef and Eldad Reef. According to the U.S. Department of Defense, in 2013 China upgraded facilities at two outposts and installed communications equipment on multiple outposts. However, between 2014-15 China paved roads on most of its features, installed a solar array on one outpost, built a large port facility on one outpost, constructed buildings and piers on four outposts, completed a 3,000 km runway on Fiery Cross Reef, and established intelligence surveillance and reconnaissance infrastructure on most outposts.[102]

---

101   Declaration on Conduct of Parties in the South China Sea; https://www.google.com.au/#q=declaration+on+the+conduct+of+parties +in+the+south+china+sea+pdf.

102   U.S. Department of Defense, *Asia-Pacific Maritime Security Strategy* (2015), http://www.defense.gov/Portals/1/Documents/pubs/ NDAA%20A-P_Maritime_SecuritY_Strategy-08142015-1300- FINALFORMAT.PDF.

On 24 July 2015, Admiral Harry Harris, Commander of the U.S. Pacific Command reported that China was building ports deep enough to berth warships and a runway on Fiery Cross Reef 915 meters longer than needed by a Boeing 747 aircraft to take off but long enough for a B-52 bomber. In addition, Admiral Harris noted that China was constructing aircraft hangars protected by revetments for tactical fighter aircraft. 'I believe those facilities are clearly military in nature', he said, and would serve as forward operating posts by China's military in combat against regional states. Also, Harris concluded that China's artificial islands 'extends a surveillance network that could be in place with radars, electronic warfare capabilities and the like.'[103]

Subi Reef. China erected a structure on Subi Reef in the 1990s more than a decade before it began converting the reef into an artificial island in 2014. 1997, Subi hosted satellite communications and a helipad; a radome was identified in 2011.[104] Subi now comprises four million square metres of land hosting radar towers, loading piers and a military grade 3,000-metre airfield. On 6 April 2016 a 55-metre lighthouse constructed on Subi became operational.[105] On 12 July a Chinese Cessna CE-680 flew to Subi to test the airstrip. A day later a China Southern Airlines Airbus A319 successfully conducted a test flight from Haikou on Hainan Island to Subi.

Mischief Reef. China took possession of Mischief Reef, a low tide elevation, in 1995 and promptly built a small covered platform on stilts. In October 1998 China added three octagon-shaped structures and two two-story concrete towers that bristle with satellite communications and High Frequency antennae. It is likely the towers house electronic intelligence equipment and radar. China later built two piers and a helipad, and installed navigational radar and anti-aircraft guns. Mischief Reef was converted to a 5.5 square kilometre artificial island in 2014-15. In September 2015 China commenced preparatory work on ca 3,000 metre

---

[103] Quotations in this paragraph are taken from Kevin Baron, 'China's New Islands Are Clearly Military, U.S. Pacific Chief Says,' *Defense One*, 24 July 2015, http://www.defenseone.com/threats/2015/07/chinas-new-islands-are-clearly-military/118591/.

[104] Ibid.

[105] Jesse Johnson, 'Beijing opens new lighthouse on man-made island in South China Sea,' *The Japan Times*, 6 April 2016, http://www.japantimes.co.jp/news/2016/04/06/asia-pacific/beijing-opens-new-lighthouse-man-made-island-south-china-sea/.

long concrete airstrip, its third in the Spratlys.[106] On 12 July 2016 a Chinese Cessna CE-680 flew to Mischief Reef to test the airstrip. The following day a Hainan Airlines Boeing 737 conducted a test flight from Haikou on Hainan Island to Mischief Reef. China is also completing a sixty metre tall lighthouse on Mischief Reef.

Fiery Cross Reef. In 2015, in the space of eight months, China transformed Fiery Cross Reef (Yongshu) into a 2.65 square kilometre artificial island. In April 2015, United States defence officials claimed they had spotted self-propelled artillery on Fiery Cross Reef that was removed later.[107] The infrastructure on Fiery Cross include seawalls, concrete roads, military barracks, a multi-story tower, a harbor, helipads, an airfield and early warning radar.[108] The 3,300 metre long airfield can be used by most support and combat aircraft in the PLAN and PLA Air Force inventory.[109] The airfield became operational in January 2016 when China conducted three test flights by an Airbus A319 and a Boeing 737 civilian passenger aircraft.[110] China also has completed building a lighthouse and is nearing completion of a hospital on Fiery Cross. In sum, Fiery Cross is

---

[106]   Asia Maritime Transparency Initiative, Center for Strategic and International Studies. 'Airstrips Near Completion,' January 2016. http://amti.csis.org/airstrips-near-completion/.

[107]   Lolita C. Baldor and Matthew Pennington, 'Pentagon chief criticizes Beijing's South China Sea moves,' Associated Press, 30 May 2015, http://news.yahoo.com/us-says-china-artillery-vehicles-artificial-island-093552171--politics.html.

[108]   Jim Sciutto, 'Exclusive: China Warns U.S. surveillance plane,' CNN Politics, 15 September 2015, http://edition.cnn.com/2015/05/20/politics/south-china-sea-navy-flight/.

[109]   Victor Robert Lee and DigitalGlobe, 'China's New Military Installations in the Disputed Spratly Islands: Satellite Image Update,' 15 March 2015, https://medium.com/satellite-image-analysis/china-s-new-military-installations-in-the-spratly-islands-satellite-image-update-1169bacc07f9#.kfjxtbfjx.

[110]   Kristine Kwok and Zhuang Pinghui, 'Chinese military aircraft likely to land at new airport in disputed area of South China Sea in coming months, says ex-PLA officer,' *South China Morning Post*, 8 January 2016. http://www.scmp.com/news/china/diplomacy-defence/article/1899036/chinese-military-aircraft-likely-land-new-airport.

fast emerging as a combined naval-air base and operational headquarters for Chinese military ships and aircraft in the Spratly islands.[111]

According to a Chinese Civil Aviation Administration official, '(t) he airport will serve as an aviation hub in the Nansha (Spratly) Islands and will offer convenience for goods and personnel transportation and emergency medical care in Yongshu Reef and adjacent areas'.[112] Chinese media reported that a number of government agencies - including fishing, maritime affairs, search and rescue, scientific research, environmental protection, tourism and garbage disposal - will be set up on Fiery Cross Reef.[113]

Other Features. China has transformed Johnson South, Cuarteron, Hughes and Gaven reefs into artificial islands on which it has constructed reinforced sea walls, gun emplacements, docks, helipads, radomes, towers, and multistory buildings.[114] In 2015 satellite imagery of Johnson South revealed the presence of two PLAN frigates.[115] China has also completed building two 50-metre high lighthouses on Cuarteron and Johnson South reefs.[116]

Each of China's three airfields are much larger than the airstrips maintained by Malaysia (1,368 m), Taiwan (1,195 m), the Philippines

---

[111]   Baron, 'China's New Islands Are Clearly Military, U.S. Pacific Chief Says'; for background consult: James C. Bussert and Bruce A. Elleman, *People's Liberation Army Navy: Combat Systems and Technology, 1949-2010* (Annapolis: Naval Institute Press, 2011), 144.

[112]   Ibid.

[113]   Ibid. The Chinese media has carried reports of future plans to construct up to twenty floating nuclear power platforms to assist in the commercial development of the South China Sea; Kathy Chen and David Stanway, 'China media again touts plans to float nuclear reactors in disputed South China Sea,' Reuters, 15 July 2016, http://www.dailymail.co.uk/wires/reuters/article-3691659/China-media-touts-plans-float-nuclear-reactors-disputed-South-China-Sea.html.

[114]   Lee and DigitalGlobe, 'China's New Military Installations in the Disputed Spratly Islands: Satellite Image Update' and Josh Rogin, 'U.S. Misses Real Threat of China's Fake Islands,' Bloomberg View, 2 April 2015, https://www.bloomberg.com/view/articles/2015-04-02/u-s-misses-real-threat-of-china-s-fake-islands.

[115]   Ibid.

[116]   Johnson, 'Beijing opens new lighthouse on man-made island in South China Sea.'

(1,000 m), and Vietnam (500m). With the exception of Vietnam, all the runways in the South China Sea will be able to accommodate jet fighters; but only China will be able to operate bombers.[117]

The harbor can accommodate the PLAN's largest warships, such as the Type-071 Landing Platform Dock. In August 2015, a U.S. Navy P8-A Poseidon observed 'a lot of surface traffic' including PLAN warships and China Coast Guard vessels with air search radar.[118] Fiery Cross provides easy access to deep waters (2,000m) that are ideal for submarine traffic.

Taiwan. Before China's construction of artificial islands Taiwan occupied the largest land feature in the Spratlys, Itu Aba (Taiping) and one smaller feature. Itu Aba was found to be a rock by the Arbitral Tribunal that announced its award on 12 July 2016.[119] It is entitled to a 12 nm territorial sea but not a 200 nm Exclusive Economic Zone.

Itu Aba is administered by Coast Guard officials who replaced regular soldiers in 2000. The island is protected by machine guns, 81mm and 210mm mortars, as well as 40mm anti-aircraft guns. The island has a 1,195 metre long runway and limited port facilities.[120]

According to the U.S. Defense Department Taiwan installed solar arrays on Itu Aba in 2013 and the following year began construction of a new pier and new buildings.[121] When construction is completed Itu Aba will have port capable of accommodating 3,000 ton naval frigates and Coast Guard cutters. The runway is also being improved for use

[117] Asia Maritime Transparency Initiative, Center for Strategic and International Studies. 'Air Power in the South China Sea,' 2015. http://amti.csis.org/airstrips-scs/.

[118] Sciutto, 'Exclusive: China Warns U.S. surveillance plane.'

[119] Steve Mollman, 'This tiny islet in the South China Sea is now officially a "rock" – and the implications are global,' *Quartz*, 25 July 2016, http://qz.com/737219/this-tiny-islet-in-the-south-china-sea-is-now-officially-a-rock-and-the-implications-are-global/, Charles Au, 'Taiwan rejects South China Sea ruling,' *Shepard Media*, 25 July 2016, https://www.shephardmedia.com/news/imps-news/taiwan-rejects-south-china-sea-ruling/, and Lynn Kuok, 'Taiwan Must Tread Carefully on South China Sea Ruling,' *The Wall Street Journal*, 25 July 2016, http://www.wsj.com/articles/taiwan-must-tread-carefully-on-south-china-sea-ruling-1469465725.

[120] Lee and DigitalGlobe, 'China's New Military Installations in the Disputed Spratly Islands: Satellite Image Update.'

[121] U.S. Department of Defense, *Asia-Pacific Maritime Security Strategy.*

by Hercules C-130 transport planes. Itu Aba will continue to serve as a support base for Taiwanese deep-sea fishermen and marine and mineral research.[122]

Malaysia. Malaysia occupies seven features in the South China Sea.[123] In 1983 the Royal Malaysian Navy took possession of Swallow Reef (Pulau Layang-Layang) and set up a naval station that is protected by anti-ship guns and the *Starburst* anti-aircraft defence system. Malaysia has also developed Swallow Reef into a tourist resort for scuba diving.[124] Swallow Reef is serviced by a 1,368 metre concrete runway, two hangars, radar, and an air traffic control tower.

According to the U.S. Defense Department, Malaysia made no visible improvements to its communications, maritime domain awareness or defensive infrastructure between 2009 and 2015. In 2013 Malaysia erected new buildings, water storage facilities, and refurbished two air hangars at Swallow Reef.[125]

The Philippines. The Philippines occupies eight reefs and islands in the Spratlys, the largest of which is Pag-asa (Thitu) that has a 1,000-metre runway. According to the U.S. Defense Department, the Philippines constructed support buildings at four outposts, and cleared a road around Thitu Island in 2013. However, between 2009 and 2015 the Philippines made no visible improvements to its communications, maritime domain awareness or defensive infrastructure.[126]

Vietnam. Vietnam occupies twenty-one features in the Spratlys of which nine are above water at high tide and twelve are low tide elevations

---

[122] Michael Gold and Greg Torode, 'As Taiwan beefs up prized South China Sea outpost, barely a peep from China,' Reuters, May 25, 2015. http://www. reuters.com/article/us-taiwan-southchinasea-idusBREA4O0E620140525.

[123] Mohd Nizam Basiron, 'Malaysia's Maritime Challenges and Opportunities: The Search for Sustainability and Security,' in Joshua Ho and Sam Bateman, eds, *Maritime Challenges and Priorities in Asia: Implications for Regional Security* (London: Routledge Press, 2012), 73-75.

[124] Asia Maritime Transparency Initiative, Center for Strategic and International Studies, 'Before and After: The South China Sea Transformed,' 18 February 2015. http://amti.csis.org/before-and-after-the-south-china-sea-transformed/.

[125] U.S. Department of Defense, *Asia-Pacific Maritime Security Strategy.*

[126] Ibid.

---

on which Vietnam has erected structures.[127] Vietnam has posted People's Army of Vietnam Navy personnel to thirty-three garrisons. Some features host more than one garrison. Six civilian households are located on Vietnamese features in the Spratlys.

U.S. officials claim that Vietnam has forty-eight outposts in the Spratlys. This discrepancy may be explained by eighteen platforms or technical support services structures (*nha gian dich vu ky thuat*) that Vietnam has erected in Vanguard Bank (Tu Chinh). Vietnam does not consider Vanguard Bank part of the Spratly islands.

Vietnam's largest feature, Spratly Island (Dao Truong Sa Lon), has a total land area of 150,000 square metres. It houses a fishing port, a 500-metre airstrip, a meteorological station, medical clinic and classrooms.

In late 2014/early 2015 Vietnam began converting Cornwallis South Reef into small artificial islands by shifting sand and dredging the seabed to enlarge the channel into the reef's lagoon.[128] By August 2015 Vietnam created a land area of 16,000 square metres and began laying the foundations for several buildings. The pre-existing infrastructure on Cornwallis South Reef consists of several pillboxes, four buildings, four docks, solar panels, communications antennae and satellite dishes.

According to Minister of National Defence General Quang Thanh, speaking in mid-2015, Vietnam recently reinforced embankments on some of its Spratly features that are above water at high tide to prevent erosion by wind and water. Minister Thanh also stated that Vietnam only built small

---

127 'Danh sach cac dao do Viet Nam kiem soat o quan dao Truong Sa' (List of islands controlled by Vietnam in the Spratly Islands), http://nguyentandung. org/danh-sach-cac-dao-do-viet-nam-kiem-soat-o-quan-dao-truong-sa.html and Address to the National Assembly by Prime Minister Nguyen Tan Dung quoted in Tien Dung and Nguyen Hung, 'Viet Nam doi chu quyen Hoang Sa bang hoa binh (Vietnam Claims the Spratlys Are in a Peaceful State),' *VNExpress*, 25 November 2011; http://vnexpress.net/tin-tuc/thoi-su/viet-nam-doi-chu-quyen-hoang-sa-bang-hoa-binh-2212051.html.

128 Asia Maritime Transparency Initiative, Center for Strategic and International Studies, 'Washed Away: Typhoon Melor Spotlights Vietnamese Island Building,' December 2015. http://amti.csis.org/ typhoon-spotlights-island-building/.

houses that can accommodate a few people on its low tide elevations. He claimed, '(t)he scope and characteristic of our work is purely civilian'[129]

According to the U.S. Department of Defense, between 2009 and 2015, Vietnam improved the civilian infrastructure on five outposts, installed communications and radar equipment on fifteen outposts, made point defence improvements on eighteen outposts and carried out quality of life improvements on nineteen outposts. The Defense Department reports that the only infrastructure improvements carried out from 2011-2015 were the construction of helipads on six outposts.[130]

Conclusion: Implications for Regional Security

There are seven major implications arising from the militarization of the South China Sea.[131]

First, the commitment by China and members of ASEAN who signed the 2002 Declaration on Conduct of Parties in the South China Sea (DOC), to 'exercise self-restraint in the conduct of activities that would complicate or escalate disputes and affect peace and stability' has been overtaken by subsequent developments, including most notably China's construction of artificial islands. ASEAN's recent efforts to get China's concurrence on operationalizing the DOC's clause mentioning 'among other' activities has not been taken up. The DOC does not explicitly mention constructing artificial islands and China has driven large dredging vessels through this loophole.

Second, all the artificial islands that China has constructed were subject to the award issued by the Arbitral Tribunal that heard the case

---

[129] David Alexander, 'Vietnam, U.S. Discuss Land Reclamation In South China Sea,' Reuters, 2 June 2015. http://www.huffingtonpost.com/2015/06/02/vietnam-us-south-china-sea_n_7482252.html.

[130] U.S. Department of Defense, *Asia-Pacific Maritime Security Strategy*.

[131] This section draws on Carlyle A. Thayer, 'New Model of Major Power Relations: China-U.S. Global Cooperation and Regional Contention,' Presentation to International Conference on ASEAN and China–U.S. Relations: New Security Dynamics and Regional Implications, co-sponsored by the Diplomatic Academy of Vietnam and the Konrad Adenauer Stiftung, Sheraton Hotel, Hanoi, 10 March 2016, http://www.viet-studies.info/kinhte/Thayer_NewModel.pdf.

of The Philippines v China on 12 July.[132] The Tribunal ruled that none of the land features in the South China Sea, including Taiwan's Itu Aba (Taiping), were islands as defined by UNCLOS Article 121 and therefore were not entitled to a 200 nautical mile Exclusive Economic Zone (EEZ) or an extended continental shelf.

The Arbitral Tribunal meticulously examined the status of land features raised by the Philippines and found that Cuarteron Reef, Fiery Cross Reef, Gaven Reef (North), Johnson Reef, McKennan Reef and Scarborough Shoal were rocks and entitled to a twelve nautical mile territorial sea but not a 220 nm EEZ. China claims sovereignty over these rocks, although this is disputed by other parties, including Vietnam and the Philippines.

The Tribunal also found that Gaven Reef (South), Hughes Reef, Mischief Reef, Second Thomas Shoal and Subi Reef were low tide elevations. As low tide elevations these features were not entitled to any maritime zones and were not subject to appropriation. In other words China cannot claim them as its sovereign territory.

One major implication of the Tribunal's finding on the status of features was that both Mischief Reef and Second Thomas Shoal fell within the Philippines' EEZ and there was no overlap with the maritime entitlements of Chinese-occupied rocks. Therefore, the Tribunal found that China's construction of structures and installations on Mischief Reef was not authorized by the Philippines. In addition, the Tribunal found that hydrocarbon rich Reed Bank was a submerged reef formation that fell within the Philippines' EEZ. Therefore, the Philippines has sovereign jurisdiction over Reed Bank.

The Tribunal found that it did not have jurisdiction to decide on Philippine complaints about China's investment (in a military sense) of Second Thomas Shoal where the Philippines beached the BRP *Sierra Madre* in 1999 in order to stake out its sovereignty claims. The Tribunal

---

[132]   This section is based on Carlyle A. Thayer, 'The Role of Arbitration in the Settlement of Maritime Disputes in the South China Sea,' Presentation to the International Conference on the Law of the Sea, Legal Issues Relating to Awards of the Arbitral Tribunal Established Under Annex VII of UNCLOS 1982, organized by the University of Law Ho Chi Minh City and the Vietnam Lawyers' Association, Reunification Palace, Ho Chi Minh City, 23 July 2016 and Carl Thayer 'After the Ruling: Lawfare in the South China Sea,' *The Diplomat Magazine*, no. 21, August 2016. 1-18, http://magazine. thediplomat.com/#/issues/-KN_NWvIeCtf3lVXufVR/read.

found that Chinese activities, such as interrupting supply to Second Thomas Shoal, were 'military activities' and thus fell outside its purview.

China refused to participate in the deliberations of the Arbitral Tribunal and after the award was issued declared it was 'null and void' and that China would not be bound by it. Since the Arbitral Tribunal has no power of enforcement, and ASEAN is divided on the issues, the result is that the United Nations Convention on the Law of the Sea, widely regarded as the constitution for the world's oceans, has been undermined as a legal basis for peace and security in the South China Sea,

Third, China has repeatedly stated that the artificial islands will provide a range of civilian support services and public goods such as improvements of the living conditions of personnel stationed on the artificial islands, marine search and rescue, disaster prevention and mitigation, meteorological observation, and navigational aids. As China completes building the infrastructure for these services and assigns personnel to carry them out, China will also provide 'some necessary military facilities' to defend its interests.

If China stations military helicopters, mobile artillery batteries, amphibious ships it will be able to exert pressure on claimants to withdraw and China will have greater capability to dislodge claimants from their features.[133] As Admiral Harris has observed, for example, '(w)hen one looks at China's pattern of provocative actions towards smaller claimant states… and the deep asymmetry between China's capabilities and those of its smaller neighbors – well it's no surprise that the scope and pace of building man-made islands raise serious questions about Chinese intentions.'[134]

An increased Chinese military presence will result in further Chinese actions to prevent intrusions into the maritime area surrounding its artificial islands. Regional fishermen, who have already felt the brunt of Chinese actions to exclude them from the area, will come under increased pressure. In addition, China's beefed up military presence will improve its capacity to intercept and ward off military vessels and aircraft from the

---

[133] Bonnie Glaser, 'Growing Militarization of the South China Sea,' *Real Clear Defense*, 30 July 2015. http://www.realcleardefense.com/articles/2015/07/30/growing_militarization_of_the_south_china_sea_108304.html.

[134] Admiral Harry B. Harris Jr., Commander, U.S. Pacific Fleet, speech to the Australian Strategic Policy Institute Canberra, Australia 31 March 2015. http://www.cpf.navy.mil/leaders/harry-harris/speeches/2015/03/ASPI-Australia.pdf.

Philippines and Vietnam. China has already ventured further south and brought similar pressure to bear on Malaysia and Indonesia. This can be expected to continue.

Fourth, China has always held in reserve the right to establish an Air Identification Zone (ADIZ) over the South China Sea. Victor Robert Lee argues, Chinese artificial island bases 'will likely serve to constrain the activities of competing militaries in the region, and appear more than adequate to support air traffic monitoring and enforcement in the event China were to declare an Air Defense Identification Zone over the South China Sea.'[135]

In some senses a nascent ADIZ already exists as noted by senior U.S. Navy admirals. Chinese Navy personnel, both on Fiery Cross Reef and on PLAN warships, constantly challenge over flights by foreign military aircraft including from the Philippines, Australia and the United States. If China deploys jet fighters and surface-to-air missiles to the airfields on its artificial islands it will enhance its capacity to enforce its ADIZ.

Fifth, China's unilateral drive to secure control over the South China Sea and the U.S. policy of military rebalancing already have created a security dilemma. Each perceives the actions of the other as inherently threatening. The United States has stated that it intends to step up the scope and complexity of its FONOPs. The U.S. may also enlist the support of Japan and Australia to join it in asserting freedom of navigation and over flight. China has countered that it will take appropriate action in response. As the China-U.S. security dilemma intensifies, it will raise the probability of incidents leading to serious tactical miscalculations and even conflict.

Sixth, if and when China decides to undertake actions at the higher end of the militarization scale – deploying tactical military aircraft, missiles, amphibious forces and warships – this will alter the naval balance of power in coming decades. China will develop an increased capacity to observe and respond to U.S. military operations in South China Sea. U.S. military forces will be held at risk further from China than at present.

Chinese military facilities on Fiery Cross will enable force projection and reduce the time for PLAN aircraft and warships to respond to incident in the southern reaches of the South China Sea. In sum, China will be able

---

[135]   Lee and DigitalGlobe, 'China's New Military Installations in the Disputed Spratly Islands: Satellite Image Update.'

to sustain larger naval deployments in the Spratly islands and lower reaches of the South China Sea for longer periods than at present.

Once China has completed its construction activities on its artificial islands and consolidated its network of radars and electronic systems, it will have an enhanced capacity for intelligence, surveillance, reconnaissance and maritime domain awareness on a 24/7 basis. This network will support the deployment of surveillance aircraft, airborne early warning and control, unmanned aircraft, transport planes, tanker aircraft, fighters, and bombers.

One of the most strategically worrying developments would be the development of facilities on Fiery Cross Reef to support the basing of conventional and nuclear submarines. Nuclear submarines would have quick access to the nearby deep waters. As Lee has noted, deep waters near all of the eight reefs are viable channels for submarines of all navies. The PLAN can be expected to deploy fixed ocean floor acoustic arrays and well as to support other forms of air, maritime and anti-submarine surveillance.'[136]

Seventh, ASEAN 's professed goal of remaining central to the region's security architecture and guardian of Southeast Asia's regional autonomy is now under serious challenge as a result of the debacle at the Special China-ASEAN Foreign Ministers Meeting in Kunming on 25 June 2016[137] and the lack of consensus evident at the 49th ASEAN Ministerial Meeting just held in Vientiane. ASEAN may well remain a putative community in coming years but ASEAN unity could be fractured further as states individually decide to accommodate to China's rise or balance against China. This would undermine the political-security pillar one of the three pillars on which the ASEAN Community is based.

---

[136] Lee and DigitalGlobe, 'China's New Military Installations in the Disputed Spratly Islands: Satellite Image Update.'

[137] Carl Thayer, 'The ASEAN-China Special Meeting Mystery: Bureaucratic Snafu or Chinese Heavy-Handedness?,' *The Diplomat*, June 17, 2016, http://thediplomat.com/2016/06/the-asean-china-special-meeting-mystery-bureaucratic-snafu-or-chinese-heavy-handedness/ and Carl Thayer, 'Revealed: The Truth Behind ASEAN's Retracted Kunming Statement,' *The Diplomat*, June 19, 2016, http://thediplomat.com/2016/06/revealed-the-truth-behind-aseans-retracted-kunming-statement/.

Land Reclamation and Militarization in the Paracel and the Spratly Islands

Go Ito
Meiji University, Japan

China's Core Interests Have Produced Its Unilateral Approaches

The South China Sea currently faces a crisis by construction of artificial islands in the maritime heart of Southeast Asia. China claims that its construction activities are legal under international law and that China is only doing what other claimants have done in previous years. In fact, China is acting with great restraint according to its officials.

However, China's artificial islands will serve as bases for search and rescue and better weather forecasting. They are also likely to serve as forward operating bases for China's fishing fleet, oil exploration and survey vessels and maritime law enforcement ships. China has also put down a marker that these bases will serve "defense needs" and holds in reserve the right to establish as Air Defense Identification Zone.

Conception of Maritime Security

The concept of security in the maritime area can be divided into three elements: (1) Freedom of Navigation, (2) Exclusive Economic Zones (EEZ), and (3) Territorial Ownership. In arguing the legitimacy of territorial (or maritime) ownership, the Chinese often say that Japan and the US are outsiders for the South China Sea.

However, this claim cannot be sustained from the perspectives of (1) above, since areas of the South China Sea are where a tremendous number of vessels pass every day for transport and other logistical purposes. Those by the Japanese, Koreans, and other countries are not an exception. The logic of maritime security should be considered not only in terms of ownership (note there is no territory on the sea), but rather as an entire concept that includes all three elements.

China has obstructed the passage of various vessels in the past, and these events challenge the existing foundations of global maritime order. In this context, it is not enough in terms of the maritime security only to observe the freedom of navigation. We can find issues of (2) and (3) by claimant countries. We should discuss these problems as a whole and look for possible solutions, or at least methods for calming down the current situation.

China's Claim of Unfairness in International Relations

In terms of territorial sovereignty, China could say:

(a) Guam and Hawaii for the United States;
(b) French Polynesia for France;
(c) The Falkland Islands for Britain;
(d) The Antilles for the Netherlands, the United States, France and Britain.

The above islands are geographically located quite far from their home countries, while China claims only the area of the South China Sea, which is in the neighborhood of China.

However, this claim cannot be sustained since China's claim on the 9-dash line argues that the whole maritime area should be owned and monitored by the Chinese. The UNCLOS does not argue ownership in the maritime areas.

Ownership of islands and rocks in the South China Sea (which is (3)) may lead to the claim on the EEZ around the island (which is (2)), and may expand the argument of obstructing the freedom of navigation (which is (1)). This argument contends that maritime areas are like an extension of land. China would seemingly like to argue this logic of territorial sovereignty over the maritime areas.

The ASEAN after the Award of the Permanent Court of Arbitration

After the PCA's award, it can be argued that China will seek to conduct such approaches as bilateral negotiations with claimant countries (the Philippines and Cambodia/Laos for different reasons), multilateral negotiations like the holding of high-level SCS meetings. The hidden intention is to get rid of the American influence, and the use of economic leverages to satisfy the wealth of the claimant countries. As a scholar, I am interested in how swing states (not anti-China nor pro-China) will respond to China's initiatives.

The PCA's award will also challenge the centrality of ASEAN as well. On issues of the South China Sea, the ASEAN is not monolithic. The award will be a litmus test for the solidarity of the ASEAN. More significantly, the PCA's award indicated that all islands within the 9-dash line have been "transient use." The islands and rocks do not belong to China, or to any other country. How then do we respond to this decision?

In this paper, I argue that the ASEAN has four options:

1. Continue on its present course of hedging and consulting with China over the implementation of the Declaration on Conduct of Parties in the South China Sea (DOC) and discuss on the basis of consensus on a Code of Conduct in the South China Sea (COC);
2. Bandwagon with China in the expectation China will be munificent and reward ASEAN and its member states for their compliant behavior;
3. Balancing with the United States to constrain China;
4. Pursue a proactive dual track approach.

The Role of the United States and Japan: How Will the Public Goods Be Protected?

The Role of the United States and Japan is to do something more than the FON Strategy. The FON indicated only an innocent passage over a sea area close to China and the ASEAN. The US was able to drop its anchor on the seabed, assuming that it could regard the areas of high sea over the South China Sea, but it didn't do so.

Based on the rule of law in the maritime area, both the US and Japan will seek to provide various methods for capacity building on the part of claimant countries. More specifically, as long as China continues to change the status quo in a coercive way, it is important for both countries to provide a certain level of deterrent capabilities to the claimant countries. Already, Japan has provided Vietnam and the Philippines with patrol vessels of the Japan Coast Guard, and similar methods will be needed to conduct countermeasures against China. This logic has stemmed from China's incessant intrusion into the Senkaku areas over years, despite the fact that China knows that the area has been disputed. China says that the intrusion is an action of sovereignty, while Japan knows and has conducted the same claim, but has voluntarily refrained from placing Japanese vessels into the disputed area because it does not want to provoke China. In this context, Japan's voluntary restraint has been regarded unilaterally by China as the absence of a sovereignty claim over the Senkaku islands.

The maritime area should be addressed not as the property of countries, but as a public good for the passage of vessels. In this context, such multilateral approaches as the existing ARF, ADMM Plus, Shangri-la Dialogues should be continued. Also, the joint military exercises by the United States, Australia, and Japan (together with other Pacific partners) could be seen as a method of deterrence against China. The 2+2 meetings have been expanded to India as well, under the banner of the "Security Diamond" argued by Japan's Prime Minister Shinzo Abe.

Conclusion

Countermeasures by military force should be a sad story, but it is not enough for us just to pray for the disappearance of changing the status quo with coercive powers. China knows that it created its isolation on maritime issues. When a country becomes isolated, it could go to strengthen its military capabilities only to justify its position (such as North Korea after Russia and China normalized diplomatic relations with South Korea in 1992), or could seek to find out a reasonable commonality with international society (such as Taiwan which has sought to democratize itself after the US normalized diplomatic relations with the PRC in 1979).

In which direction will China go? Pre-war, Japan failed to look for the maintenance of international collaboration and marched into war with the United States. History teaches us important lessons. Now, it is time for China to learn from history.

Developments related to Chinese Assertiveness in SCS

Shekhar Dutt

There is much that can said about the South China Sea. However, history has to be avoided, and the current situation viewed as the ipso facto reality of the day. Chinese assertion in the South China Sea is a reality and so is the verdict of the Permanent Court of Arbitration. The claims and position of China have been internationally and legally declared unreasonable and illegal. The challenge before us is about the implementation of the verdict and whether a possibility exists to change the status quo. While the ruling is in favour of the Philippines and it affects all countries concerned with the South China Sea, the power and status quo is with China. This is what impacts not only all countries that share maritime boundaries with China but also those who are concerned about the attitude and assertion of China both on land and at sea. As an Indian and as a global citizen, my worries spring from this dilemma of the future.

I do not need to elaborate that the situation in the South China Sea remains grim with rising tension because of militarization, growing nationalism and massive changes being made artificially to the geographical features of the region. These do not augur well for the peace and stability of the region. At this initial stage let me touch on the crux of this problem because all other diagnosis and prognisis spring from it. The problem actually is in the zone of ambiguity that shrouds Chinese intentions. Allow me to elaborate. During the whole course of protest against Chinese actions of creation of artificial land in the sea, it has always been promising an agreed Code of Conduct (COC) as well as efforts to resolve the issue through negotiations. Its actions are quite the contrary, and indicate readiness to use a muscular approach. China has insisted on her sovereignty over the area indicated in the nine-dash lines and has refused to be flexible on this self perpetuated view. Its policy of assertion has mutated to indications of aggressiveness. While China mentioned her historical and legal claims she refused to participate in the arbitration or even give credence to it. This despite being a signatory to all connected international conventions. The ambiguity therefore stems from an approach that rests on soft talk and hard line actions.

China's policy towards the South China disputes raises several questions. Is China interested in talks to resolve the issue, or not? Why is China behaving aggressively and is this behavior going to be limited to countries who are disputants in the South China Sea or will it perpetuate towards all other neighbouring countries? Is China following a well-crafted expansionist policy? Is the Chinese diplomatic projection of her interest in talks to resolve the issue meant only to buy time and wait for an opportunity to dictate its own terms? Is China utilising this time to acquire more features in the South China Sea and strengthen its position?

If one was to analyse the incidents related to the issue, no satisfactory explanations for the Chinese approach would emerge. The peaceniks would argue that it is merely a structural problem and the fragmented policy-making structure of China leads to competing and at times contradictory narratives. Considering its present power structure it would remain a falacy. Another view is that there is a long term strategic shift driven by the Chinese anxiety about a US role in the region. This perspective emerges out of Xinhua's fiery editorial of April 2015. It echoed earlier statements by Chinese officials that accused the US of arbitrarily exercising military power, stoking tensions between China and its neighbours - including nudging its ally the Philippines to engage in provocations against China. To gain a greater and clearer understanding, one needs to examine Chinese behavior with all her claims in its periphery, including its land borders.

Before I venture into anlysing Chinese attitude, let me mention the momentous change that it has brought about in the very fundamentals of the domains of future conflicts. Oceans and seas have seen conflict and contests in the past as well. Power in the sea has been defined by the destruction that a country can cause to its adversary whenever it attempts to use it. Control over the use of sea has been the essential measure of power. It is for this reason that international norms evolved simultaneously to keep pace with emerging technologies that created greater capabilities of reach and economic exploitation of the seas. To avoid conflict the limits of rights over contiguous waters was defined. Freedom of the high seas was always the guiding principle of global commons. What China has done is to bring in a new factor of **territory at sea** and thus involve claims over **every right** within the understanding of **global commons**. Artificial territory within the oceans has emerged as a new phenomenon. The PCA obviously does not wish to constrict the global commons and aims at precluding the growth of such claims in the future. International norms would obviously wish to preclude creating precedence for the future. The relevance and credibility of international norms and ruling is being tested. The issue is, **do countries have equal rights?** Or have we moved back to rudimentary human norm of **might is right?**

This implies that future human existence is of little concern as we play with nature and destroy emergence of marine life and maritime stability. Global norms and concerns are under threat. Can we accept it?

Similarities in Chinese policies in all the disputed areas in the periphery

I will attempt to closely examine the Chinese disputes in three regions in its periphery. Regions that China claims, namely the Sino-Indian land border, East China Sea and South China Sea. One can discern that China has similar approaches in all of these regions. Three factors support this.

First, in all three areas, contradictory signals are witnessed from soft talks and hard line actions. While diplomatically China suggests that the issues would be resolved through negotiations, simultaneously it is pursuing aggressive activities to assert its claims. This dual approach is common in all of the three regions. It is gradually actualising its claim through continuous and progrssive 'nibbling at it. Second, in all of these regions, the aggressive activities by the Chinese started in 2006. And third, China organized a major work conference on periphery diplomacy sometime in October 2013. This reflected Beijing's common approach. Xi Jinping stated that the period extending to 2020 is a "period of strategic opportunity" for China's growth and development. During this time,

China needed to maintain a stable external environment that is conducive to domestic economic reform and growth. To achieve this goal, Xi exhorted that China must strive to make China's neighbours "more friendly in politics, economically more closely tied to us, and have deeper security cooperation and closer people-to-people ties." "The neighbouring countries should be treated as friends and partners and China should make them feel safe and help them to develop." The narrative is therefore common and is a part of regional and international posturing. While the narrative is about peace, the actions are all about muscular exploitation of a perceived strategic opportunity.

If all of us see China's behaviour as part of a larger strategic design of expansion and power projection, all of us can come together to conceive a common response. Let me first piece together the Chinese Design.

The Sino–Indian border

Although India and China agreed in 1993, 1996 and 2005 to maintain peace at the border and resolve boundary issues – tensions continue because of the actions of the Chinese. In 2005, China and India signed approved guidelines to resolve the border dispute and it was expected that a framework would be signed soon after and the issue finally resolved. However, contrary to expectations, since 2006 the Chinese began to demand India's Arunachal Pradesh State, declaring it as Southern Tibet.

Since then they have routinely objected to the visit of Indian leaders to the state. In February 2015 Liu Zhenmin, Chinese vice-foreign minister, said the Indian prime minister's trip to Arunachal Pradesh, which Beijing considers part of Tibet, "infringes on China's territorial sovereignty and magnifies the border dispute." In May 2015, just before the Indian Prime Minister's visit to China, the Global Times published a scathing editorial entitled, "Can Modi's visit upgrade Sino-Indian ties?" and accused the India government of playing "little tricks" on the border dispute. It criticised the Prime Minister's visits to Arunachal Pradesh and called on India to "stop all support to the Dalai Lama."

The Chinese PLA increasingly began to intrude into Indian borders. Their patrols became aggressive. The Chinese PLA troops began to come in greater numbers and began to stay for longer periods of time. Since 2012, they began to write on Indian rocks that they said belonged to China. They also destroyed Indian patrol shelters. In April 2013 Chinese troops entered the Indian Territory in the Daulat Beg Oldi (DBO) sector in eastern Ladakh and erected a tented post, setting the stage for a face-off with Indian troops. On 16th July 2013, 50 Chinese troops, riding on horses and ponies, intruded into the Indian territory of Chumar in Ladakh staking their claim over the area. They remained until 17th July 2013. In August 2013 the Chinese troops intruded into Arunachal Pradesh and stayed there for four days. Again the Chinese troops came to Chumar area in Ladakh in December 2013. India, however, exercised restraint and acted per the agreements between the two countries.

These incidents were not mere stray local initiatives. They were timed strategically. In 2014 several intrusions took place when either the Special Representatives were meeting or the Indian PM was meeting Xi Jinping. Chinese troops were reported to have entered into Indian Territory in the Burtse area of Ladakh. They put up tents about 1.5 kilometers away from the Indian border post. According to reports, the PLA personnel were sitting on the ground with flags reading "this is Chinese territory, go back." In September 2014, Chinese troops entered Ladakh (Chumar) and left after a strong protest from the Indian side. Again, in December 2014, Chinese troops intruded into Indian Territory and left after a confrontation. Moreover, when Indian PM Modi visited Arunachal Pradesh in February 2015, the visit was harshly criticized by the Chinese. China has chosen to target highly strategic areas along the line of Actual Control. In Ladakh, it has chosen Despang and Chumar region where India otherwise has a tactical military advantage. In the east it has shown agression in Arunachal Pradesh that leads to a narrow corridor between Bangladesh, Nepal and India. Cartographic aggression is a connected assault. This intensity of transgression of India's borders and violation of agreements is a recent phenomenon and is reflective of what China is doing on its other borders.

The strategy also covers Pakistani-occupied Kashmir (PoK) with a cover story of providing assistance by way of road improvements. China has cemented its "all-weather ties" with Pakistan by agreeing to build a strategic $46 billion (Rs 2.9 lakh crore) economic corridor through Pakistan-occupied Kashmir (linking China with the port of Gwadar). The militarization of Tibet is another significant activity. The demography of Tibet is forcefully being altered by settling a Han majority in this ethinic Tibetan homeland.

The Sino–Japanese conflict on Senkaku Islands

China is involved in a dispute with Japan over the Senkaku Islands. Despite the Treaty of Peace and Friendship between Japan and the People's Republic of China that was signed on August 12, 1978 by Deng Xiaoping and Fukuda Takeo, and which came into effect on October 23, 1978, the dispute continues. Its aggressive activities in this region also began in 2006. Vessels from China and Hong Kong have entered into the Japanese EEZ many times. On several occasions activists, backed by the Chinese Coast Guard ships and boats have tried to forcibly gain entry into the Japanese islands.

A perceptible intention to change the status quo is obvious even in this case. Chinese jets and patrol boats have been aggressively visiting the area, resulting in Japan responding similarly to protect its territory. In its dispute with Japan over the Senkaku/Diaoyu Islands, China took the first step to change the status quo in its favour in December 2008 when it dispatched law enforcement vessels into the 12 nm territorial waters around the islands for the first time. After the Japanese government purchased three of the five islands in September 2012, China reacted by conducting patrols in the contiguous and territorial waters on a nearly regular basis. Establishing a routine presence is aimed at challenging Japan's administrative control over the islands and bringing it under Chinese jurisdiction.

On November 23rd, 2013, China demarcated a maritime Air Defence Identification Zone (ADIZ). While other countries also have ADIZs, the Chinese zone is special in a couple of ways. First, China's ADIZ encompasses the air space above Japan's Senkaku Islands and it overlaps with Japan's ADIZ. An unfettered and direct challenge to Japanese sovereignty became obvious. We should remind ourselves about the tension in May 2014 when a Chinese Su-27 flew close to Japan's Self Defence Forces. I am sure the similarity in the Chinese pattern and the time lines are obvious.

Similarity with China and the South China Sea

In the South China Sea, China mantains cordial diplomatic relations with the disputants but simultaneously asserts its claims through imposing fishing bans, sending out its maritime forces and carrying out naval exercises and gradually occupying areas. Even here, agreements exist.

With Vietnam, China signed two agreements; one in 1993 and another in 2011. It also has party-to-party relations with Vietnam. Its diplomatic relations with the Philippines are also continuing. All this is reinforced through multilateral platforms like ASEAN.

The Narrative of Peace has been the underlying theme, regardless of China's action. The Chinese PM Li Keqiang stated in November 2014 soon after the APEC Summit that China and ASEAN have reached consensus on a "dual track approach", wherein the issues involved in specific disputes are discussed bilaterally, but ASEAN as a whole is given a role in upholding "peace and stability". While this is not the first time that China has agreed to give some role to ASEAN, this could be seen as its willingness to provide a little more space to ASEAN. President Xi Jinping, while addressing the Australian Parliament in the same month after the G20, stated that China would not use force to achieve its objectives. He offered that, "It is China's longstanding position to address peacefully its disputes with countries concerned and territorial sovereignty and maritime interests through dialogue and consultation." Earlier in the year, Chinese Foreign Ministry spokesman, Qin Gang, on 7th March, 2014 announced China's willingness to work with the Association of Southeast Asian Nations (ASEAN) to formulate a Code of Conduct (COC) for the South China Sea. Significantly Philippine president Benigno Aquino III said he and Chinese counterpart Xi Jinping had a "meeting of minds" during talks in Beijing where he went to attend the APEC Summit. In April 2015, China's ministry of foreign affairs reiterated that Beijing wants relevant disputes resolved through negotiation and consultation by countries directly concerned. The foreign ministry argued Beijing is committed to safeguarding regional peace and stability and pushing for mutually beneficial win-win arrangements with countries concerned. "The situation of this region is generally stable and relevant cooperation has been moved forward with positive results," foreign ministry spokesman Hong Lei said in a press conference in Beijing. One notices the smooth diplomatic shift towards a bilateral format instead of a multi-lateral uniform settlement. A divided oppposition suits China.

In contrast to these stated positions of peace and conflict avoidance, since 2006, China began to change its approach towards the South China Sea. In December 2006, China placed new markers in the Paracel Islands, which Vietnam protested calling them invalid. In 2007, China established the city of Sansha for administering Paracel and Spratly Islands that obviously hurt Vietnam. In 2008, the Chinese State Council authorised Chinese Maritime Surveillance (CMS) to commence regular patrols over all the maritime areas claimed by China. In 2010, CMS ships also established a sovereignty marker on James Shoal. In the same year, China established local governing bodies in Paracel Islands and developed the islands for tourism. In 2011, China cut off the cable of Vietnamese seismic ships. China took further steps to tighten its control over the disputed areas when in June 2012 the Chinese Cabinet approved the establishment of the prefectural level city of Sansha to strengthen its administration over the Xisha (Paracel), Zhongsha and Nansha (Spratly) island groups. China also occupied Scarborough Shoal, threatened Second James Shoal and placed an oil rig in the Vietnamese EEZ which was accompanied by 7 military ships and 33 Chinese marine patrol boats and surveillance ships, along with many other vessels. The new fishing regulations issued by China's Hainan provincial authorities from 1st January 2014, cover not only China's EEZ but also disputed areas, as well as international waters. China has shown scant regard to the Philippines appeal to the International Court. The position paper issued by China in December 2014 not only dismisses the grounds for the Filipino appeal; it also forcefully states that the arbitration case will not 'shake China's resolve and determination to safeguard its sovereignty and relevant maritime rights and interests.'

China is also making assiduous efforts to strengthen its hold over the disputants through diplomatic and economic manoeuvres. China is promoting the establishment of a new maritime silk route for the 21st century linking the Pacific and Indian oceans; China is trying to connect more than 20 countries along the ancient Silk Road under a grandiose program christened "One Belt, One Road."; the creation of free trade zones along China's periphery; deepening regional financial cooperation by creating an Asian infrastructure bank; and pushing for the conclusion by the end of 2015 of the Regional Comprehensive Economic Partnership (RCEP), a free trade agreement that would include the ten ASEAN member states and its FTA partners (Australia, China, India, Korea, and New Zealand). In addition, China is focussing on improving connectivity with South East Asian countries. It has funded major infrastructure projects in Southeast Asia such as the Nanning-Singapore economic corridor that envisions an integrated road and railway transportation system linking China, Vietnam, Laos, Cambodia, Thailand, Malaysia, and Singapore. It is also supporting the Great Mekong Sub-region, to link China's Yunnan Province, with the six nations of the Mekong River basin. While these are being presented as initiatives for trade and development, their major strategic purpose is to establish Chinese indespensability. There are suspicions about China's real intent. The hegamonic design is somewhat obvious. China's efforts have obviously divided the ASEAN. The greator worry is the increasing militarisation of the region. There is no need to go into the details of the increased military expenditure of all the countries involved. That is well known.

Commonality in the deductions

In my view, China has decided to disturb the strategic balance in the region. All of its actions are directed at changing the status quo. It has expanded the scope and expanse of its assertion. It has done so through gradual but continuous effort. It has a plan and it is working towards this plan. China is not only occupying reefs and shoals but also placing oil rigs, cutting cables, denying other disputants to carry on normal exploration in their own EEZs, stopping ships of other countries going to their own reefs, as well as harassing fishermen of other countries.

There does not appear there's any likelihood of China changing its strategy. The status quo suits China eminently.

I could also venture to mention that Chinese aggressive nationalism and irredentism has become a potent feature of China's foreign policy.

China has little doubt that the developments in the South China Sea are an escalatory step towards a rivalry between China and US. Notwithstanding some Chinese scholars saying that China is unlikely to wage war in the South China Sea, it is using its military power to deter other claimants from opposing China in the South China Sea.

The Chinese approach towards the South China Sea is part of its policy towards all areas in periphery. Chinese approach reflects its duplicity. It is showing scant regard for the treaties made with other countries to maintain peace and tranquillity and also towards the International Court of Justice.

China feels its economic relations with the claimants would not allow the disputants to go beyond a limit to oppose China. Moreover it feels that it can use its economic relations and influence to keep the ASEAN divided. Hence, there is no real commitment towards a Code of Conduct.

The Indian Perspective

India has always respected international conventions and accepted decisions of legal international bodies. The acceptance and implementation of the verdict with respect to the maritime dispute with Bangladesh is testimony to that fact. India'sposition is clearly based on statements emenating from India and her Prime Minister. They are as follows:

1. **Freedom of navigation and overflights in the South China Sea.** Soon after the placing of oilrig in the South China Sea, the Indian Foreign Ministry's spokesperson Syed Akbaruddin stated, "India maintains that freedom of navigation in the South China Sea should not be impeded and India calls for cooperation and strengthening of maritime security. Later in the US-India Joint Strategic Vision for Asia-Pacific and Indian Ocean Region (January 2015) specific mention was made on South China Sea. It said, "Regional prosperity depends on security. We affirm the importance of safeguarding maritime security and ensuring freedom of navigation and overflight throughout the region, especially in the South China Sea."

2. **Status quo to be maintained and opposition to expansionist policy and use of force.** Indian PM Modi in Japan in 2014 stated that "everywhere around us, we see an 18th century expansionist mind-set: encroaching in other countries, intruding in others' waters, invading other countries and capturing territory."

3. **Primacy of International Law of the Sea and emphasis on Code of Conduct.** At the 12th India-ASEAN Summit, Indian PM Modi delved into the South China Sea dispute in a little more detail in his closing statement. "For peace and stability in South China Sea, everyone should follow international norms and law. This includes the 1982 United Nations Convention on the Law of the Sea. We also hope that you will be able to successfully implement the guidelines to the 2002 Declaration on Conduct and that the code of conduct on South China Sea can be concluded soon on the basis of consensus."

Conclusion

Given the the efforts that concerned nations have already made, and the fact that there is a ruling by the Permanent Court of Arbitration in place, it is not easy to offer any suggestions. Obviously the first suggestion is to get the ruling implemented. However, the challenge is how to go about that? The main thrust should be to reduce tensions and the chances of a conflict. Given economic relations among the disputants with China and rising ultra-nationalism, coupled with militarisation, there is a need to work out pragmatic solutions. While the Code of Conduct has been accepted by all, ways need to be found for its finalisation and implementation.

There is a need for ASEAN unity in the matter. Any bi-lateral understanding will dilute the impact of international opinion. A much stronger joint push from the international community is needed for changing the Chinese approach so that the status quo ante is restored.

The US should take steps in coordination with other outside powers interested in the region and also with other disputants to build pressure on China. Separate diplomatic statements and efforts have not yielded any results.

Russia, which has an interest in South East Asia and has developed ties with nations in the region in energy and defence, should also be brought in so that bi-polarity does not develop on this issue because of Russia siding with China. Russia's bilateral ties with Malaysia, Indonesia, and Vietnam need to be leveraged against its strategic partnership with China.

Finally, all international forae and all connected issues should be comprehensively synergised to highlight the challenge to our global future. Ecology and preservation of marine life is a major concern, and cannot be ignored.

A Study on the China's "Nine-Dash" Line: The Award of PCA (July 12, 2016)

Jeong Gab Yong

Maritime Disputes of the South China Sea

The South China Sea (SCS) is the dominant term used in English, but it is sometimes called by different names (for instance, Vietnam calls it "The East Sea"). SCS is a part of the Pacific Ocean, through which one-third of the world's shipping passes and it is believed to hold huge oil and gas reserves beneath its seabed. Joint development authorities have been set up in areas of overlapping claims to jointly develop the area and divide the profits equally without settling the issue of sovereignty over the area.

It's mostly maritime features (islands, islets, rocks, shoals, atolls, banks, etc.) are subject to competing claims of sovereignty by several countries, namely Vietnam, China, the Philippines, Malaysia, Indonesia, Taiwan and Brunei. These countries have made competing territorial claims over the SCS, and such disputes have been regarded as Asia's most potentially dangerous point of conflict.

By Notification and Statement of Claim, dated 22 January 2013, the Philippines initiated arbitration proceedings against China pursuant to

Articles 286 and 287 of the Convention and in accordance with Article 1 of Annex VII of the Convention. On Tuesday, July 12th 2016, the Permanent Court of Arbitration (PCA) in The Hague issued its long-awaited ruling in the South China Sea disputes between the Philippines and China.

China's "Nine-Dash Line" in the SCS

In the 1940s, the "Nine-Dash Line" appeared on a map of islands in the SCS published by China, and the "Eleven-Dash Line" first published the "Map of Location of the South China Sea Islands" in 1946 and 1949. In 1953, two "dash lines" were removed from the "Eleven-Dash Line", when the territorial title to the Gulf of Tonkin was transferred from China to Vietnam.

In 2009, the map of the "Nine-Dash Line" formally appeared again, and the map was attached to the *Notes Verbale* presented by China in response to the Viet Nam/Malaysia Joint Submission to the United Nations on 7 May 2009.

In this *"Notes Verbale"*, China presented its position concerning the "Nine-Dash Line" as follows:

> "China has indisputable sovereignty over the islands in the South China Sea and the adjacent waters, and enjoys sovereign rights and jurisdiction over the relevant waters, as well as the seabed and subsoil thereof. The above position is consistently held by the Chinese Government, and is widely known by the international community."

China is claiming a large portion of the disputed territories in the SCS including the Spratly and Paracel Islands based on the so-called "Nine-Dash Line" and argues that these islands were part of its territory centuries ago, and it is using a 1947 map to support its claims.

In 2013, China released a new map of China, adding a 10th dash on the eastern side of Taiwan. In its 2013 map, China claims the "Ten-Dash Line" is its "national boundaries" without explaining the legal basis or giving the fixed coordinates for the Dash Line.

The "Nine-Dash Line" in the South China Sea (SCS) claimed by China covers most of the SCS and overlaps Exclusive Economic Zone (EEZ) claims of Vietnam, the Philippines, Indonesia, Malaysia, Taiwan, and Brunei. China claims sovereignty or sovereign rights over the SCS on the basis of discovery, and historic titles.

Award of the PCA on the "Nine-Dash Line"

The Award of PCA was a milestone decision in an attempt to peacefully settle the South China Sea disputes in accordance with international law. This is the first international ruling for disputes in the South China Sea, creating the basis to settle disputes in the sea in accordance with international law, specifically the United Nations Convention on the Law of the Sea (1982 UNCLOS).

One of the most important aspects is that the ruling rejected China's claim of historic rights within the "Nine-Dash Line" based on the 1982 UNCLOS and Annex VII of the Convention.

China has stated its view that its "relevant rights in the South China Sea, formed in the long historical course" are "protected under international law including the United Nations Convention on the Law of the Sea (UNCLOS)."

The 1982 UNCLOS does not include any express provisions preserving or protecting historic rights that are at variance with the Convention. On the contrary, the Convention supersedes earlier rights and agreements to the extent of any incompatibility. The Convention is comprehensive in setting out the nature of the exclusive economic zone and continental shelf, and the rights of other States within those zones. China's claim to historic rights is not compatible with these provisions.

The Tribunal concludes that China's claim to historic rights to the living and non-living resources within the "nine-dash line" is incompatible with the Convention to the extent that it exceeds the limits of China's maritime zones as provided for by the Convention.

Finally, the Tribunal concludes that, between the Philippines and China, China's claims to historic rights, or other sovereign rights or jurisdiction, with respect to the maritime areas of the South China Sea encompassed by the relevant part of the 'nine-dash line', are contrary to the Convention and without lawful effect in that they exceed the geographic and substantive limits of China's maritime entitlements under the Convention.

Legal Effect of the China's "Nine-Dash Line"

China's "Nine-Dash Lines" are illegal and contrary to international law and the 1982 United Nations Convention on the Law of the Sea(1982 UNCLOS), for the following reasons;

First, China has no "Historic Titles" in the SCS.

To obtain territorial sovereignty of a state or historic titles, for example, discovery, pre-occupation, effective control, prescription, or acquisition should be considered by international law.

China insisted that from the ancient dynasty of Han, or Ming, China had explored and had effective control over the South China Sea and argued that any other coastal countries never protested or raised any objection to China's claims to the SCS.

However, China's historic titles to territory are very uncertain and protested by other countries, so it cannot be recognized as historic title. And other coastal countries, including Vietnam, have also insisted that they had rights on the East Sea (SCS) many years ago.

Second, The SCS is not "historical waters".

China claims sovereignty over the SCS by holding so-called "historic rights" on the grounds. To meet the international standard for establishing a claim to historic waters, a State must demonstrate its open, effective, long term, and continuous exercise of authority, coupled with acquiescence by foreign States.

China's claims to sovereign rights and jurisdiction, and to "historic rights" do not meet the international standard for establishing a claim to "historical waters".

Third, China's claims are very ambiguous.

China insists that it has indisputable sovereignty over the islands in the SCS and attached "Nine Dash Lines' map in its *Notes Verbale* of 2009. However, China has not clarified the legal basis or nature of its claim associated with "Nine Dash Lines" map. However, he legal nature of the water or maritime area enclosed by it remains unclear.

Vietnam and other coastal countries objected to China's claims reflected in the "Nine Dash Lines" map as being without basis under the international law of the sea.

The "Nine Dash Line" is invalid.

Generally, the act would have the legal effect, its intention is to be clear and unambiguous, and the legal act itself should be obvious.

China's "Nine-Dash Line" is one of the legal acts. If it can be seen as justified and legally valid, its intention and geographic indications should be clear and obvious. But it merely crossed the line without a geographical indication that cannot be seen as justified or valid. Furthermore, it is uncertain whether the map has any legal relevance to the delimitation of China's boundaries in the SCS, because China has never provided any explanation as to the exact meaning of the "Nine-Dash Line".

Therefore, it should be determined to be invalid because of the geographical indication in itself is unclear and false.

<Fig.> 1947 Lines and 2009 Lines are not coincident

Source; U.S. Department of State, *LIMITS IN THE SEAS*, No.143 (5th Dec., 2014)

The "Nine-Dash Line" is illegal in light of the 1982 UNCLOS.

The legal nature and meaning of the "Nine-Dash Line" is very ambiguous, and its validity under the 1982 UNCLOS is highly controversial. The 1982 UNCLOS provides for the conditions of the islands having EEZ or continental shelf, as well as the limit of EEZ. Accordingly, China's claim to the wide maritime area, the islands and features in the SCS cannot be justified under the 1982 UNCLOS.

The question regarding the legality of the "Nine-Dash Line" should not be judged in light of the 1982 UNCLOS.

The "Nine-Dash Line", and China's land reclamation and militarization violated the 1982 UNCLOS and international law.

Since China's land reclamation and militarization efforts began in December 2013, it has repeatedly stated that what it's doing is legal. In a statement, China's Foreign Ministry said that the country's activities were "completely within the scope of China's sovereignty", and the outposts will have undefined military purposes, as well as help with maritime search and rescue, disaster relief and navigation.

However, the land reclamation and militarization, which began in late 2013, have turned submerged reefs into islands, and their locations are in "disputed areas". The areas within the SCS under dispute include a number of islands and other rock formations, so the problem is that much of the territory claimed by China overlaps with the EEZs of other countries.

China's reclamation and militarization activities are disturbing the free navigation of the seas. The ASEAN 2002 Declaration stated China should refrain from inhabiting currently uninhabited areas and to handle their differences in a constructive manner.

For these reasons, China's land reclamation and militarization activities in the "Nine-Dash Line" violated the 1982 UNCLOS and the international law.

Conclusion

As discussed above, China's "Nine-Dash Line" did not meet the international standards for establishing sovereignty or sovereign right to the SCS, and China's so-called "Nine-Dash Line" is contrary to the general principles of international law and the 1982 UNCLOS.

International law is consent-based governance, and is the set of rules generally regarded and accepted as binding in relations between nations. It serves as a framework for the practice of organized international relations. Furthermore, international law is concerned with the rights and duties of states in their relations with each other.

Our international community has realized through many historical experiences the miserable consequences of war between countries. The United Nations was established in order to maintain global peace and security.

As one of the five permanent members of the United Nations Security Council, China is a country that has a primary responsibility to maintain international peace and security of the international community and to develop friendly relations among nations, based on respect for the principle of equal rights.

From the accumulated wisdom of clamant countries, China needs to resolve international disputes not by force or war, but through peaceful methods or means.

The most fundamental cause of these conflicts is the "Nine-Dash Line" that China claims.

In order to solve the SCS disputes peacefully, China should to give up and withdraw its "Nine-Dash Line" voluntarily - and immediately.

The South China Sea Conflict: Impact of the Paracel Oil Rig Incident and the PCA Award relevant to Three Warfares

Koichi Sato

Introduction

The three warfares were named by the China's People's Liberation Army (PLA) in 2003, and its original source was Sunzi (孫子) in 5th Century B.C.,[138] though some ASEAN nations, such as Vietnam and

---

[138] Senryaku Kenkyu Gurupu (戦略研究グループ：Strategic Study Group), Zhugoku ni yoru Sansen No Teigitou Oyobi Ea Pawa Ni Kansuru Sansen No Jirei (中国による三戦の　定義等およびエア・パワーに関する三戦の事例：China's Definition of Three Warfare and Some Cases of Three Warfare on Air Power), *Ea Pawa Kenkyu* (エア・パワー研究： Research on Air Power), Staff College, Air-Self Defense Force, No. 2, January 2016, p. 113.

the Philippines skillfully utilize three warfares to cope with China in the South China Sea conflict.

The Chinese government sent the oilrig Haiyang Shiyou 981 off the Paracel Islands on 2 May 2014.[139] China dispatched China Coast Guard (CCG) patrol vessels, transportation ships, and fishery boats to defend the oilrig against Vietnamese government ships. The Vietnamese government used the international mass media to denounce China's "unlawful" energy detection and violent activities against the Vietnamese law enforcement agencies' vessels and fishing boats.[140]

The Vietnamese government gained political support from Japan, the United States of America, and many Western countries in the diplomatic and media arenas. Under significant psychological pressure, Chinese leaders let the Chinese oilrig and vessels pull out more than a month ahead of schedule from the disputed waters. This was considered a victory by Vietnam in its media warfare with China.

On 22 January 2013, the Philippines government initiated arbitration proceedings with the Permanent Court of Arbitration (PCA) in The Hague, the Netherlands, to clarify its conflicting claims with China in the South China Sea.[141] And on 12 July 2016 the PCA decided overwhelmingly in favor of the Philippines in its ruling against China over its expansive claims and aggressive behavior in the South China Sea.

The Tribunal concluded that, between the Philippines and China, there was no legal basis for China to claim historic rights to resources, in excess of the rights provided for by the Convention, and within the sea areas falling within the 'nine-dash line'.[142] The award has strong legal and psychological impacts on the Chinese government.

---

[139] "Remarks by FM Spokesman Le Hai Binh on 4th May 2014" http://mofa.gov.vn/en/tt_baochi/pbnfn/ns140505232230/newsitem_print_preview, accessed September 13, 2014.

[140] Author's interview with a Vietnamese diplomat on 15 December 2015.

[141] The Philippines' Submission, *ASEAN Focus: Special Issue on the South China Sea Arbitration*, ISEAS Yusof Ishak Institute, July 2016, p.2.

[142] *Press Release: The South China Sea Arbitration (The Republic of the Philippines V. The People's Republic of China)*, Permanent Court of Arbitration, The Hague, 12 July 2016, pp. 1-11.

This short paper looks into the impact of these two dramatic incidents on the structure of the South China Sea conflict relevant to China's three warfares: media warfare, psychological warfare, and legal warfare.

Structure of the South China Sea Conflict

The Chinese Prime Minister Zhou Enlai (周恩来) declared the Chinese claim on four South China Sea archipelagos on 15 August 1951, and the Chinese government drew the nine-dash line in the South China Sea Map in 1953.[143] It claims all the maritime features in the line, though their assertion of the first discovery and effective occupation does not seem to be superior to the other claimants such as the Philippines, Vietnam, Malaysia, Taiwan, and Brunei.[144]

Table-1: Conflicting Claims in the South China Sea

States and a Party	No of Claimed (Claimed Year)	No of Occupation
Taiwan	All (1947)	1
China	All (1951)	8
Philippines	53 (1956)	8
Vietnam	All (1956)	8
Malaysia	17 (1979)	21
Brunei	1~2 (1982)	0

---

[143] Han Zhenhua (韓振華), et al, *Woguo nanhai zhudao shiliao huibian* (我国南海諸島史料・編), Dongfang Chubanshe (東方出版社) Publisher, 1985, Xiamen (厦門), p. 444, Li Guoqiang (李国強), Zhugoku To Shuhenkokka No Kaijoukokkyou Mondai (中国と周辺国 家の海上国境問題：The Frontier Issue between China and its Neighboring Countries), Slavic Research Center, Hokkaido University, *Kyokai Kenkyu* (境界研究：Japan Border Review), No. 1, 2010, p.51.

[144] The Permanent Court of Arbitration has determined that there is no legal basis to China's expansive claims to the South China Sea. Goh Sui Noi, "Tribunal rejects China's sea claims," *The Straits Times*, July 13, 2016.

Source: Tatsuo Urano, Nankaishoto Kokusai Funsoushi (南海諸島国際紛 争史：History of the International Conflict on the South China Sea Islands), Tosui Shobo Publisher, Tokyo, 1997. Some data amended by the writer.

Is it true that small ASEAN nations cannot cope with China? Physically, it is true that they have difficulty coping with China in terms of naval engagement. However, naval engagement is only a part of the maritime conflict. From external observation, current maritime conflict in the South China Sea is composed of three parts: high intensity conflict, middle intensity conflict, and low intensity conflict, and three warfares: media warfare, legal warfare, and psychological warfare[145] in the diplomatic and political fields including ASEAN's Conference Diplomacy.

The high intensity conflict is relevant to nuclear war; a matter between China and the United States of America (U.S.A). The People's Liberation Army (PLA) navy constructed an underground submarine base to hide strategic submarines from spy satellites in 2008.[146] The PLA navy dispatches the strategic submarine, which carries Submarine-Launched Ballistic Missiles (SLBM), for nuclear patrol every day.

China wants to make the South China Sea a sanctuary for its submarines so that China can maintain the Second Strike Capability against the U.S. nuclear attack. The U.S. navy dispatched anti-submarine and maritime surveillance airplanes such as the EP3, and ocean surveillance ships to watch the PLA strategic submarines' activities. These maritime disputes led the EP3's collision in April 2001, and the incident involving the USNS Impeccable in March 2009.

The middle intensity conflict is relevant to naval engagements and naval exercises. Vietnam has had two naval engagements with China. The Vietnamese navy encountered the PLA navy in the area around the Paracel Islands in January 1974.[147] In 1988, the Socialist Republic of Vietnam navy had a similar encounter with the PLA navy in the seas surrounding the

---

[145] Peter Navarro, China's Non-Kinetic Three Warfares Against America, http://www.huffingtonpost.com/peter-navarro-and-greg-autry/chinas-nonkinetic-three-w b 8914156.html, accessed July 27, 2016, Senryaku Kenkyu Gurupu, op. cit., pp. 113-124.

[146] Thomas Harding, "Chinese nuclear submarine base," Telegraph, 1 May 2008, http://www.telegraph.co.uk/news/worldnews/asia/china/1917167/Chinese-nuclear-submarine-base.html, accessed August 2, 2016.

[147] M. Taylor Fravel, *Strong Borders Secure Nation*, Princeton, 2008, pp. 267-299.

Spratly Islands, during which the PLA navy seized seven reefs including Johnson South Reef.[148]

The PLA navy currently conducts naval exercises in the areas of the Spratly Islands, the Paracel Islands and Scarborough Shoal in the Macclesfield Bank to intimidate the ASEAN claimants such like Vietnam, the Philippines, Malaysia, and Brunei. This, in spite of the Vietnamese navy purchasing six Russian Kilo class Hunter-Killer submarines in a large effort to develop a deterrent capability. The PLA navy has also reclaimed reefs of the Spratly Islands, and constructed airstrips. The U. S. navy conducts Freedom of Navigation Operations (FNOPS) to check the Chinese offensive, although current FNOPS only mean the innocent passage.[149]

The Low Intensity Conflict relates to maritime law enforcement agencies, transportation ships, and fishery boats.[150] It is actually the main conflict in the South China Sea between China and ASEAN claimants, as the Chinese government tries to avoid U.S. naval intervention. If China dispatches PLA navy gunboats to defeat small navies of ASEAN claimants, it would become a serious security issue of the sea lane of communications (SLOC) in the South China Sea, and is relevant to the national interests of the U.S., as well as its ally, the Philippines.

The Low Intensity Conflict and the Three Warfares

1.   The Paracel Oil Rig Incident

If China wants to avoid U. S. intervention, it should concentrate on the low intensity conflict with ASEAN claimants in the South China Sea. The China Coast Guard (CCG) vessels collided with smaller Vietnamese Marine Police vessels in the Paracel Oil Rig incident, and the CCG vessels chased and collided with Vietnamese fishery boats in the area surrounding

---

[148]   Ibid.

[149]   Joseph Bosco, After the South China Sea Ruling, Time for More FONOPs, Diplomat, July 29, 2016, http://thediplomat.com/tag/freedom-of-navigation-operations-south-china-sea, accessed August 5, 2016.

[150]   "China sends more military ships to defend illegal oil rig," Vietnam+ (June 5, 2014), http://en.vietnamplus.vn/china-sends-more-military-ships-to-defend-illegal-oil-rig/61403.vnp, accessed September 14, 2014.

the Paracel Islands repeatedly.[151] The Vietnamese government appealed the CCG's violent activities to the Japanese, the U.S. and many other western governments.[152] The Vietnamese Marine Police invited foreign reporters to their vessels and let them observe the CCG's violent activities at sea.[153]

The collision of the CCG vessels with the smaller Vietnamese marine police vessels and fisheries boats was shown on TV programs, YouTube, and Western news outlets.[154] The incident shocked many people, because it flew in the face of how we perceive maritime law enforcement agencies, such as those of Japan and U.S. Coast Guard authorities, which are charged with navigation safety, search and rescue operations, the prevention of illegal activities, and marine pollution at sea.

Quite unexpectedly, Western nations supported the Vietnamese brave resistance movement, and Western governments denounced China in various international conferences including the Shangri-La Dialogue in Singapore.[155] Chinese leaders were under psychological pressure, resulting in the Chinese oilrig and vessels puling out more than a month ahead of

---

[151] "Chinese ship sinks Vietnamese fishing vessel," Vietnam+ (May 26, 2014), http://en.vietnamplus.vn/chinese-ship-sinks-vietnamese-fishing-vessel/60909.vnp, accessed September 17, 2014, Sasaki Manabu (佐々木学), "Sekkin 30 meters, Isshoku Sokuhatsu Zhugoku-Betonamu, Minamisinakai Genkai" (接近 30m、一触即発中国・ベ　トナム、南シナ海厳戒：Access 30m, An Explosive situation Sino-Vietnamese Maritime Conflict, Alert in the South China Sea), Asahi Shimbun (朝日新聞), May 28, 2014, p. 1.

[152] Author's interview with the Vietnamese diplomatic resource, March 3, 2015.

[153] Sasaki Manabu, "Sekkin 30 meters, Isshoku Sokuhatsu Zhugoku-Betonamu, Minamisinakai Genkai," op. cit.

[154] The photo of the CCG 37102's collision into the Vietnamese ship was appeared in the front page of *Sankei Shimbun*, May 11, 2014. Kyodo, "Ugokanu Shoko" (動かぬ証拠：Indisputable evidence), *Sankei Shimbun* (産経新聞), May 11, 2014, p. 1.

[155] "Major Power Perspectives on Peace and Security in the Asia-pacific: Lieutenant General Wang Guanzhong (Shangri-la Dialogue 2014, Fourth Plenary Session)," International Institute for Strategic Studies (IISS) (June 1, 2014), https://www.iiss.org/en/events/shangri%20la%20dialogue/archive/2014-c20c/plenary-4-a239/wang-guanzhong-2e5e, accessed January 30, 2016.

schedule from the disputed waters.[156] The Vietnamese government got the victory in the media and in the psychological warfare against China.

2. The PCA Award

The parties of the low intensity conflict lack the decisive blow, and the conflict has continued. If so, the weak and small countries can do many things in the context of three warfares. The Philippines' arbitration proceedings of 22 January 2013 can be classified in it. The Philippines' submissions requested the Tribunal to clarify its conflicting claims with China, namely: China's historic rights in the South China Sea, the legal effect of the Chinese "nine-dash line," several reefs' maritime status, the Chinese violation of the duties to protect the marine environment in relation to reclamation activities, the CCG vessels' dangerous activities against the Philippines' vessels, and so on.[157]

China submitted a *Note Verbale* rejecting the claim made by the Philippines in the Notification and Statement of Claim, and calling on the Philippines to resolve the dispute through bilateral negotiations.[158] China stated that "the Arbitral Tribunal lacks jurisdiction in the case," but it seemed that China never believed it, because the Chinese Ambassador to the United Kingdom requested a meeting with the President of the Tribunal on November 14, 2013, and the Tribunal sent a letter to remind the Parties to refrain from *ex parte* communications with the members of the Tribunal.[159] The Philippines' arbitration proceedings had some legal and psychological impacts on China before the award.

---

[156] Teddy Ng & Kristine Kwok, "Oil rig stops exploration work near disputed Paracel Islands a month early," South China Morning Post, July 16, 2014, http://www.scmp.com/print/news/china/article/1555221/china-says-oil-rig-finishes-mission-waters-vietnam, accessed July 27, 2016.

[157] The Philippines' Submission, *ASEAN Focus: Special Issue on the South China Sea Arbitration*, ISEAS Yusof Ishak Institute, July 2016, p.2.

[158] Philippines files case against PRC, http://amti.csis.org/ArbitrationTL/, accessed August 7, 2016.

[159] Arbitral Tribunal, *PCA Case N°2013-19 In the Matter of an Arbitration before An Arbitral Tribunal Constituted under Annex VII to the 1982 United Nations Convention on the Law of the Sea between the Republic of the Philippines and the People's Republic of China, Award on Jurisdiction and Admissibility*, Permanent Court of Arbitration, 29 October 2015, p. 18.

The award in the *Philippines versus China Arbitration* of 12 July 2016 was a sensational decision, because it denied not only most of China's claims but also the importance of the shape of maritime features above the waters in the Spratly Archipelago.[160] The award attached more importance to the islanders' community, and their historical economic activity. The award concluded the activity of the Japanese enterprises in the Spratly Islands in 1930-40 was transient and it never constituted inhabitation by a stable community and that all of the historical economic activity.[161]

It seems the reason that some prominent maritime law scholar called the award a "game changer."[162] The Tribunal concluded that historical navigation and fishing by China in the waters of the South China Sea represented the exercise of high seas freedoms, rather than of historic right, and that there was no evidence that China had historically exercised exclusive control over the waters of the South China Sea or prevented other States from exploiting their resources.[163] China didn't accept the award, though its legal base for nine-dash line and the historical rights were lost. The Philippines government got the victory in legal and psychological warfares against China.

Conclusion

The Paracel Oil Rig Incident and the PCA Award served as a lesson for all of the ASEAN claimants. They can utilize the media and psychological warfares against every Chinese maritime offensive in the South China Sea in the same way Vietnam did in its case, and the legal and psychological warfares, utilizing the Philippines' award against the Chinese assertion in the diplomatic arenas including ASEAN's conference diplomacy, though

---

[160] *Press Release: The South China Sea Arbitration (The Republic of the Philippines V. The People's Republic of China)*, Permanent Court of Arbitration, The Hague, 12 July. 2016, pp. 1-11.

[161] *Press Release: The South China Sea Arbitration (The Republic of the Philippines V. The People's Republic of China)*, Permanent Court of Arbitration, The Hague, 12 July 2016, p. 2.

[162] Robert Beckman, The South China Sea Ruling: game Changer in the Maritime Disputes, *RSIS Commentary*, No. 180 – 18 July 2016, pp. 1-6.

[163] Press Release: The South China Sea Arbitration (The Republic of the Philippines V. The People's Republic of China), Permanent Court of Arbitration, The Hague, 12 July 2016, p. 9.

ASEAN countries have no power to stop the low intensity conflict in the South China Sea. Further, with respect to the PCA award, the ASEAN claimants should consider some political by-products.

Firstly, the denouncement of China by the PCA award is not enough to construct the new regional order the award established. The ASEAN claimants should reconsider their delimitation of the boundaries in the South China Sea, and their own reclamations, if they really respect the PCA award. If reconsideration by ASEAN claimants of the current boundaries and the reclamations is not persuasive enough the effect of the award will be weakened. The writer considers this to be a difficult problem for all of the ASEAN claimants.

Secondly, the ASEAN claimants should be careful to utilize the award at future ASEAN conferences, if only because the ASEAN foreign ministers have experienced many hardships because of the joint statements and the Chairman's statements in relation to South China Sea issues. If ASEAN claimants stress the PCA award's logic too much, pro-China ASEAN nations will rebel. Thus, ASEAN's unity cannot be realized, and it will weaken the ASEAN's centrality in the Asia Pacific Region.

Thirdly, if the Philippines attach importance to the PCA award, China will attach importance to the bilateral negotiations with other claimants.[164] China may use the large amount of development and financial assistances as a counter to the PCA award. This will lead to disunity among the ASEAN claimants.

How can ASEAN cope with issues around a lack of unity and still pressure China effectively? The writer's recommendation to the ASEAN claimants is: utilize the influence of the external dialogue partners (Japan, the U.S.A, Australia, and India) and the dialogue sessions with them: hold an ASEAN Regional Forum (ARF), ASEAN+1 Summit, and East Asia Summit (EAS). The ASEAN claimants should also take more positive attitudes for the maritime consultations with them.[165]

---

[164]   Barry Desker, The South China Sea Ruling: Rising China Confronts Maritime Southeast Asia, *RSIS Commentary*, No. 179 – 15 July 2016, pp. 1-3.

[165]   It may be a time for Vietnam to abandon three no's defense policy. Ngo Di Lan, "Vietnam's Foreign Policy after the 12th National Party Congress: Expanding Continuity," cogitASIA, http://cogitasia.com/vietnams-foreign-policy-after-the-12th-national-party-congress-expanding-continuity, accessed August 8, 2016.

Further, the writer recommends Vietnam and other ASEAN claimants ask the dialogue partners for a helping hand to find the materials which will support them in legal warfare. Here's an example. The Chinese government repeatedly asserted that former Vietnamese Prime Minister Pham Van Dong had sent a letter to the Chinese government on 14 September 1958, recognizing Chinese territorial sovereignty of the Spratly and Paracel Islands. China continues to utilize the letter as a kind of estoppel.

The writer found the Chinese translation of Prime Minister Pham Van Dong's letter in the collection of the Sino-Vietnamese historical records.[166] There is no description of the concrete names of the Spratly and Paracel Islands, and that Prime Minister Pham Van Dong merely accepted the Chinese statement of the territorial waters. This is just an example, but the writer is sure many contradictions exist between the Chinese historical statements and current assertive ones. These materials may submit another weapon of legal warfare for the ASEAN claimants against China.

---

[166] Guo Ming, Luo Fangming, Li Baiyin (郭明、羅方明、李白茵), Xiandai Zhongyue Guanxi Ziliao Xuanbian (現代中越関係資料選編 : Modern Sino-Vietnamese Relation Materials Collection), Shishi Chubanshe (時事出版社) Publisher, Beijing (北京), 1986, pp. 348-349.

The Permanent Court of Arbitration's Award on the South China Sea Dispute between the Philippines and China: Views from America

Nguyen Manh Hung

The June 12, 2016 PCA award on the South China Sea dispute between the Philippines and China, prompted different reactions from the United States. It is customary to say that, in foreign policy, the United States speaks with one voice. But that is not always the case, even between the two branches of the government. Official Government reactions tend to be more nuanced because their statements have to be backed by concrete actions; members of Congress can afford to be more straightforward and in the discussion among scholars and experts a difference of opinions is normal and encouraged. This paper sets out to examine and analyze the variety of views from the American policy elite.

KEY RULINGS OF THE PCA AWARD

1. China's nine-dash line claim has neither a basis in contemporary international law, nor in historical fact.
2. None of the features in the Spratly are islands eligible of an exclusive economic zone and a continental shelf. Those rocks and reefs can only claim at best a 12-mile territorial sea.
3. The Mischief reef, which China took from the Philippines in 1995, the Scarborough Shoal which China has cordoned off since 2012, and the Second Thomas Shoal where China blockaded Philippine marines garrisoned on an old ship that was deliberately run aground there, are all within the EEZ of the Philippines.
4. China has violated international law by preventing Philippine fishermen to fish in their traditional fishing area and by causing environmental damages to part of the South China Sea.

PRESS REACTIONS

American press reactions were reflected in editorials in major newspapers such as *The Washington Post*, *The New York Times*, and *The Wall Street Journal*. They may be listed under the following headings:

On the implications of the ruling

1. "A major blow to Mr. Xi's attempt to establish Chinese hegemony in the region and presents him with a fateful choice: embark on a dangerous escalation, or slowly and quietly back down."[167]
2. "How China reacts to the sweeping legal defeat over its claims to the South China Sea will tell the world a lot about its approach to international law, the use of its enormous power, and its global ambitions. It would be foolish for President Xi to take provocative actions that could inflame regional tensions and conceivably lead to a military confrontation with its neighbors or the United States."[168]

---

[167] *The Washington Post* Editorial Board, July 13, 2016.

[168] *The New York Times* editorial, July 12, 2016

Warnings of Chinese reactions

1. "China suffered a humiliating loss in arbitration, and now it's more dangerous than ever."[169]
2. "China may attempt to declare an air defense identification zone or militarize the Scarborough Shoal, which is clearly in the Philippines' EEZ and within 123 miles of important U.S. military and naval base like the Subic Bay."[170]

Policy recommendations

1. "Any such action "must be contested" by the United States for its own interests."[171] If the administration fails to stop a Chinese buildup on Scarborough Shoal, its allies are likely to conclude that, "alliance with Washington is useless."[172]
2. "The claimant nations in the region need to join the Philippines in endorsing the tribunal decision, negotiating jointly with China and then proceed, if necessary, with their own arbitration cases."[173]
3. "U.S. freedom of navigation operations (FONOPS) have been spared and timid. With the Hague verdict, these operations should "increase in frequency and scope."[174]

VIEWS OF SCHOLARS AND EXPERTS

In general, scholars and experts at liberal think tanks tend to stress caution and the importance of U.S.-China relations. Their counterparts at conservative think tanks tend to advocate more forceful responses to further Chinese assertive behavior.

---

[169] *Business Insider*, July 21, 2016

[170] *The Washington Post* editorial, July 13, 2016; *The Wall Street Journal* editorial, July 12, 2016; *Business Insider*, July 21, 2016

[171] *The Washington Post* editorial, July 13, 2016; *Business Insider*, July 21, 2016

[172] *The Washington Post* editorial, May 8, 2016

[173] *The New York Times* editorial, July 12, 2016; *The Wall Street Journal* editorial, July 12, 2016

[174] *The Wall Street Journal* editorial, July 12, 2016

Views on the implications of the ruling

Conservative scholars from the American Enterprise Institute, Michael Austin, Dan Blumenthal, and Jim Talent, opined:

1. The PCA decision marks "a legal watershed in Asian international relations."
2. It put in "sharp relief" the real dispute between China and its neighbors. China believes that, at least in its sphere of influence, the "biggest dogs get the biggest benefits;" its neighbors and the United States believe in a world where nations, big or small, have equal rights under international law.
3. It "legitimates" the U.S. and its allies' view of what constitutes just and reasonable maritime rules and practice.[175]

   Add to these, Mira Rapp-Hooper of the centrist think tank, Center for a New American Century, pointed out that:
4. China's defeat was "so crushing that it has left Beijing few ways to save face."[176]

Possible Chinese reactions

Chinese officials have declared China's willingness to enter into "provisional arrangements of a practical nature," pending final settlement of dispute. Under UNCLOS, such provisional "arrangements" set aside issues of sovereignty and promote joint development of resources.[177]

Mira Rapp-Hooper developed a comprehensive list of what China might possibly do:

1. China might declare an air of defense identification zone in the South China Sea;
2. It could start to reclaim land at Scarborough Shoal;

---

[175] Michael Austin; Dan Blumenthal; Jim Talent, "Reactions to the Hague's South China Sea ruling," *AEIdeas*, June 12, 2016

[176] Mira Rapp-Hooper, "Parting the South China Sea: How to uphold the rule of law," Foreign Affairs online, July 22, 2016

[177] *The Washington Post*, July 21, 2016

3. Chinese forces could attempt to intercept a U.S. ship or plane as it conducts freedom of navigation operation;
4. It could apply new domestic laws to the area it controls;
5. It could draw straight baselines around the Spratlys, then declaring for itself an EEZ that covers most of the waters of the South China Sea;
6. It could withdraw from UNCLOS.[178]2

Dean Cheng, of the conservative Heritage Foundation, added three more possibilities:

1. China could create a diplomatic counterweight to the PCA. On the one hand, it could attack the judgment and impartiality of the court. On the other, it could create the impression that many other states stood with it;
2. It could use economic leverage to incur costs to its opponents and provide benefits to its supporters;
3. It could put on a show of force by deploying the new aircraft carrier *Liaoning* to the area.[179]

What should the United States do?

Caution:

From the liberal think tank Brookings Institution, Richard C, Bush III, explained what China could do based on its long-term strategy, while Joseph Chinyong Liow issued words of caution to both China and the United States.

On China's grand strategy, Bush pointed out:

1. In the early 2000s Chinese leaders judged that China would only be secure if it expanded its eastern and southern strategic perimeters into the East and South China Seas. Thus began a program to build the capabilities to project power into the maritime domain and then use them to press its claims.

---

[178] Hooper, *op.cit*

[179] Dean Cheng, "South China Sea after the Tribunal Ruling: Where Do We Go From Here?" *The Heritage Foundation Commentary*, July 20, 2016

2. Contrary to the Tribunal's ruling, China could treat the Spratly Islands as islands under international law; define them as a single unit for purpose of defining maritime boundaries; draw straight baselines around them; declare for itself an EEZ that covers most of the waters of the South China Sea; and, over time, challenge the rights of other countries to freedom of navigation and the exploitation of natural resources.[180]

On the need for caution, Liow suggested:

For China -

1. It should do its part to bring the Code of Conduct to conclusion as a demonstration of its commitment to regional order and stability, and the peaceful settlement of disputes.
2. It should continue to engage concerned states in dialogue. However, such dialogue cannot be conducted on the premise of Chinese "unalienable ownership" of and "legitimate entitlements" in the South China Sea.

For the United States:

1. While the South China Sea issue has become a definitive point of reference of America's Southeast Asia policy, the U.S. must take into account the fact that Southeast Asian states have expressed their desire that the South China Sea issue should not overshadow or dominate the regional agenda.
2. In pushing back Chinese assertiveness, the U.S. must be careful not to inadvertently contribute to the militarization of the region, and must be mindful of the fact that China's South China Sea claim is also informed by a deep sense of vulnerability.[181]

---

[180] Richard C. Bush III, "The South China Sea and China's grand strategy," *Brookings*, July 13, 2016.

[181] Joseph Chinyong Liow, "What does the South China Sea ruling mean, and what's next?" *Brookings*, July 12, 2016

Provisional arrangements

Commenting on China's "provisional arrangements" proposal, Bonnie Glasser, senior adviser for Asia at the centrist Center for Strategic and International Studies, warned it could be "a trap for the Philippines." She argued that since the arbitration ruling declared that China has no legal basis to claim historic rights in the South China Sea, if the Philippines accepted the provisional arrangements, that might acknowledge that China had some form of resource rights despite the ruling to the contrary."[182]

Regional and Global Responses

Dean Cheng of the conservative Heritage Foundation suggested:

1. "The U.S must help coordinate regional and global responses and reactions; and,
2. The U.S. should help Brunei, Malaysia, the Philippines, and Vietnam must devise a common approach together.[183]

FONOPS

Conservative scholars tended to advocate for more intrusive FONOPS. From the Heritage Foundation, Dean Cheng deplored U.S. freedom of navigation operations (FONOPS) saying they have been anemic, and they have been limited to "innocent passage." He suggested the U.S. should conduct "more robust" FONOPS in the disputed area.[184]

Dan Blumenthal of the American Enterprise Institute, and Paul Gerwirtz, of Yale Law School, were more emphatic.

Blumenthal said the U.S. should conduct FONOPS within 12 nautical miles of all features not entitled to territorial seas.[185] Gerwirtz thought the U.S. should continue regular freedom of navigation operations, taking

---

[182] "China's Call for South China Sea talks faces challenge, *The Washington Post*, July 21, 2016

[183] Cheng, *op.cit.*

[184] Cheng, *op.cit.*

[185] Dan Blumenthal, "The Hague Tribunal: The hard work starts now," *AEIdeas*, July 12, 2016

advantage of any additional navigation rights produced by the tribunal's decision.[186]

Role of Diplomacy and Power Politics

Conservative scholars stressed the importance of quiet diplomacy backed by power in support of the arbitration decision.

Paul Gewirtz maintained that:

1. Law cannot solve all the conflicts in the South China Sea. After the court's ruling, there is an "urgent need to move ahead with negotiations, supported by prudent power politics";
2. The U.S. Senate should advance ratification of UNCLOS as "an urgent national security priority";
3. Negotiating an enforceable, rule-based code of conduct among the ASEAN nations and China should also be a top priority;
4. The U.S. must guard against escalation and reach out to other countries for quiet diplomatic discussion of our options. The U.S. and its allies must be ready if China seeks to use force to get its way.[187]

Jacques de Lisle, director of the Foreign Policy Research Institute at the University of Pennsylvania, talked about the challenge for the United States of "neither pushing too much nor pushing too little" for China to adhere to applicable international law.[188]

The need to avoid entrapment

Furthermore, Lisle warned that, "encouraging U.S. friends or allies to be more assertive and intractable in dealing with China over the South China Sea may impede the U.S. ability to find compromise with Beijing

---

[186] Paul Gerwitz, "Why law can't solve the South China Sea conflict," *The Washington Post*, July 12, 2016

[187] *Ibid.*

[188] Jacques de Lisle, "The South China Sea Arbitration Decision: China Fought the Law and the Law Won... or Did it?," Foreign Policy Research Institute, July 2016.

or some relatively face-saving path for China that might better serve the U.S. and the goals of regional peace and stability."[189]

Scarborough Shoal, a dangerous flashpoint

Fishermen as potential disrupters of peace -

The neo-conservative private intelligence firm, *Stratfor,* advised the U.S. to pay attention to the possible danger of unintended consequences caused by fishermen around Scarborough Shoal after the PCA ruling. He warned:

"Philippine fishermen are clamoring for government protection, saying the court's decision justifies more assertive action. Chinese media reports on fishermen in Hainan province highlight the economic dependence of Chinese fishing villages on the sea, suggesting that similar pressures exist in China. Though Beijing and Manila intend to keep things calm, it is not clear they are capable of entirely policing their fishermen, who appear eager to assert their rights and protect their livelihoods. The fishermen will be the greatest potential disrupter in the South China Sea in the wake of the ruling. Unlike protesters on the street, fishermen at sea, particularly in large numbers are beyond the easy control of law enforcement."[190]

Strategic importance of Scarborough Shoal

Rear Admiral Michael McDevitt (retired), senior fellow at the Center for Naval Analyses, a think tank closely associated with the Navy, emphasized the strategic importance of Scarborough Shoal to the U.S., stating that "Scarborough is ideally located to 'control' the northeast exit of the South China Sea and is only 150 nautical miles west of Subic Bay, if it was turned into a PLA base with a jet capable airfield it would enable among other things a credible Chinese South China Sea Air Defense Identification Zone."

Secretary of Defense Ash Carter was quoted as saying Scarborough is "a piece of disputed territory that, like other disputes in that region, has

---

[189] *Ibid.*
[190] "The South China Sea Ruling: Who Cares," *Stratfor,* July 13, 2016

the potential to lead to military conflict. That's particularly concerning to us, given its proximity to the Philippines."

McDevitt also pointed out that U.S. activities regarding Scarborough from March through May 2016 sent a clear signal that the U.S. sees "Scarborough as being different from the Paracels and Spratlys."[191]

CONGRESSIONAL REACTIONS

Immediate reactions to the PCA decision from leaders of both parties in both houses of the U.S. Congress are reflected in the "Statement from Foreign Affairs and Armed Services Democrats on South China Sea Decision;" remarks by Representative Mac Thornberry, Chairman of the House Armed Services Committee; statement of House Foreign Affairs Committee Chairman Ed Royce; and a joint statement by Senator McCain, Chairman of the Senate Armed Services Committee, and Senator Sullivan, committee member. Their views may be summarized as follows:

1. We welcome the Tribunal's ruling.
2. We urge other South China Sea claimants, including Vietnam, to seek similar peaceful resolution of maritime disputes.
3. The ruling presents an opportunity for ASEAN to speak with one voice on a matter of deep political and strategic importance ... to its entire membership.
4. Beijing's refusal to participate in PCA proceedings is disappointing. Its efforts to control critical international shipping lanes should be rejected.
5. China faces a choice. China can choose to be guided by international law, institutions, and norms. Or it can choose to reject them and pursue the path of intimidation and coercion. Too often in recent years, China has chosen the latter.
6. China has moved with impunity in the past few years because the consequences of doing so have been minimal so far.
7. The U.S. must continue to be clear and consistent in its policy to oppose unilateral actions by any claimant seeking to change the

---

[191]   Michael McDevitt, "Is it Time for the U.S. to Take a Position on Scarborough Shoal? *USNI News*, July 19, 2016

status quo in the South China Sea through the use of coercion, intimidation, unilateral declarations or military moves.

8. The U.S. must regularly challenge China's excessive maritime claims and maintaining a persistent presence of surface combatants and rotational aviation assets inside the first-island chain.

9. We will continue to uphold our commitment to the Philippine Mutual Defense Treaty of 1951.

10. We should take steps to ratify UNCLOS.

11. We must continue to maintain a favorable military balance in the Asia-Pacific region, and strengthen our alliances and develop new partnership with countries in the region.

12. We must clearly communicate our interests before Chinese activity begins. This should include diplomatically and militarily signaling to deter attempts to expel another country from disputed territory like Second Thomas Shoal, conducting further reclamation and militarization at strategic locations like Scarborough Shoal, or declaring an Air Defense Identification Zone in all or part of the South China Sea.

GOVERNMENT REACTIONS

On July 12, 2016, immediately after the tribunal decision, State Department spokesman John Kirby, issued a five-point press statement:

1. The PCA decision is an "important contribution" to the shared goal of a peaceful resolution to disputes in the South China Sea.

2. The decision of the Tribunal is final and binding on both China and the Philippines.

3. All claimants should avoid provocative statements or actions.

4. The decision serves as a new opportunity to renew efforts to address maritime disputes peacefully.

5. The U.S. encourages claimants to clarify their maritime claims in accordance with international law and to work together to manage and resolve their disputes.

In a keynote address on the same day at the Center for Strategic and International Studies, Daniel J. Kritenbrink, Senior Director for Asian

Affairs of the National Security Council, laid out U.S. long-term interests and commitments in the South China Sea. He stated:

1. Our security commitments to allies are iron-clad.
2. America's long-term interests in the South China Sea will continue for generations.

Before leaving for China to discuss the issue with Chinese leaders, U.S. National Security Adviser Susan Rice made three additional points:

1. U.S. relations with China are "the most consequential relationship." I travel to China "to advance our cooperation."
2. We would not allow crises in other parts of the world, from Syria to Turkey to Ukraine, to distract from President Obama's signature policy of "rebalancing" toward Asia.
3. The U.S. military would continue to sail and fly and operate in the South China Sea (despite a Chinese warning that such patrols could end in "disaster")[192]

In terms of actions, both public and quiet diplomacy is practised.

1. Susan Rice made a high-level visit to China, July 24-27, 2016, to urge Beijing to avoid escalation in the South China Sea.
2. Secretary of State John Kerry went to Laos and the Philippines, July 24-27, 2016, to attend AEAN meetings, and reassure Southeast Asian partners of U.S. commitment and urge restraint.
3. In Laos, on June 25, 2016, the U.S. joined with Japan and Australia to issue a statement voicing opposition to "large-scale land reclamation and the construction of outpost as well as the use of those outposts for military purposes" In the South China Sea.
4. Chief of U.S Naval Operations, Admiral John Richardson, visited China on July 17-20, 2016, to "improve mutual understanding and encourage professional interaction" between the two navies,

---

[192]   *Asia Times*, July 22, 2016

but insisted on the "rights, freedoms, and lawful uses of sea and airspace guaranteed to all."[193]

5. Earlier, at the Nuclear Security Summit in March 2016, President Obama warned President Xi of "serious consequences" if China reclaimed land at Scarborough Shoal.[194]

KEY POINTS OF CONSENSUS

With varying degree of differences, it may be said that the following points constitute a general consensus of the American policy elite form both inside and outside of the government on U.S. reactions to the PCA decision:

1. The PCA decision is now part of contemporary law of the sea. It must be observed.
2. The U.S. should not push China too hard, but must be firm and persistent in calling for the management and resolution of South China Sea dispute through negotiation and other procedures of peaceful settlement of conflict based on international law.
3. The U.S. should continue to maintain a favorable military balance in the Asia-Pacific region, and strengthen our alliances and develop new partnership with countries in the region.
4. The U.S. and its allies must be prepared to respond to further unilateral attempts to change the status quo through intimidation and coercion.
5. The Scarborough Shoal is of strategic importance to the U.S.; militarization of the shoal must be contested.
6. The U.S. must clearly communicate our interests before Chinese activity begins.
7. FONOPS must be conducted more regularly but quietly based on the result of the PCA decision.

---

[193] Christopher Bodeen, "Top U.S. admiral says China exchanges conditional on safety," Associated Press, July 20, 2016.

[194] Financial Times, July 12, 2016

India's Approach to Strategic and Legal Implications of PCA's Award (Abridged)

Vinod Anand

India's policy on the South China Sea has been articulated consistently by its political leadership and it emphasizes peace and stability in the Asia Pacific, and in particular in the South China Sea, as being of critical importance to India. Furthermore, countries in the region should make efforts to resolve their disputes in an amicable manner through the instruments of diplomacy and international law, as enunciated in the 1982 United Nations Convention of the Law of the Sea (UNCLOS) as also adherence to Declaration on Code of Conduct in the South China Sea.

According to India's Maritime Strategy document, the South China Sea is a strategic 'area of interest'. One of the main reasons for this is that over 50% of India's trade passes through the SCS. New Delhi has said that it "supports freedom of navigation (FoN), right of passage and access to resources in accordance with accepted principles of international law and these should be respected by all."

Long before the PCA Award of 12 July 2016, Foreign Minister Sushma Swaraj, speaking at the Third India-Philippines Joint Commission on Bilateral Cooperation in October 2015, reiterated India's support for a peaceful solution of the dispute, adherence to international norms including UNCLOS 1982, favours the freedom of navigation and over flight in the SCS. India also supports expeditious conclusion on a Code of Conduct and full and effective implementation of the 2002 Declaration of the Code of Conduct of Parties in the SCS. India's interests lie in unimpeded trade through SCS, security of SLOCs, strengthened relations with ASEAN and East Asian countries, and cooperation with countries.

Vietnam has been a party to the South China Sea (or the East Sea) dispute and has claims of sovereignty over the Paracel Islands (Hoang Sa) and the Spratly Islands (Truong Sa). Vietnam currently has in its possession eight features in the Spratlys. Vietnam's dispute with China started in 1974 when the Chinese evicted the then South Vietnamese Garrison from the Pattle Island in the Western Paracels, and again forced the Vietnamese out of Johnson South Reef in the Spratlys in 1988. There have also been long periods of inaction, interspersed with the odd incident like that of when China towing the oil rig HS 981 into the waters of Vietnam's EEZ in May 2014, and the establishment of an exclusion zone around it. However, China is also Vietnam's largest trading partner with bilateral trade expected to be close to $100 billion in 2016.[195] This trade, however, is skewed in China's favour, giving it economic leverage vis-à-vis Vietnam.

The Communist parties of the two countries also share close relationships with regular visits being exchanged, the most recent being that of the Chinese State Councilor Yang Jiechi to Vietnam.[196] While relations between the two countries are improving, China's aggressiveness while dealing with regional issues has caused alarm in the region and Vietnam has been no exception. The current Vietnamese president, Tran Dai Quang, had, in fact, raised this issue when he said "Activities that caused destabilization, altered the status quo, violated international laws...have undermined the confidence and increased tensions" and added that "many countries in the region, and the international community

---

[195] 'China, Vietnam to fulfil trade target of $100b in 2016'. Xinhua, 2016-03-09. http://www.chinadaily.com.cn/business/2016/03/09/content_23791827.htm. Accessed on 03 Jun 16.

[196] 'President, Party Chief welcome Chinese State Councilor', 28/06/2016. http://english.vietnamnet.vn/fms/government/159556/president--party-chief-welcome-chinese-state-councilor.html. Accessed on 17 Jul 16.

feel insecure, have repeatedly raised voices expressing deep concerns."[197] Vietnam's recent defence expenditure has been focused on addressing these concerns as it buys submarines, aircraft, artillery and missile systems, fast-attack ships and a host of other military platforms.

The recent award by the Permanent Court of Arbitration (PCA) in the *Philippines vs. China* case has once again brought the South China Sea into the limelight. The PCA decided the following in response to the 15 submissions by the Philippines.[198]

(a) There was no legal basis for China to claim 'historic' rights to resources within the sea area falling within the 'nine-dash line';

(b) None of the Spratly Islands is capable of generating extended maritime zones, not can they generate the same collectively as a unit since they are basically rocks;

(c) Certain sea areas are within the EEZ of Philippines, and China had violated Philippines' sovereign rights in its EEZ';

(d) China's recent large-scale land reclamation and construction of artificial islands in the Spratly Islands has caused severe harm to the coral reef environment.

The award by the PCA has put to rest the issue of historic rights to maritime resources, especially in the maritime zones accruing to a coastal state under UNCLOS. The implications of this ruling on Vietnam's claims to the Paracels and the seas surrounding them need to be studied to assess the viability of legal options in this dimension.

It is important to note that the PCA has said that '**historic rights to land features'** are distinct from similar rights to maritime resources and hence some claim remain unaffected by this ruling.[199] Hence the question of sovereignty over the features of the Spratlys and the Paracel islands still continues to hang in the balance.

---

[197] 'Vietnam's president calls for peace and stability in S. China Sea'. Hanoi, 21 May 16, Kyodo. https://english.kyodonews.jp/news/2016/05/412480.html. Accessed on 31 May 16.

[198] Read 'Press Release: The South China Sea Arbitration (The Republic of the Philippines V. The People's Republic of China)'. The Hague, 12 July 2016. https://pcacases.com/web/sendAttach/1801. Accessed on 12 Jul 16.

[199] PCA Case N° 2013-19 In The Matter Of the South China Sea Arbitration. Pg 115.

However, the maritime zones accruing to these features can no longer be an issue of dispute since **the PCA tribunal has categorically stated that none of the features in the Spratly, either individually or collectively, is entitled to maritime zones under UNCLOS**. Consequently the utility of such features, on account of the maritime zones supposedly entitled to them, requires reconsideration in light of this award by the PCA.

The Tribunal also viewed Chinese actions as violating the rights of the Philippines in the continental shelf and the EEZ under the strictures of UNCLOS. The tribunal has clearly said that **China does not possess sovereign rights to the resources of some of the areas, namely Mischief Reef, Second Thomas Shoal, the GSEC101 block, Area 3, Area 4, or the SC58 block - all of which fall within the EEZ of the Philippines.**[200]

This holds great significance for a number of countries since China has been vociferously objecting to the maritime activity of various nations, including that of India, in the EEZ of Vietnam, and elsewhere in the area.

Considering the Tribunal's view on drawing a distinction between the 'historic rights to land features' and similar rights to maritime resources, India needs to review its policy, especially with respect to its interests in the EEZ of Vietnam, which have been contested by China. The PCA award thus strengthens not only Vietnam's case but India should now pro-actively push for exploration in additional areas offered to it by Vietnam.

Vietnam has consistently maintained its position of resolving the existing dispute by peaceful means and in line with international law, including the 1982 UN Convention on the Law of the Sea (UNCLOS), in order to maintain peace, stability in the East Sea and the region. After the release of the PCA award, the spokesperson of the Ministry of Foreign Affairs issued a statement welcoming the award and re-iterated Vietnam's sovereignty over the Paracels and the Spratlys.[201] He also stated that, "Viet Nam strongly supports the settlement of disputes in the East Sea by peaceful means, including legal and diplomatic processes, refraining from the use or threat of use of force". In December 2014, during the course of the arbitration by the PCA, Vietnam requested the Tribunal to pay due interest

---

[200] *Ibid.* Pg 279.
[201] Remarks of the Spokesperson of the Ministry of Foreign Affairs of Viet Nam. http://www.mofa.gov.vn/en/tt_baochi/pbnfn/ns160712211059. Accessed on 12 Jul 16 at 2050 h

to its '*legal rights and interests.*'[202] *Vietnam had also then rejected China's claims over the Paracels and the Spratlys as well as its claim to 'historic rights' to the waters, sea-bed and subsoil within the "dotted line."*[203] *Vietnam had also attended the hearings of the Tribunal as an observer along with other concerned states like Australia, Indonesia, Japan, Malaysia, Singapore and Thailand.*

Vietnam's abiding interest in the progress of the case is a reflection of its concerns on the issue, especially regarding China. Vietnam has been insisting on full and effective implementation of the Declaration on the Conduct of Parties in the East Sea (DOC), which was signed between the ASEAN and China in Nov 2002, as well as the development of the Code of Conduct (COC) in the South China Sea. Vietnamese concerns about Chinese actions were clearly reflected by its Deputy Minister of National Defense, Senior Lieutenant General Nguyen Chi Vinh, at the recent Shangri-La Dialogue, when he said "The problem does not just stop there, but brings with it actions of unilateral imposition, changes to the status quo along with the threat of militarization to create a deterrent strength; negative impacts on aerial, maritime and submarine security and safety; environmental destruction; and obstruction of peaceful maritime labour activities."[204] Considering the level of tensions prevalent in the region with respect to Chinese assertiveness, more so because of the recent award, Vietnam will be required to tread cautiously on this issue.

Starting another legal battle with the Chinese does seem an enticing proposition since the geographical location of the Paracels puts the Chinese on their back foot when viewed in the light of the PCA award. However, it may not bear fruit considering the ground realities and recent Chinese policy. The settlement of the Sino-Vietnamese dispute in the Beibu Gulf provided some precedent to the approach to be adopted without disturbing regional sensibilities and stability. Vietnam's warming relations with Japan and the US will also provide a necessary 'nudge to the Chinese to adopt a

---

[202] Remarks by MOFA Spokesperson Le Hai Binh on the South China Sea Arbitration case. 11 Dec 14. http://www.mofa.gov.vn/en/tt_baochi/pbnfn/ns141212143709/view. Accessed on 12 Jul 16.

[203] *Ibid.*

[204] 'The Challenges of Conflict Resolution: Senior Lieutenant General Nguyen Chi Vinh, IISS Shangri-La Dialogue 2016 Fourth Plenary Session.
http://www.iiss.org/en/events/shangri%20la%20dialogue/archive/shangri-la-dialogue-2016-4a4b/plenary4-6c15/chi-vinh-f701. Accessed on 13 Jun 16

more accommodating approach; although the Chinese are hypersensitive to such maneuvers.

As for India, it should enhance its existing oil prospecting activities in the EEZ of Vietnam and look for other areas where the potential for discovery of hydrocarbons is good. In any event, India needs to strengthen its economic, defence and strategic relationship with Vietnam and also work on trilateral cooperative arrangements with like-minded ASEAN and other countries in the region like Japan, the US and Australia. India also needs to work towards bringing equilibrium in the South China Sea in concert with these countries. The credibility of China in international forums has taken a beating. Though China has been defiant and rejected the PCA Award, it is difficult to say how China will behave in the near future.

The Award on the Marine Environment of the South China Sea in the Philippines vs. China Arbitration Case

Nguyen Chu Hoi

Summary

On July 12, 2016, after nearly 3 years under consideration, the Arbitral Tribunal in The Hague, in the Netherlands, issued an award in the Philippines vs. China case. In the award, the Arbitral Tribunal clarified the damages to the South China Sea's marine environment, caused by China's construction and reclamation activities on seven features in the Spratly Islands. This paper analyses the reasons leading up to the Tribunal's award on those environmental issues; and the impacts of China's activities on the marine environment, marine biodiversity, and the South China Sea (SCS) regional fisheries. In addition, the paper further explains why China's actions not only violated the United Nations Convention on the Law of the Sea 1982 (UNCLOS 1982), but was also in non-compliance with the "Declaration on the Conduct of Parties in the South China Sea" (DOC).

The award itself has provided enough principles and legal basis to the parties involved in the SCS arbitration to deal with China after the ruling.

Introduction

The Philippines vs. China arbitration case concluded on July 12, 2016, with the final awards of the Arbitral Tribunal under Annex VII of the UNCLOS 1982. This could be considered as the "lawsuit of the century" because, for the first time in history, China, one of world's largest nations, and a member of the United Nations Security Council, was taken to court by a small country for maritime disputes. The ruling affected not only all parties involved in the arbitration case, but other countries in the region as well, and beyond, not to mention the implementation and development of maritime and international law.[205] After 17 years of failed bilateral negotiations, and 3 years of trial preparation, the awards were seen as a victory for the Philippines. The Arbitral Tribunal itself also confirmed in the ruling that the Philippines had completed all legal procedures; thus, the country's right to unilaterally bring the case to the arbitral tribunal was recognized.[206]

The damage to the SCS's marine environment was clarified through questions relating to China's behaviour that the Philippines deemed to be inconsistent with the UNCLOS 1982, violating the rights that the Convention assigned to the Philippines and the SCS marine environment; with the focus on China's construction and reclamation activities in the Spratly Islands. This paper analyses the reasons leading to the awards on environmental issues and the impacts of China's activities on the marine

---

[205] Viet Long (2016). *[The lawsuit of the century: a turning point in the SCS]*, *VietnamNet*, July 14, 2016.

[206] Nguyen Thi Lan Anh (2016). "Dự báo quan trọng về Biển Đông sau phán quyết của Tòa" *[Important predictions about the SCS after the Arbitral Tribunal's ruling]*, *VietnamNet*, July 11, 2016.

Annex VII of the UNCLOS 1982 provides that in order to complete the procedures of bringing an arbitration case to court, the Philippines must satisfy the following conditions: (i) prove that there exists a dispute over the interpretation and application of the UNCLOS between the Philippines and China; (ii) prove that the two parties have previously exchanged views on settling the dispute without success; (iii) prove that the two parties do not choose any other dispute settlement mechanism aside the UNCLOS.

environment, marine biodiversity, and fisheries in the SCS; thus, proposing solutions/measures to implement the award in accordance with the spirit of The Hague's Arbitral Tribunal.

1. The SCS's Marine Environment: Importance and Status

The SCS is one of the four largest seas in the world, with more than 7000 large and small islands situated in its coastal waters and concentrating into large offshore island clusters, such as Vietnam's Truong Sa and Hoang Sa Islands (Spratly and Paracel Islands) or Dongsha Islands (Pratas Islands) claimed by Taiwan. These offshore islands are made up of coral reefs developed on ancient volcanic rocks, and include geographical features such as islets, reefs, rocks, shoals and atolls. Coral reefs are among the most important and most vulnerable marine ecosystems, and are home to around 3000 species living in the SCS. In particular, the Southern part of the SCS, the marine waters surrounding the Spratly Islands, expanding to the coasts of Philippines' Luzon, Brunei, and Vietnam's coasts from Khanh Hoa to Ninh Thuan, have the most diverse coral species (about 517 species, nearly as many as that of the Coral Triangle (566 species, the core of which lies in the Indonesia – Philippines marine waters (Picture 1).[207]

The offshore coral reefs in the SCS not only serve as the "common house" of many marine living species, but they are also the "factory" that provides nutrients and seafood breeds, including shrimp and fish larvae. In addition, there exists in the SCS a strong seasonal circulation, which disperses the nutrients and seafood breeds from the offshore coral islands, especially around the Spratly Islands, to remaining marine waters in the SCS; even to the Coral Triangle. Thus, the SCS has always had a high biodiversity and conservation value rich in fisheries resources. According to the United Nations Environment Programme (UNEP), the SCS accounts for 1/10 of total fish catch in the world; and by 2030, China will account for 40% of global fish consumption.[208]

---

[207] Vo Si Tuan (2014). *Reef-building corals in Vietnam's sea], Proceedings of the 2nd National Science Conference on Marine Biology and Sustainable Development* (The Natural Sciences and Technology Publisher, 2014), Ha Noi: p. 315 – 322,

[208] James Borton (2016). *From the Arbitral Tribunal's ruling to the marine environmental issues. Tien Phong Newspaper,* August 4, 2016, 217.

The SCS is also one of the most important large marine ecosystems (LME) in the region and the world. About 300 million people in 9 countries (China, Vietnam, the Philippines, Brunei, Indonesia, Singapore, Malaysia, Thailand and Cambodia), and one territory (Taiwan) surrounding the SCS depend on the marine natural resources, especially the fishery resources which are a daily livelihood source for the coastal communities and islanders. According to the evaluation by Gomez and his colleagues,[209] a hectare of coral reefs yields US$350 thousand per year in total economic value. Therefore, if the marine environment and the ecosystems around these offshore islands are given appropriate protection, the environmental security and biodiversity resources throughout the SCS will be maintained.

The above-mentioned offshore coral reef islands also contain the interwoven strategic interests of the countries around the SCS and beyond. Therefore, it is no coincidence that political powers have set their sights on these marine waters. With unilateral and unjustified claims of the "nine-dash line" that covers more than 80% of the entire SCS, China has, step by step, been illegally occupying the entire Paracel Islands and 7 shoals in Vietnam's Spratly Islands. More seriously, China's unilateral claims and recent reclamation and construction of artificial islands have been threatening ecological and environmental security in the SCS.

2. China's actions and the environmental destruction in the South China Sea

According to Professor E.D. Gomez from the Marine Science Institute, University of the Philippines, while in a rush to seize control of the SCS, governmental and military leaders of China seem to have had little concern over the fact that the coral reefs, sea grass beds and shallow marine ecosystems in the SCS are being destroyed so quickly.[210] To date, China has not only constructed about 1500 hectares of "artificial islands" from the shoals of the Spratly and Paracel Islands, but it has also destroyed thousands of hectares of coral reefs, sea grass beds and other shallow marine ecosystems in order to get sandy materials for such reclamation

---

[209] Edgardo D. Gomez (2015). Potential danger to biodiversity and economic productivity in the East Sea. Paper presented at the Seminar on "The East Sea environment and human behaviour", Hai Phong City, August 8, 2015

[210] See (6)

and construction. This action has caused serious damage, amounting to almost US$4 billion per year to the littoral countries around the SCS; including China itself. If China does not stop construction, the local marine environment will suffer further damage.[211]

China's reclamation and construction not only alter the structure and natural functioning of the shoals, rocks and atolls in the Spratly Islands, but also "cut off" the ecological connectivity between the offshore coral islands and the rest of the SCS. The actions of the Chinese have a broad negative impact on the ability to provide nutrients, seafood breeds and marine living resources for the majority of the SCS and adjacent waters. Vietnamese, Filipinos, Malaysian, Indonesian, and the Chinese themselves, will suffer the consequences. Professor John McManus from Miami University, USA, also warned about a major disruption in the marine fisheries and an environmental disaster affecting the lives of millions of people.[212]

In addition, the destructive fishing activities of Chinese fishermen in the SCS have led to the degradation of the ecosystems and there is now a danger of extinction for several species such as sea turtles, sharks, some other fish species, and especially giant clams. Marine fish reserves around the Spratly Islands and the western marine waters of the SCS have decreased by 16% compared to the period before 2010.[213] The destruction of the giant clams in the Scarborough Shoal (which China seized control from the Philippines in 2012), plus large volume exploitation of shell species in the surface of the shoal has caused prolonged ecological disturbance, killing many benthos.[214] Furthermore, the number of coral reefs and fish species in the disputed waters of the SCS has also dropped from 460 to

---

[211] Marie Antonette Juinio-Meñez and Edgardo D. Gomez, 2016. Rock-Island-Reef: the high stakes in the South China Sea. Paper presented in 2nd International Seminar on Environmental and Maritime Security for a Blue SCS. Haiphong, Vietnam (11-12 Oct. 2016).

[212] See (5)

[213] Nguyen Quang Hung and Vu Viet Ha (2015). *Fishery resources in Vietnam's sea and some of the impacts on the renewability of these resources.* Paper presented at the Seminar on "The East Sea environment and human behaviour", Hai Phong City, August 8, 2015.

[214] See (1)

261, and the list of endangered species have welcomed new additions such as green sea turtles, giant clams and hawksbill sea turtles.[215]

For that reason, China has seriously violated many relevant international conventions, including the UNCLOS 1982, the Convention on Biological Diversity (CBD), the Convention on International Trade in Endangered Species of Wild Fauna and Flora (CITES), and Article 6 of the DOC, in which China itself has pledged commitments. China's disrespect for international law and bilateral commitments has received a strong international response. However, despite the protests of regional countries and the world, China still continues its illegal reclamation and infrastructure construction in the Spratly and Paracel Islands, and increases its military presence, thus, increasing tensions in the SCS. This situation has led to an inclination to "internationalise" and create change of the state of affairs in the SCS, which is clearly not what China aims to achieve.[216]

3. The Arbitral Tribunal's award on the SCS's marine environmental issues

Within this context, the Philippines brought an arbitration case against China to the Arbitral Tribunal in January 2013, to clarify historical rights, a source to determine rights to the waters of the SCS, the regulations on a number of specific maritime features and their surrounding marine waters, and the legality of China's actions which the Philippines deemed a violation of the UNCLOS 1982. In accordance with the framework of the dispute settlement mechanism specified in the UNCLOS 1982, the Arbitral Tribunal emphasised that it did not purport to make any ruling as to which state enjoys sovereignty over any land territory in the SCS, or to delimit any maritime boundary between the Parties.[217]

During the 3 years that the case was under consideration, the world witnessed intense verbal and nonverbal reactions from Beijing. China, on the one hand, urged the Philippines to withdraw its case, but deliberately

---

[215]   See (5)

[216]   Nguyen Chu Hoi (2016). *How's China 'waiting' for the verdict on the 'nine-dash line'?.*, *World Overview – Journal of Science and Strategies*, 65 (Ministry of Public Security, 2016): 7 – 9. ISSN: 0866-7446, Ha Noi.

[217]   Permanent Court of Arbitration (2016). Press release of the South China Sea arbitration (The Republic of The Philippines V.S The People's Republic of China).

dodged the lawsuit on the other hand; refusing to participate in the arbitration despite the fact that this friendly, open and peaceful dispute settlement mechanism could provide a long term solution to the situation in the SCS. This move by China, along with its application, citations and interpretation of relevant provisions in the international laws in their favour, are enough to make the international public sense China's anxiety.

Finally, on July 12, 2016, the Arbitral Tribunal under Annex VII of the UNCLOS 1982 rendered an arbitration award that was unanimously approved by all arbitrators. Among the 15 submissions made by Manila, the Tribunal found that the disputes that the Philippines had placed fell broadly within 4 categories.

First, the Philippines asked the Tribunal to resolve a dispute concerning the source of maritime rights and entitlements in the SCS, particularly the legality of China's "nine-dash line", based on the UNCLOS 1982.

Second, the Philippines sought a declaration from the Tribunal about the maritime features that both China and the Philippines laid claims to, including islands, reefs, rocks, shoals, submerged banks and low-tide elevations, and about the legal status of these features and their adjacent waters according to the UNCLOS 1982.

Third, the Philippines sought conclusions concerning the legality of China's action in the SCS, which includes interfering with the exercise of the Philippines' rights under the Convention, and inflicting severe harm on the marine environment by tolerating harmful fishing methods and constructing artificial islands.

Fourth, the Philippines asked the Tribunal to find that China had aggravated and extended the disputes between the parties during the course of the arbitration by engaging in large-scale construction of artificial islands and land reclamation at seven coral features in the Spratly Islands.

In the end, with respect to China's destructive actions towards the local marine environment, an objective and transparent award was given. Based on expert reviews of the environmental impacts of China's actions, the Tribunal found that "China's recent reclamation and construction activities have and will cause environmental harm to coral reefs at seven features in the Spratly Islands; beyond the pre-existing damage to reefs that resulted from destructive fishing and the collection of corals and clams, storm damage, Crown-of-Thorns starfish, and the human presence on small garrisons on the reefs";[218] that "China, despite its rules on the protection of giant clams, and on the preservation of the coral reef environment generally, was fully aware of the practice and has actively tolerated it as a means to exploit the living resources of the reefs". The Tribunal also noted that the large-scale island-building activities of China is inconsistent with the obligations of a member country in the UNCLOS 1982 when settling a dispute, for China has caused irreparable damage to the marine environment, constructed a large artificial island in the exclusive economic zone of the Philippines, and destroyed evidence of the natural conditions of the maritime features that are involved in the SCS arbitration.[219]

The award has provided enough international legal principles not only for parties involved in the SCS dispute, but also other countries and environmental organisations in the region and the world, to fight against China's destructive actions to the SCS's marine environment. Although China still firmly rejects the ruling, the country is also being looked at by the whole world to see whether it respects justice or not.

After the Tribunal's ruling, many solutions have been proposed to force China to abide the above-mentioned award. According to Dr. James Borton (University of South Carolina and the US–Asia Institute), overfishing and the growing number of damaged reefs requires scientific intervention.[220] He suggested that since there are increasingly more cases of fishing vessels collision happening in the disputed waters, the ASEAN leaders should:

- Seek measures to reduce the frequency of these incidents instead of sending more vessels out.
- Establish a regional marine science advisory council to handle issues of environmental degradation.
- Promote dialogues to build a Peace Marine Park in the SCS.
- Propose a Scientific Committee to review and research into the Antarctic Treaty for the possibility to apply to the situation in the SCS.

---

[218] See (13)

[219] See (5)

[220] See (5)

China and relevant parties should consider a number of trust-building measures in compliance with Articles 5 and 6 of the DOC.[221] Strengthening of scientific cooperation between marine scientists in the ASEAN, and conducting independent scientific investigation in the disputed marine waters and artificial islands are also necessary moves.

Conclusion

Peace and stability in the SCS can only be maintained if international law is respected and the ruling of the Arbitral Tribunal is strictly adhered to.

The destruction of coral reefs to expand and construct artificial islands is not only unable to alter the legal positions of the shoals, but is also destructive to the marine environment in the SCS.

Solutions to this environmental issue can only be effective when all relevant parties are willing to build trust, negotiate and be cooperative in exchanging information.

First and foremost, China should stop its illegal reclamation and construction in the 7 maritime features in the SCS, and comply with its legal obligation to protect the environment, of which transparency of information and cooperation with relevant parties in supervising the offshore marine environment should be the focus.

---

[221] Declaration on the Conduct of Parties in the South China Sea (2002).

Giant Clams in Despair: The Urgent Need for Environmentally Conscious Cooperation in the South China Sea and Implications for ASEAN and Concerned Countries Around the Globe

Dai Trang Nguyen

Abstract

A Chinese proverb says, "One word goes out, four horses can't pull it back," and by the same token, certain environmental damages cannot be reversed. Over the past decades, there have been strong concerns about environmental degradation in the South China Sea. The July 12, 2016 ruling of the Permanent Court of Arbitration in The Hague with findings of "irreparable harm to the marine environment" and the harvesting of "endangered sea turtles, coral, and giant clams" has brought more attention to the seriousness of the issue. This paper focuses on the danger of inaction and indifference towards the protection of the marine environment in the South China Sea caused by the complexity of territorial disputes, land reclamation, construction of artificial islands, and illegal poaching.

The paper suggests that (1) it is in the interests of ASEAN members to consider environmental protection as a strategic issue of national and regional economic development, and to cooperate with each other and with other countries to prevent further environmental damages; (2) it is in the interests of many countries around the world to address the importance of protecting the environment in the South China Sea at national, regional and global levels; to support international and local NGOs, civil society organizations and environmental groups to raise awareness and find solutions; and to reach out and cooperate with ASEAN countries through assistance and investment for environmental protection and sustainable economic development.

Introduction

It takes political will and much more to change the way we think in order to achieve a green planet. Many parts of the world are cities with bicycles[222] rather than cars because they would cause serious environmental pollution. A higher stage of development would mean promoting bicycles, not cars. It is, however, a challenge to convince many people about taking action to reduce car pollution and the need to have more bicycles, not cars.

The damage to the marine environment in the South China Sea is one of the emphases in the July 12, 2016 ruling of the Permanent Court of Arbitration in The Hague. While China insists that it has ensured the protection of the ecological environment based on scientific proof,[223] the reality of protecting the marine environment in the South China Sea will continue to be plagued by the complexity of territorial disputes, land reclamation, construction of artificial islands, and illegal poaching.

---

[222] Sibinski (2015). Cycling Is Everyone's Business. *World Bank.*

[223] Foreign Ministry Spokesperson Hong Lei's Regular Press Conference on May 6, 2015. Ministry of Foreign Affairs of the People's Republic of China. See also Hong (2016), The U.S.-China Battle in the Post-Arbitration South China Sea: Diverging and Converging Interests. Maritime Awareness Project.

This paper looks at how geopolitical complexities in the South China Sea would likely lead to inaction and indifference towards the protection of the marine environment despite many concerns voiced by researchers. It suggests that to overcome this inaction and indifference, ASEAN countries and especially Southeast Asian claimants need to consider the strategic link between the environment and economic development, and to work collaboratively with each other and with other countries to prevent further environmental damages. The paper also suggests that, besides important issues that concern many other countries including freedom of navigation for trade and global security, environmental issues in the South China Sea need to get the attention of international and local NGOs, civil society organizations and environmental groups. At the same time, it is in the interests of these countries to cooperate with ASEAN countries through assistance and investment for environmental protection and sustainable economic development.

Why inaction and indifference?

On July 12, 2016, The Hague ruling specifically mentioned that -

Harm to Marine Environment: The Tribunal considered the effect on the marine environment of China's recent large-scale land reclamation and construction of artificial islands at seven features in the Spratly Islands and found that China had caused severe harm to the coral reef environment and violated its obligation to preserve and protect fragile ecosystems and the habitat of depleted, threatened, or endangered species. The Tribunal also found that Chinese authorities were aware that Chinese fishermen have harvested endangered sea turtles, coral, and giant clams on a substantial scale in the South China Sea (using methods that inflict severe damage on the coral reef environment) and had not fulfilled their obligations to stop such activities.[224]

---

[224]   Press Release - *Permanent Court of Arbitration*. July 12, 2016.

Various sources explain the severity of the problem. According to *National Geographic*, "More than 40 square miles (104 square kilometers) of coral reefs – some of the most biodiverse on Earth – have been destroyed by giant clam poaching in the South China Sea."[225] The illegal poaching of giant clam is due to the demand of their shells to be used as interior décor and jewelry in China. Dr. John McManus, a professor of marine biology and ecology at the University of Miami who researched the Spratlys in early 2016, explains that construction of artificial islands in the South China Sea could lead to permanent ecocide.[226] The danger of irreversible environmental damages in the South China Sea lies with the possibility of prolonged inaction and indifference.

The fight against climate change has been seen as becoming more urgent every day if actions are not taken soon enough.[227] According to Tom Rand, a clean-technology venture capitalist in Canada, there are many reasons for the inaction and indifference, including vested interests in business and politics, the complexity of climate science, "the fact that climate change happens over the long term but we think and act over the short term," and the classic tragedy of commons: "the problem is global but action is local."[228]

Rand discusses the notion of the "siren song of denial", and it is not just *active denial* that is loud and up-front by the extremist "sceptics"[229] but also *passive denial* that is more subtle by many who "accept that climate disruption as both real and dangerous yet still turn a blind eye",[230] caused by feelings of powerlessness and overwhelming, by fear of what it means for our children, and wanting to avoid feelings of guilt.[231]

He suggests that instead of fighting our shared cognitive biases, we could take advantage of them by starting a new conversation such as about "a bright future of clean energy abundance, underwritten by an economic

[225] Bale (2016). Giant Clam Poaching Wipes Out Reefs in South China Sea. *National Geographic.*

[226] Beech (2016). The Environment Is the Silent Casualty of Beijing's Ambitions in the South China Sea. *Time.*

[227] Greenpeace Canada. Our Campaigns.

[228] Rand (2014). *Waking the Frog: Solutions for our Climate Change Paralysis. p. 13*

[229] Ibid, p. 52.

[230] Ibid, p. 57.

[231] Ibid, p. 58.

stimulus package that rebuilds our infrastructure."[232] This way, we "shoot for the heart and get past our biases, defenses, and feelings of fear."[233]

In parallel, we can derive the causes of active and passive denial when it comes to the issue of environmental damages in the South China Sea. Countries with interests in preventing activities that cause these damages would be more vocal, while others with lesser interests might stay with inaction. This paper places emphasis on states and stakeholders with passive denial and suggests the need to start conversations at global, national and local levels on topics that "shoot for the heart" and at the same time, work to protect the marine environment in the South China Sea.

The Case for ASEAN's Sustainable Economic Development

ASEAN members can have very different interests in the South China Sea, given that some of them are claimants and others are not, and China's strong economic influence in the region. The Association left out the international court ruling in favor of the Philippines in a joint statement on July 25, 2016. While a lack of consensus on a joint statement on this sensitive topic might be considered a lack of unity, ASEAN has in fact sought to strike a balance between unity and maintaining trust of superpowers "in new ways that are both principled and practical."[234]

Moving forward, a strategic conversation with ASEAN and within ASEAN on the issue of environmental protection in the South China Sea would need to steer away from discussion of unity or seeking consensus, and from the complexity of territorial disputes. Rather, the conversation needs to switch to positive outcomes of a protected marine environment, and link them to practical gains such as improved livelihood opportunities, stronger economic development, and enhanced international cooperation with other countries around the world.

As ASEAN Vision 2025 calls for "clean and green ASEAN to achieve sustainable development by ensuring protection of the region's environment,"[235] there is an opportunity to bring forward a conversation that would motivate stakeholders to consider environment protection as

---

232 Rand (2015). Climate denial's siren song.
233 Rand (2014). p. 80.
234 Tay (2016). What ASEAN did right. *The Jakarta Post.*
235 ASEAN (August 2016). ASEAN reaffirms call for clean and green environment.

---

a strategic issue of national and regional economic development, and to cooperate with each other and with other countries to prevent further environmental damages.

Southeast Asian claimants specifically would have higher motivation to bring forward the conversation on the protection of the marine environment in the South China Sea. The economic and environmental benefits of cooperating with countries outside the region to learn from their experience in environmental protection in similar circumstances around the world would help bring forward conversations that lead to solutions to environment problems in the region.

The Case for Other Countries to Engage in Discussion and Action towards Environmental Protection in the South China Sea

The United States has been engaging in the discussion of environmental issues in the South China Sea through research and workshops, while other countries such as Australia and New Zealand have been more cautious not risking their economic relationships with China.[236] Canada would have to consider a similar balance, however nine days after the ruling, Canada's Minister of Foreign Affairs issued a statement which concludes: "Canada is committed to the maintenance of international law and to an international rules-based order for the oceans and seas, as well as to the peaceful management and settlements of disputes."[237]

In Canada, there have been discussions on why the country should have an interest in the South China Sea. Suggesting that Canada should help prevent war in the region, former Ambassador to Vietnam, Marius Grinius, stated, "It's in Canada's highest interest to ensure that the South China Sea remains a zone of peace, stability, prosperity and open international passage."[238] *Gordon Houlden, director of the China Institute at the University of Alberta*, explains why the Hague decision should matter to Canada: the risk of being drawn into coalition warfare on disputes when security has broken down, economic consequences in case of waters for

---

[236] Wright (2016). The South China Sea: A battle of narratives. *Open Canada.*

[237] Global Affairs Canada (July 21, 2016). Canadian statement on South China Sea Arbitration.

[238] Grinius (2016). South China Sea and the New Great Game. Policy Paper. *Canadian Global Affairs Institute.*

commerce being closed, fishing stocks and the ecological system at risk, and Canada's abiding interest in negotiation and arbitration according to international law, specifically UNCLOS.[239]

Deanna Horton, another former Ambassador to Vietnam, explains why the South China Sea has significance for Canada: the concerns about the impact on Canada's growing trade and investment in Asia and environmental degradation of island building. "As a Pacific nation, Canada should be willing to shoulder more of the burden to avoid a costly miscalculation that could lead to conflict and further environmental damage." With a reputation of respect for international law, Canada can "support its partners in Asia, but also to engage China to promote further economic integration, confidence-building on security for all stakeholders, and on climate change mitigation."[240] This view is related to Arnold Wolfers' notion of "milieu goals," where Canada as a middle power can help maintain regional and global stability and peace, and an international order beyond national interests.

However, the discussions above could be in direct conflict with commercial interests with China, thus could drown any discussion about the South China Sea including environmental issues. While the business sector in countries like Canada would pursue economic interests, the government can choose to adopt policy favoring either economic or environmental interests (for example, the current Liberal government has more environmental interests compared to the previous Conservative one).

The civil society sector, especially environmental groups, would be a very important sector with strong environmental interests. They need to be empowered at national, regional and global levels to address the importance of protecting the environment in the South China Sea. It is in the interests of many countries around the world to support international and local NGOs, civil society organizations and environmental groups to raise awareness and find solutions, and to reach out and cooperate with ASEAN countries through assistance and investment for environmental protection and sustainable economic development.

---

239 Houlden (2016). Why the South China Sea Decision Matters to Canada. *The Edmonton Journal*.

240 Horton (2016). Of Dashed Lines and Diplomacy. *Asia-Pacific Foundation of Canada*.

Conclusion

Canadian environmental activist David Suzuki once said: "Human beings are often at their best when responding to immediate crises – car accidents, house fires, hurricanes. We are less effective in the face of enormous but slow-moving crises such as the loss of biodiversity or climate change."[241] Both active and passive denial both work to cause inaction and indifference among many stakeholders at a global, regional, national, local, and individual level. The geopolitical complexities of the South China Sea will continue to play out conflict and negotiation at different levels, but the protection of the marine environment cannot afford to wait. The countries involved as well as other countries, and especially civil society groups, need to raise awareness, start conversations and build development cooperation that would help prevent irreversible environmental damages in the area.

Bibliography

ASEAN (August 2016). *ASEAN reaffirms call for clean and green environment.* Retrieved on August 9, 2016 from http://asean.org/asean-reaffirms-call-for-clean-and-green-environment/.

Bale, Rachael (July 12, 2016). *Giant Clam Poaching Wipes Out Reefs in South China Sea.* National Geographic. Retrieved on August 8, 2016 from http://news.nationalgeographic.com/2016/06/south-china-sea-coral-reef-destruction/.

Beech, Hannah (June 1, 2016). *The Environment Is the Silent Casualty of Beijing's Ambitions in the South China Sea.* Time. Retrieved on August 8, 2016 from *http://time.com/4353292/south-china-sea-environment-destruction-coral-giant-clams/.*

Ministry of Foreign Affairs of the People's Republic of China. *Foreign Ministry Spokesperson Hong Lei's Regular Press Conference on May 6, 2015.* Retrieved on August 8, 2016 from http://www.fmprc.gov.cn/mfa_eng/xwfw_665399/s2510_665401/t1361284.shtml.

Global Affairs Canada (July 21, 2016). *Canadian Statement on South China Sea Arbitration.* Retrieved on August 8, 2016 from http://news.gc.ca/web/article-en.do?nid=1102379.

---

[241] Suzuki (2004). *From Naked Ape to Superspecies: Humanity and the Global Eco-Crisis.*

Grinius, Marius (June 2016). *South China Sea and the New Great Game.* Policy Paper. Canadian Global Affairs Institute.

Greenpeace Canada. *Our Campaigns.* Retrieved on August 8, 2016 from http://www.greenpeace.org/canada/en/campaigns/.

Hong, Nong (June 8, 2016). *The U.S.-China Battle in the Post-Arbitration South China Sea: Diverging and Converging Interests.* Maritime Awareness Project.

Horton, Deanna (July 12, 2016). *Of Dashed Lines and Diplomacy.* Asia-Pacific Foundation of Canada. Retrieved on August 8, 2016 from http://www.asiapacific.ca/blog/dashed-lines-and-diplomacy.

Houlden, Gordon (July 15, 2016). *Why the South China Sea Decision Matters to Canada.* The Edmonton Journal. Retrieved on August 8, 2016 from http://edmontonjournal.com/opinion/columnists/opinion-why-the-south-china-sea-decision-matters-to-canada.

McManus, John. *The Spratly Islands: A Marine Park?* Journal of the Human Environment 23(3):181-186. May 1994.

Permanent Court of Arbitration. *Press Release.* Retrieved on August 8, 2016 from https://pca-cpa.org/wp-content/uploads/sites/175/2016/07/PH-CN-20160712-Press-Release-No-11-English.pdf.

Rand, Tom (2014). *Waking the Frog: Solutions for our Climate Change Paralysis. Toronto: ECW Press.*

Rand, Tom (May 11, 2015). *Climate Denial's Siren Song.* National Observer. Retrieved on August 8, 2016 from *http://www.nationalobserver. com/2015/05/05/opinion/climate-denial%E2%80%99s-siren-song*

Sibinski, Leszek (February 4, 2015). *Cycling Is Everyone's Business.* World Bank. Retrieved on August 8, 2016 from http://blogs.worldbank.org/publicsphere/cycling-everyone-s-business.

Suzuki, David and Holly Dressel (2004). *From Naked Ape to Superspecies: Humanity and the Global Eco-Crisis.* Greystone Books.

Tay, Simon (2016). *What ASEAN Did Right.* The Jakarta Post. Retrieved on August 8, 2016 from http://www.thejakartapost.com/academia/2016/08/09/what-asean-did-right.html.

Vu Hai Dang (2004). *Marine Protected Areas Network in the South China Sea: Charting a Course for Future Cooperation.* Leiden, Boston: Martinus Nijhoff Publishers.

Wolfers, Arnold (1962). *Discord and Collaboration: Essays on International Politics*. Baltimore: The Johns Hopkins Press.

Wright, Gerald (July 14, 2016). *The South China Sea: A Battle of Narratives*. OpenCanada. Retrieved on August 8, 2016 from https://www.opencanada.org/features/south-china-sea-battle-narratives/.

New challenges and new reality in the conflict in the South China Sea

Dimitry Mosyakov

It is regrettable that it is necessary to recognize that forecasts of further escalation of the situation in the South China Sea have proven to be true. China will not stop, but will actually strengthen the process of an arms race on the Paracel and Spratly area, trying to turn these islands, which it occupies illegally under international law, into unsinkable aircraft carriers. The images from American satellites made on February 14, 2016, show that the Chinese military have already placed a division of a modern surface-to-air missile system, named HQ-9, on Woody's island of the South China Sea; part of the Paracel Islands. It is reported that on Woody's island there are also two fire batteries deployed as a part of a total of eight launchers of the HQ-9 antiaircraft complex (Live Journal 18 February 2016).

When Pentagon chief, Ashton Carter, received this information he immediately accused China of constructing artificial islands, unprecedented on scales and rates, in the South China Sea. The official representative of the Ministry of Foreign Affairs of the People's Republic of China, Hua Chunying stated, "that construction activities of the Chinese side on Nansha's islands (the Chinese name of the Spratlys) were conducted within Chinese sovereignty, is legal and reasonable and not directed against any country". (The official representative the Ministry of Foreign Affairs of the People's Republic of China, Hua Chunying, then answered a question of the journalist concerning the statement of the Minister of Defence of the USA on the South China Sea.

There is serious exaggeration in the words of the official representative of the Chinese Ministry of Foreign Affairs, i.e. China's sovereignty over the Spratly and Paracel islands is not acknowledged anywhere in the world. Now, after the decision of The Hague Tribunal for the South China Sea, which was made public on July 12, 2016, Chinese demands and claims in the South China Sea have become even more elusive.

According to the court decision, China cannot claim territory within the so-called "nine dash line", which Beijing has referred to as its territorial claim, because this is more than 80% of the South China Sea. Construction on the reefs and shoals of the Spratly archipelago, all artificial structures and all attempts by Chinese authorities to pass them off as high-grade natural islands, have been declared illegal. In addition, the Tribunal acknowledged the illegal actions of China to restrict access of Philippine fishermen on Scarborough Reef, located off the coast of the Philippines. Beijing's actions on the Spratly Islands are also recognized as detrimental to the ecosystem of the region.

The Court's decision received full support from ASEAN countries and the international community. As for Russia, after the court decision there was a very serious change in its position in resolving international conflict in the South China Sea, despite the fact that a Foreign Ministry spokesman declared on the 13th of July, 2016 that "Russia's position on the situation in the South China Sea is consistent and unchanging". In reality, when compared with the Russian point of view before the ASEAN-Russia summit in May 2016, new trends could be seen. Foreign Ministry spokesman said that "we advocate that those involved in territorial disputes in these waters should strictly follow the principle of non-use of force, continue to search for ways of political and diplomatic settlement of existing differences on the basis of international law, and bove all the UN Convention on the Law of the Sea 1982, as well as in the spirit of ASEAN-Chinese documents." "We support the efforts of ASEAN and China to develop a code of conduct in the South China Sea", - added the diplomat (коммерсант) on July 14, 2016. As we know, in the first half of 2016 during the summit Russia-ASEAN there was another position; Russia supported attempts to resolve the conflict between the countries and participants in the conflict on the basis of bilateral negotiations without any interference from the outside. International law and the UN Convention on the Law of the Sea 1982, as the foundation for negotiations and code of conduct as the guarantee of good behavior were not in use.

So now we can say that Russia not only recognized the legitimacy of the decision of the tribunal in Hague, but did so despite the fact that China rejected it. We also can state that Russia returned to the position that it held in 2013. At that time, during an official visit to SRV on November 13, 2013 by V.V. Putin, "The joint statement on further strengthening of the relations of comprehensive strategic partnership between the Russian Federation and the Socialist Republic of Vietnam" has been signed. In the Statement, V.V. Putin and the President of Vietnam, Truong Tan Sang, noted that territorial and other disputes in the Pacific should be solved peacefully, without the use of force or threat of force according to international law, based on the Charter of the UN on a maritime law of 1982. They have jointly supported accomplishment of the Declaration on behavior of the parties in the South China Sea of 2002 and the fastest adoption of the legally binding Code of conduct in the region.

Serious changes in Russia's position can be decisive for the success of future negotiations to resolve current contradictions in the South China Sea because China now stands alone before the international community that recognizes the results and decisions of the Hague Tribunal. We can see that in this issue Russia took an opposing position to China that rejected not just the verdict, but also the right to arbitration to decide on this issue, thus taking an important step towards rapprochement with ASEAN countries and Vietnam in particular. However, Russia understands the success of bilateral consultations and negotiations between China and individual ASEAN countries can easily be elusive.

Past experience shows us that bilateral negotiations are not effective in resolving contradictions in the South China Sea. For example, we can take the fact that in its relationship with Vietnam, China does not carry out even two-way deals between the People's Republic of China and the SRV. During a visit to China in October 2011 by Secretary General of the Communist Party of Vietnam, Nguyen Phu Trong, a preliminary agreement was reached concerning ways of resolving the conflict of the South China Sea. The two sides decided that they would not take actions that could complicate a conflict further, without having entered into a dialogue previously with the other party. After that, at the APEC summit in Vladivostok in September 2012, during a meeting with the president of SRV Truong Tan Sang, Chinese President Hu Jintao declared that, "China and Vietnam shall calm down and show restraint in questions of the South China Sea, disputes to postpone and begin joint operation". The Chinese leadership also stated that China wanted to realize the following peace purposes: fulfill the international responsibility and liabilities in such areas as search and rescue transactions at the sea; prevention and simplification of consequences of natural disasters; sea scientific research; meteorological supervision; protection of the ecological environment; safety of navigation; provision of services to fishery". (The official representative of the Ministry of Foreign Affairs of the People's Republic of China, Hua Chunying, had answered a question from a journalist concerning the statement by the U.S. Minister of Defence on the South China Sea.)

However, after these statements were made no positive shift towards "joint cooperation and restraint" in the South China Sea have happened, despite the constant readiness of the Vietnamese side for negotiations. It is quite probable that in due course, in spite of the under which China expands its military presence at South China Sea will be implemented. Until now China continues to send all of its new military contingents equipped with increasingly modern arms, fighting ships and air defense complexes to the islands.

What can we expect in the future with respect to the decision of The Hague Tribunal?

It is possible that China could change its position despite the fact that Beijing now rejects the verdict and speaks about "indisputable sovereignty." With the arbitral tribunal ruling against China's "nine-dash line," and the impact on China's foreign policy, Beijing is in no position to reject regional efforts. A collective security mechanism in the region will offer China a way to renew negotiations with ASEAN and settle issues with the SCS claimants, allowing it to save "face" by taking account of the arbitral tribunal decision without formally acknowledging it.

At present, China has taken a position that the decision is illegitimate. All interested countries and the international community still have a challenge ahead, which is to try to work to make sure that resolving the issues of the South China Sea is only possible through diplomacy and the rule of law, and through the diplomatic process. It will also come about through available legal institutions connected with fishing, natural resources, with the free movement of vessels, and protection of the economic and political rights of all claimants. After The Hague Tribunal decision, the way forward to resolving contradictions in the South China Sea can be realistic and can be implemented in the future.

The Award by the Permanent Court of Arbitration: Challenge or Chance for China?

Gerhard Will

The recent award of the Permanent Court of Arbitration (PCA) in The Hague, regarding the South China Sea (SCS) case came as a surprise to many politicians and political observers. It decided nearly 100 per cent in favour of the Philippines, and denied nearly 100 per cent of all the claims made by China. In addition, the award accused China of encroaching illegally into the Philippine's Exclusive Economic Zone (EEZ), violating the UNCLOS by blocking Philippine fishing boats and oil exploration vessels, and causing "severe harm" to the habitats of endangered species in the SCS.

Accordingly, only few politicians and political observers were not surprised when China declared: the award is "null and void and has no binding force". China neither accepts nor recognizes it. In a 13,900-word White Paper, published just one day after the PCA decision, Beijing once again emphasized its historic rights and claimed that the Philippines had "distorted facts, misinterpreted laws and concocted a pack of lies" in order to undermine China's interests. Other Chinese commentators and newspapers were even more outspoken. The People's Daily qualified the PCA as a "lackey of some outside forces" that would be remembered as a "laughing stock" in human history.[242] Prof. Sen Dingli from Fudan University demanded that his country revise its stance and "employ a more effective approach". The Chinese newspaper "Global Times" reassured its readers that "Chinese law enforcement forces have been well prepared" and "Chinese people will firmly support our government to launch a tit-for-tat counterpunch."[243]

But this tough language was not followed by equally militant actions. Though China's vice-foreign minister stated one day after the decision of The Hague that its government reserved the right to declare an "Air Defence Identification Zone" (ADIZ) over the SCS, China did not impose it. No flights of the Chinese Air Force were reported in the contested area between Mischief and Subic Reefs. Moreover, China did not begin construction of an artificial island on Scarborough Shoal, nor did it announce any intent to withdraw from UNCLOS. Unlike the 2012 Japanese nationalization of the disputed Senkaku/Diaoyutai-islands, China has not allowed managed public protests to take place near the Philippines or US embassies.

China's Strategic Options

These different and sometimes contradictory signals given by China may indicate the country needs time to digest the tribunal's award and to develop a strategy to cope with this grave challenge to its international reputation. Generally speaking, there are three strategies at China's disposal.

1. Staying on course

Some analysts argue that China's refraining from militant actions is only a tactical move to be revised after September, when the high-level segment of the 2016 UN-General-Assembly and the meeting of the G-20-Summit. After that, Beijing would again adhere to its old strategy "pushing towards the bottom-line without breaking it"[244] by fortifying its position

---

[242]   New York Times, July 12, 2016

[243]   The Guardian, July 12, 2016

[244]   Shi Yinhong (Renmin-University Beijing) Shi Yinhong 2015 „China's Complicated Foreign Policy." European Council on Foreign Relations, March 31. http://www. ecfr.eu/article/commentary_chinas_complicated_foreign_policy311562

in the SCS with both non-military and military means: building and expanding artificial islands, dispatching fishery flotillas protected by para-military maritime forces, and strengthening its navy and air force units.

On the diplomatic front, Beijing has already started some initiatives. Though the Chinese government has repeatedly rejected an "internationalization" of the conflicts in the SCS, it has again launched an international campaign to support its stance against dispute settlement by supra-national institutions such as the PCA. In June, Beijing claimed that it had won support for its position from 60 countries, but so far only Sudan, Gambia, Kenya, Russia, South Africa, Zimbabwe and Cambodia have explicitly endorsed China's position.

In ASEAN, Cambodia is the staunchest and most important ally of Beijing. For the past several years, Phnom Penh has successfully prevented ASEAN from passing a common resolution openly criticising China's policy towards the SCS. A new Chinese aid package of almost 600 Mio. US$ was given to Cambodia shortly after the PCA announced its award. Though Prime Minister Hun Sen denied any political strings attached to this package, outside observers were not surprised, when at the ASEAN Foreign Ministers' meeting in Vientiane (July 24, 2016), Cambodia blocked a joint statement endorsing the award of The Hague. The official statement of this meeting only expressed serious concerns over artificial land reclamations and escalations of activities in the SCS, and added that such actions had "eroded trust and confidence, increased tensions and may undermine peace, security and stability in the region."

These diplomatic victories notwithstanding, Beijing has also had to take into account the negative effects of a policy based on its economic and military power. With a carrot-and-stick approach, China can force most of the governments of the ASEAN members into some kind of cooperation. It cannot, however, foster the image of a benign hegemon, which selflessly promotes the economic success and national sovereignty of its neighbours in the South. Vice versa, the ASEAN governments face grave difficulties in explaining to their nationalistically inclined populations why following China's lead is in the interest of their country.

To balance China's growing military power, most of the ASEAN states have increased their military budgets, and more or less openly welcomed the deployment of military forces from the US, Japan and even India. But a further militarization of the conflicts in the SCS will inevitably jeopardize the comprehensive and intensive economic cooperation between China and Southeast Asia that Beijing is aiming for.

2. Complying with the International Law

After being a pariah state for over two decades, China's integration into the world market and the acceptance of the international order made it possible for the PRC to become one of the world's leading economic and political powers. Not only has Beijing signed most UN-conventions and agreements – last not least the UNCLOS – but it also acceded to the WTO and has participated pro-actively in many UN peacekeeping missions.

In stark contrast to other Asian nations such as India, Bangladesh, Singapore, Malaysia, Myanmar and others which, in their respective maritime areas, accepted dispute settlement by international courts, the PRC has boycotted the PCA's proceedings and rejected its ruling. Some analysts interpreted this move as a rejection of the entire system of international law, instead opting for the law of the strongest.

But Beijing's attitude to international law is much more ambiguous and contradictory. Though the PRC refused to participate, it did not ignore the proceedings in The Hague. In December 7, 2014 the Chinese Ministry of Foreign Affairs released the Chinese government's response defining the Chinese position, and referring to the UNCLOS. The Chinese White Paper published after the announcement of the award in The Hague in 2016 pursues this approach in more detail.

"This novel form of 'non-participating participation' must be seen against the backcloth of a strategic ambition by China to develop a greater mastery of international law." to quote a report of Chatham House in London. According to this, the Chinese leadership took "impressive steps" to promote compliance with international law by hiring international lawyers and by educating and training Chinese experts in international law.[245]

To show its willingness to comply with international law, and with substantial parts of the award, "all China has to do is – nothing", as Bill Hayton put it.[246] China does needs not publically abandon its claims in

---

[245] China's fury over south China Sea belies its legal insecurities? Aug 7, 2016
[246] Bill Hayton, What will follow China's legel defeat in South China Sea? NIKKEI Asian review, July 13, 2016

the SCS. It can show that it respects the Exclusive Economic Zone of the other claimant states with practical steps, such as stopping oil exploration or fishery.

Even if that is done in a low-profile, discreet and face-saving way, it will not be easy to pass this message to a Chinese public who, over the past decades, have come to view China's sovereignty and territorial integrity in the SCS as non-negotiable, undisputed. For them, any compromise could come close to high treason. Last not least, power, influence and resources of organisations and institutions like the navy and the air force, the governments of the coastal provinces, the coast guards, the fishery protection flotillas etc. have grown enormously in size in these years of conflict. It is only logical then that they would be more than reluctant to agree with a form of conflict settlement that might be a serious blow to their power, influence and resources.

3. Establishing new international rules and practices

China's rise took place in an international system which is coming under growing criticism, because it is based on "Western" dominance, and therefore unfair to countries like China. The Chinese Communist Party (CCP) considers itself as the front-rank in a fierce ideological confrontation with the "West". CCP's general secretary Xi Jinping began an ideological campaign at home and abroad to create and promote a "Chinese ideology". "An important part of the strategy is to discredit Western ideas and institutions, both in order to make China's alternative model seem more attractive ..."[247]

The most important message of this campaign means: "Democracy with Chinese characteristics" is superior to "Western Democracy" because it is "real democracy" with a better economic performance.

But what does that mean for the realm of international relations?

So far, Beijing did not present an alternative vision of an international order. The PRC has launched and supported some initiatives and cooperation formats in which the US have no say, such as the "Shanghai Cooperation Organization", the BRICS group, or, in the economic, the "One Belt One Road Initiative" and the "Asian Infrastructure Investment

---

[247] Mareike Ohlberg, Boosting the Party's Voice. China's quest for global ideological dominance. MERICS China Monitor, July 21, 2016

Bank". These have been conceived to transform old power constellations. It is, however, quite unclear which role existing international law would play in these cooperation agreements, and how far conflicts would be settled by referring to international law or via bilateral or multilateral consultations.

It is obvious that such new or modified international norms and procedures cannot be worked out on the drawing board. They have to be developed in a closely linked process between theory and practice. In this process, the SCS could become a new testing ground for China's ability to build a new regional order and cooperative security architecture to find the consent of its neighbours in South East Asia.

For almost 20 years, Beijing has declared that the conflicts in the SCS should be settled by bilateral negotiations, and by the joint development of the shared resources. In the summer of 2016, Foreign Minister Wang Yi stated that bilateral negotiations could be complemented by multilateral negotiations and arrangements. But till now, there has been only one case of such a bilateral agreement regarding maritime delimitation and fishery cooperation. These are the agreements on the Gulf of Tong King, which were signed on December 25, 2000, and ratified more than three years later (June 30, 2004). Other projects of common development with Chinese participation failed, and Beijing did not give prominence to the above-mentioned Tong King – agreements as examples of China's willingness and ability for compromise and cooperation.

Therefore, the award of The Hague could and should be a reminder, a last call for Beijing to demonstrate its willingness and ability to settle conflicts via bilateral agreements and cooperative arrangements. Since the competition for dwindling fish-stocks is one of the most critical drivers of conflict in the SCS, endangering not only the livelihood but the very lives of many fishermen in cooperation projects, fishery should be given absolute priority.

Successfully concluded and implemented cooperation agreements could pave the way for further steps in building regional security architecture and for a comprehensive conflict settlement in the SCS. Beyond that, they could form important components of the new regional and international system the PRC is striving for. If Chinese proposals of bilateral and multilateral consultations and negotiations do not show any positive results in the near future, they will be seen as nothing but a fig-leaf for China's assertive pursuit in the SCS, casting grave doubts in China's sincerity.

4. Concluding remarks

When we look at recent speeches and statements of Xi Jinping and his advisers, a military approach to the conflicts in the SCS appear to get priority, whereas diplomatic efforts would only play a secondary, auxiliary role. One of Xi's senior advisers described his strategy as follows: "China's leaders have exhibited different types of leadership. Mao took great risks as he crashed repeatedly against immovable 'walls' to achieve his goals. Jiang Zemin and Hu Jintao shunned risks and tiptoed away from the walls. Xi like Mao takes bold risks, fearlessly attacks a well-chosen wall, and adjusts when the wall won't budge or cracks."[248] In February 2016, the seven existing military regions were replaced by five externally oriented theatre commands. One of them, the new "Southern Theatre Command" with a "main strategic direction towards the South China Sea will be the "core of China's national defence."[249]

Xi himself speaks of a renaissance of the Chinese Nation, restoring it to its old strength, magnitude and splendour. He called this "China's dream". But contrary to old imperial China whose power rested on a flourishing, auto-centric economy, the power of modern China rests on flourishing economic relations with regional and international partners. An indispensable precondition for flourishing economic relations is an international order and norms accepted by the members of the international community.

Therefore, the SCS will be a litmus-test or a very decisive testing-ground for China's ability either to comply with the existing international order or to modify it or to create a new international order which will get the consent of as many countries as possible. In any case, China will be confronted with a huge task. Whether China can master this task will depend to a great deal on the willingness and capacity of non-Chinese actors to engage China with firmness, flexibility and constructiveness.

---

[248] John W. Lewis a. Xue Litai, China's security agenda transcends the South China Sea, Bulletin of Atomic Scientists, 2016, Vol. 72, No.4., p. 219 http://dx.doi.org/10.1080/00963402.2016.1194056

[249] Op. cit. P. 217

ASEAN's STRATEGIES AFTER THE PCA DECISION

Kavi Chongkittavorn

Following the ruling by the Permanent Court of Arbitration (PCA) last month, ASEAN's overall positions on the South China Sea have been strengthened.

Although the grouping's dialogue partners - the US, Japan and Australia - tried hard to push ASEAN to mention the decision in its joint Vientiane communiqué, the group's foreign ministers disregarded the suggestion.

Ironically, granted the current status, the outcome unexpectedly generates a win-win situation for concerned parties, especially the Philippines and China, albeit the latter's consistent objection to the ruling to further engage bilaterally to resolve their common problems. With Manila's return to the ASEAN fold, the group's bargaining power has increased. Furthermore, it has renewed the process of mending ASEAN-China relations, and the 25-year anniversary of ties will be commemorated in Vientiane next month.

Four ASEAN documents at the Vientiane meeting

To assess ASEAN's next move - as well as its latest strength emerging from the 49th ASEAN Ministerial Meeting last month - it is necessary to make a comprehensive examination of all the papers issued at Vientiane on the current regional situation.

There were four documents - the ASEAN Foreign Ministers' Statement on the Occasion of the 40th Anniversary of the Treaty of Amity and Cooperation in Southeast Asia (TAC), the annual Joint Communiqué, the Joint Statement of the Foreign Ministers of ASEAN Member States on the Maintenance of Peace, Security and Stability in the Region, and finally, the ASEAN-China statement on the Declaration of the Code of Conduct and the early conclusion to the code of conduct (COC).

As it turned out, all these statements implicitly reinforced the ASEAN positions and commitment to solve the maritime conflict with a full respect for legal and diplomatic process.

Following Thailand's proposal to reiterate the importance of TAC on the eve of the 40th anniversary of this historic treaty, the ASEAN foreign ministers agreed without any hesitation to come out with a statement to pay tribute to TAC's promotion of peace and stability in the region for the past four decades.

In addition, in the statement, ASEAN called on the TAC signatories - including key major powers - to continue to "fully respect and promote the effective implementation of the TAC, especially the purpose and principles contained therein."

It is interesting to note that for the first time, ASEAN's foreign ministers agreed to explore "a legally binding instrument" building upon the TAC for the wider region. ASEAN is more confident than ever that the TAC is an excellent instrument to engage external powers and secure peace and stability so its application should be widely promoted. In the ASEAN Vision 2025, the grouping vows to strengthen respect for and recognition of the TAC among high contracting parties.

The TAC joint statement jump-started all ASEAN members to work on the content of 49th ASEAN joint communiqué, which was released on schedule despite unfavorable predictions. As in previous years, the section on the South China Sea continued to serve as an indicator of overall ASEAN solidarity.

The 388-word document - with its eight-paragraph section in the 32-page communiqué - signaled a united ASEAN position on the dispute, which it said must be resolved through peaceful means, based on "friendly consultations and negotiations by sovereign states directly concerned in accordance with the universally recognized principles of international law including the UN Law of the Sea of 1982".

ASEAN reaffirmed its longstanding policy to fully implement the 2002 Declaration on the Conduct of Parties in the South China Sea and the early conclusion of the Code of Conduct (COC) to ensure freedom of navigation and over flight in the South China Sea region. It also agreed to non-militarization and to "undertake self-restraint in the conduct of activities that would complicate or escalate disputes and affect peace and stability" in the region.

The statement expanded the concept of self-restraint to include "refraining from action of inhibiting the presently uninhabited islands, reefs, shoals, cays and other features". This has always been the Philippine position.

At the Vientiane meeting, Philippines Foreign Secretary Perfecto Yasay displayed leadership in consistently urging ASEAN for "restraint and sobriety" followed the PCA award. At one point, Myanmar's Foreign Minister Aung San Suu Kyi responded, commenting that ASEAN should not shy away from mentioning a major decision of international rules of law which would reflect on the group's own self-respect. After the award, Myanmar released a statement touching on the decision, the first stand-alone diplomatic statement on the South China Sea, with a well-crafted response bearing Suu Kyi's advocacy at the ASEAN meeting.

Role of Lao as the ASEAN chair

Kudos for this rare display of unity must go to the Lao chair, Foreign Minister Saleumxay Kommasith, who steered the group to reach a consensus, despite different views among ASEAN members. From the very beginning, Laos reiterated that the chair would protect the grouping's interest and solidarity. This time around, Manila's magnanimity and reengagement with ASEAN, Phnom Penh's assertiveness, as a non-conflicting party, did not have as much impact as before. To firm up the ASEAN position, the chair also backed Indonesia's proposal for the ASEAN foreign ministers to issue an additional statement on the maintenance of peace, security and stability in the region - in reference to the South China Sea.

Indonesia, which kept low profile until recently, is not a direct conflicted party in the South China Sea. It wants to ensure that major powers do not interfere in the region and urged them to follow all ASEAN-led mechanisms and endorsed principles. The document mentioned the Indonesia's initiative back in 2011, which led to the Declaration of the East Asia Summit on the Principles for Mutually Beneficial Relations. Obviously, the latest Jakarta initiative indicated the desire to reinvigorate Indonesia's regional profile as well as the Indo-Pacific Treaty of Amity and Cooperation, which was proposed by the previous government under President Susilo Bambang Yudhyono. The proposal is now under consideration by ASEAN.

ASEAN-China reconfirmation of DOC

Finally, there was a joint statement from ASEAN and China that reaffirmed their commitment to the full implementation of DOC as well as freedom of navigation in and overflight above the South China Sea. The statement did not mention the July 12 decision.

At a glance, all of these affirmations about principles and international rules of law relating to the South China Sea dispute appear to be hollow and meaningless given the past bitter experiences. But in reality, that is not the case. ASEAN foreign ministers have to work hard to come up with their declarations one after another. They are not given much time, as outsiders might have thought, granted the fasting-changing strategic environment.

After the Vientiane meeting, ASEAN is confident there could be substantial progress on the ongoing process to complete the code of conduct in the South China Sea (CoC). Chinese Foreign Minister Wang Yi indicated that Beijing is now ready to conclude the CoC by sometime next year. On this, some new tangible progress has been made over agreement to observe the Code of Unplanned Encounters at Sea (CUES) in the area. ASEAN and China earlier discussed the CUES, which was put forward by Singapore as the coordinating country for ASEAN-China relations at a previous working group meeting in April. This new measure will further reduce tensions and the risk of accidents and misunderstandings in these busy waters. Laos and Myanmar are preparing to accede to the CUES.

The grouping also wants to establish hotlines between the foreign ministries of China and ASEAN members to promote trust and confidence, which reached an all-time low ahead of the ASEAN annual meeting. Senior officials on both sides are now discussing the modalities. At the upcoming ASEAN-China commemorative summit, two joint-statements on the CUES and guidelines for the hotlines would be release.

Sea of peace, stability and sustainable development

Both sides are also exploring the possibility of undertaking cooperative activities in the South China Sea, such as navigation safety, search and rescue, marine scientific research, environmental protection, and combating transnational crimes at sea.

All in all, the four ASEAN documents renewed the ASEAN centrality and laid a new foundation for a much-needed conducive atmosphere to improve ASEAN and China relations. Early next month, their countries' leaders are due to meet in Vientiane to celebrate 25 years of bilateral relations. In a series of exchanges of letters between the leaders of China and ASEAN on this special occasion, Premier Li Keqiang pledged to bring their relations to "a higher plane and make greater contribution to peace, stability and prosperity of this region and beyond". China regards ASEAN as "the priority in neighborhood diplomacy and will continue to support the ASEAN integration process and ASEAN's centrality in regional cooperation".

Near the end of his letter in July, Premier Li expressed his wish that mutual relations with ASEAN will "go from strength to strength" and his hope that the friendship between people in the region would be "everlasting". It remains to be seen how quickly these expressions of goodwill can be materialised. But if this is the path China and ASEAN have indeed chosen to travel, they will need extraordinary political will and patience to overcome their differences and forge a new foundation for trusting relations for the next 25 years. As Foreign Minister Don Pramudwinai aptly summed up at the ASEAN meeting - ASEAN and China now have to the opportunity to transform the South China Sea into "a sea of peace, stability and sustainable development."

LEGAL BASES FOR MOVING FORWARD

Ngo Vinh Long

The ruling of the Permanent Court of Arbitration in The Hague on the case made by the Philippines against China's South China Sea (SCS) claims has provided a number of legal bases for the coastal countries in Southeast Asia to move forward on several fronts. The road ahead, however, is still treacherous and possibly threatened by crouching tigers (臥虎 wó hú), hidden dragons (藏龍 cáng lóng), and raging bulls (憤怒的 公牛 fènnù de gōngniú).

In light of this situation, it is necessary to review briefly below some of the legal bases provided by the PCA ruling in order to see areas in which the coastal Southeast Asian countries could move forward together in the interests of all parties involved.

First, the PCA ruling unequivocally reaffirms the status of the EEZs, and the resources therein, of the coastal countries according to UNCLOS. It states specifically [Press Release-English] that "…to the extent China had historic rights to resources in the waters of the South China Sea, such rights were extinguished to the extent they were incompatible with the exclusive economic zones provided for in the Convention." Furthermore, the "Tribunal concluded that there was no legal basis for China to claim historic rights to resources within the sea areas falling within the 'nine-dash line'." For the reasons stated, it is in the mutual interests of the coastal

SEA countries to abide by this ruling and to cooperate in the common defense of each other's EEZs against threats and encroachments.

The second ruling of the PCA has to do with "entitlements to maritime areas and the status of features" in the Spratlys. Since this has implications beyond the disputes between China and the Philippines as well as beyond the Spratly area itself, an extensive quote from the English press release is necessary here as a basis for further discussion [emphases added]:

Features that are above water at high tide generate an entitlement to at least a 12 nautical mile territorial sea, whereas features that are submerged at high tide do not. The Tribunal noted that the reefs have been heavily modified by land reclamation and construction, recalled that the Convention classifies features on their natural condition, and relied on historical materials in evaluating the features. The Tribunal then considered whether any of the features claimed by China could generate maritime zones beyond 12 nautical miles. Under the Convention, islands generate an exclusive economic zone of 200 nautical miles and a continental shelf, but "[r]ocks which cannot sustain human habitation or economic life of their own shall have no exclusive economic zone or continental shelf." The Tribunal concluded that this provision depends upon the objective capacity of a feature, in its natural condition, to sustain either a stable community of people or economic activity that is not dependent on outside resources or purely extractive in nature. The Tribunal noted that the current presence of official personnel on many of the features is dependent on outside support and not reflective of the capacity of the features. The Tribunal found historical evidence to be more relevant and noted that the Spratly Islands were historically used by small groups of fishermen and that several Japanese fishing and guano mining enterprises were attempted.

The Tribunal concluded that such transient use does not constitute inhabitation by a stable community and that all of the historical economic activity had been extractive. Accordingly, the Tribunal concluded that none of the Spratly Islands is capable of generating extended maritime zones. The Tribunal also held that the Spratly Islands cannot generate maritime zones collectively as a unit. Having found that none of the features claimed by China was capable of generating an exclusive economic zone, the Tribunal found that it could—without delimiting a boundary— declare that certain sea areas are within the exclusive economic zone of the Philippines, because those areas are not overlapped by any possible entitlement of China.

Specifically, the Tribunal (p. 10 of the Press release) declares:

Having found that Mischief Reef, Second Thomas Shoal and Reed Bank are submerged at high tide, form part of the exclusive economic zone and continental shelf of the Philippines, and are not overlapped by any possible entitlement of China, the Tribunal concluded that the Convention is clear in allocating sovereign rights to the Philippines with respect to sea areas in its exclusive economic zone. The Tribunal found as a matter of fact that China had (a) interfered with Philippine petroleum exploration at Reed Bank, (b) purported to prohibit fishing by Philippine vessels within the Philippines' exclusive economic zone, (c) protected and failed to prevent Chinese fishermen from fishing within the Philippines' exclusive economic zone at Mischief Reef and Second Thomas Shoal, and (d) constructed installations and artificial islands at Mischief Reef without the authorization of the Philippines. The Tribunal therefore concluded that China had violated the Philippines' sovereign rights with respect to its exclusive economic zone and continental shelf.

In light of the above, it could be reasonably stated that other submerged features that are within the EEZ and continental shelves of the Philippines and other coastal SEA states belong to each of them respectively and not to outside claimants. Hence consultations and/or negotiations should be made to resolve claims with respect to rocks that are in the EEZ of another country. In this connection, the SEA states could perhaps cooperate in the effort of defining and classifying features in the Spratlys according to the definitions stated by UNCLOS (submerged features at high tide and rocks) as the PCA has performed for some of them. One example mentioned in the Press Release (p.9) says "… the Tribunal concluded that all of the high-tide features in the Spratly Islands (including, for example, Itu Aba, Thitu, West York Island, Spratly Island, North-East Cay, South-West Cay) are legally 'rocks' that do not generate an exclusive economic zone or continental shelf." They are entitled to at most 12 nautical miles of territorial sea each, given that they do not overlap with territorial sea of other rocks. But the areas beyond are international waters.

Another example provided by the PCA shows "that Subi Reef, Gaven Reef (South), Hughes Reef, Mischief Reef, and Second Thomas Shoal, are low-tide elevations, within the meaning of Article 13 of the Convention," [p. 473 of the Award] and hence generate no entitlement to maritime zones of their own. Hence, one cannot build on low-tide elevations or submerged rocks, reefs and shoals in order to claim 12 nautical mile territorial sea around them. In fact, one can only declare "safety zones" of only 500 meters around installations built on such low-tide features within one's own EEZs as defined by Article 60 of UNCLOS on "Artificial islands, installations and structures in the exclusive economic zone" and Article 260 on "Safety zones."

The first example has important implications since Itu Aba, which is the largest feature not only in the Spratlys but also larger than any in the Paracels, is defined only as a rock then the same definition could be extended to the features in the Paracel archipelago. On the basis of the PCA ruling Vietnam itself could perhaps make China an offer to negotiate a bilateral code of conduct in the Paracel area before the sovereignty issue is settled. If China refuses, then Vietnam could ask the PCA to make a ruling on the characteristics of the features in the Paracel group as it has done in the Spratlys. Vietnam could also bring China to the Permanent Court of Arbitration, the International Court of Justice and other relevant legal institutions as well as the court of public opinion for all the harms that China has inflicted on Vietnamese fishermen in violation of UNCLOS and the PCA recent ruling.

Coastal SEA nations should cooperate with one another in rallying international support on this issue since China has used its occupation of the Paracels to claim an EEZ as well as to have established the Sansha prefecture on it expressly for administering and controlling the South China Sea. As a result, peace and security in the area have been threatened by China's increasing aggressive activities in the last decade or so.

For the time being a common effort by the Southeast Asian coastal states to come up with a clear account of the features in the Spratlys, identifying high tide and low tide ones, would make it easier for them to agree on the sovereignty of the structures claimed. In general the claimants should take the high road with regard to low tide features and not try to split hair with hatchets, thereby possibly allowing disputes to be intensified to the detriments of all. One possible solution that would benefit all people, including those outside Southeast Asia, is for the coastal SEA states to declare all low tide areas in the open sea as maritime environmental reserves that could be used for scientific researches and experiments.

The status of low tide and high tide features that are in the EEZs of each coastal state should already be clear according to the PCA ruling. Hence states with conflicting claims should try to resolve them amicably through consultations and negotiations according to the spirit of the law.

Big states think that they could get away with being defiant, but small states should be brilliant.

To this end, perhaps Vietnam and the Philippines should consult each other on the status of the following features (by coordinates from north to south) since they seem to be in the EEZ of the Philippines: Petly Reef (coordinates 10.41/114.58, Sand Cay (10.37/114.48), Namyit Island (10.18/114.37), Discovery Great Reef (10.05/113.85), Sin Cowe Island (9.89/114.33), Sin Cowe East Island (9.87/114.47), (Lansdowne Reef - 9.78/114.37), Collins Reef (9.77/114.26), Pearson Reef (8.96/113.68), Tennent Reef (8.86/114.65), Alison Reef (8.82/113.98), and Cornwallis South Reef (8.72/114.18). Likewise, Vietnam and Malaysia could start talking with each other on the status of the following features that are in the EEZ of Malaysia: Barque Canada Reef (8.18/113.31), Amboyna Cay (7.89/112.92). In this connection it might be wise to reconsider the claims of sovereignty for rocks in another country's EEZ that have never been actually occupied and/or administered.

Southeast Asian coastal states could take the initiatives on the issues mentioned above among themselves without having to wait for ASEAN to act as a group or for it to come up, along with China, with a COC (Code of Conduct) in the South China Sea. However, after having made a concerted effort on the above issues the SEA coastal states could then be in a better position to rally diplomatic and international support for their common positions as well as for compliance to the PCA ruling and international law.

BUILDING A NEW SECURITY ARCHITECTURE IN THE SOUTH CHINA SEA AND BEYOND

Harry Krejsa

Openness and inclusion are the keys to both security and prosperity in the modern strategic and economic environment. In the security realm, information sharing, clarity of intent, and constant communication reduce the risk of unintended conflict. Rules built through consensus and adhered to regardless of whether they serve a nation's short-term interests are critical for a harmonious world. In the economic realm the importance of these values are similarly clear. The ability to trade openly, compete effectively, and transport energy and goods unfettered has been crucial to global prosperity generally and many coastal countries in particular.

China is most frequently mentioned when discussing the developmental power of secure and open global commons. Over the last few decades, China has harnessed global market norms and institutions, international trade, and safe access to maritime shipping lanes to transform its economy and move hundreds of millions out of poverty. Vietnam seems poised to pursue a similar path. Since economic liberalizations in the 1990s, Vietnam has enjoyed the second-fasted rate of economic growth per person in the world (with only China ahead of it). Recent years have seen Vietnam average 5-6% annual GDP growth, tantalizingly close to rates of expansion that brought so-called economic miracles to South Korea and Taiwan.

Vietnam has pursued a robust endorsement of foreign investment, local control across its various provinces, and an embrace of multiple engines of growth. As a result, Vietnam enjoys a strong and diversified economy resistant to shocks while making parallel investments in education to allow its workforce to still benefit from an increasingly automated manufacturing industry. International trade has grown to represent 150% of Vietnam's GDP, more than any of its similar middle-income peers. [250] Its geography has become an asset, providing Vietnam with access to significant offshore energy reserves and the world's busiest sea lanes.

That is, as long as that access remains safe and unhindered. While openness and inclusion are keys to both security and prosperity, the tensions among them are highlighted most clearly in the maritime domain, and most critically in the South China Sea. The region is resource-rich and key to many of the area's economies. One-third of the world's commercial shipping, worth about $5 trillion, passes through the Sea each year. It holds proven reserves of at least 7 billion barrels of oil and 900 trillion cubic feet of natural gas. Yet the South China Sea is also one of the world's most contested regions, with persistent disputes between countries such as Vietnam, the Philippines, Taiwan, Malaysia, and Brunei over legions of reefs, rocks, islands, and reclaimed land.[251] The largest source of tension, coercion, and ongoing provocation in the region, however, is China.

While the Philippines have borne the brunt of China's aggression and coercive behavior, Vietnam has also seen these issues first hand. 2014 saw perhaps the most dramatic such example, when Chinese oil rig HD-981 crossed into Vietnam-claimed waters south of the Paracel Islands and began extraction operations. Though China has long disavowed any attempt to militarize the South China Sea, the rig was accompanied by eighty Chinese Coast Guard and Navy vessels, which repelled Vietnamese attempts at interdiction. Though the rig was eventually withdrawn in July of that year, the effort was seen as a strategic test case, allowing Beijing to gauge the pushback it could encounter when asserting its ownership over

---

[250] "The Other Asian Tiger: Vietnam's Success Merits a Closer Look," *The Economist*, August 6, 2016, http://www.economist.com/news/leaders/21703368-vietnams-success-merits-closer-look-other-asian-tiger.

[251] Van Jackson, Mira Rapp-Hooper, Paul Scharre, Harry Krejsa, and Jeff Chism, "Networked Transparency: Constructing a Common Operational Picture of the South China Sea," Center for a New American Security, March 2016.

disputed territories and resources.[252] Earlier this year, the very same rig returned to waters claimed by Vietnam and resumed operations. When Hanoi protested and lashed out at China, Beijing belittled their neighbor and expressed hope that Vietnam would not take the incident so seriously, urging Hanoi to "view it calmly."[253]

After the first Chinese oil rig incursion in 2014, Vietnam came out in support of the Philippines' taking their case against China at the Permanent Court of Arbitration. In a statement, Hanoi urged the court to reject China's claims based on its so-called Nine-Dash Line and that the court give "due regard" to Vietnam's rights and interests.[254] Since a leadership shuffle in the Communist Party of Vietnam earlier this year, however, a somewhat less-U.S. friendly government seems less likely to take legal action in the short term.[255] This has not stopped China from continuing to disregard Vietnam's claims, however, As evidenced by the return of oilrig HS 981.

These of course are just a few of the many ways Beijing is seeking to change the South China Sea. Rather than an area of safe, open inclusion, China is seeking to turn the waterway into one of coercive exclusion. By building artificial islands, Beijing is expanding its strategic reach (if not its dubious legal claims following the arbitration ruling). The Chinese Coast Guard has been a persistent source of harassment for civilian ships and other nations' coast guards alike. China's movement of weapons platforms

---

[252] Ankit Panda, "Why Did China Set Up an Oil Rig Within Vietnamese Waters?," The Diplomat, May 13, 2014, http://thediplomat.com/2014/05/why-did-china-set-up-an-oil-rig-within-vietnamese-waters.

[253] Mike Ives, "Vietnam Objects to Chinese Oil Rig in Disputed Waters," New York Times, January 20, 2016, http://www.nytimes.com/2016/01/21/world/asia/south-china-sea-vietnam-china.html?_r=0
Vu Trong Khanh, "Vietnam Tells China to Remove Oil Rig From Disputed Waters," Wall Street Journal, April 8, 2016, http://www.wsj.com/articles/vietnam-tells-china-to-remove-oil-rig-from-disputed-waters-1460042757.

[254] Prashanth Parameswaran, "Vietnam Launches Legal Challenge Against China's South China Sea Claims," The Diplomat, December 12, 2014, http://thediplomat.com/2014/12/vietnam-launches-legal-challenge-against-chinas-south-china-sea-claims.

[255] Matthew Pennekamp, "The End of Vietnam's Pivot to America?" The National Interest, March 4, 2016, http://nationalinterest.org/feature/the-end-vietnams-pivot-america-15398.

among the Paracels and, likely soon, among the Spratlys are furthering the regional militarization it claims to abhor. All the while, Beijing is seeking to prevent the region's actors from acting in concert, doing all they can to atomize and isolate the South China Sea's claimants.[256]

At the same time that China pursues its campaign of intimidation and isolation, the PLA is engaging in an ambitious military modernization effort. The last two decades have been marked by annual double-digit percentage increases in military spending, making China now the world's second-largest military.[257] Within the next twenty to thirty years, some expect China's military spending to exceed even that of the United States.[258] With a more geographically constrained scope than the United States, however, China will be able to exert tremendous influence over its neighbors and regional competitors far more quickly.

Consequently, Asian nations are becoming more and more interested in regional cooperation over security. Increasingly, this interest is not just with existing major powers, but among regional actors themselves. Australia has begun boosting maritime domain awareness and improving equipment stocks through its Pacific patrol boat program.[259] Japan has similarly sought to boost equipment and surveillance among Southeast Asian partners.[260] The United States is currently standing up its ambitious Maritime Security Initiative, which seeks to grow security cooperation and capabilities among

[256] Patrick Cronin and Harry Krejsa, "How Will China React to the Gavel Coming Down in the South China Sea?," War on the Rocks, June 26, 2016, http://warontherocks.com/2016/06/how-will-china-react-to-the-gavel-coming-down-in-the-south-china-sea/.

[257] Richard A. Bitzinger, "China's Double-Digit Defense Growth: What It Means for a Peaceful Rise," Foreign Affairs, March 19, 2015, https://www.foreignaffairs.com/articles/china/2015-03-19/chinas-double-digit-defense-growth.

[258] China's Military Rise: The Dragon's New Teeth," The Economist, April 7, 2012, http://www.economist.com/node/21552193.

[259] Shahryar Pasandideh, "Australia Launches New Pacific Patrol Boat Program," The Diplomat, July 1, 2014, http://thediplomat.com/2014/07/australia-launches-new-pacific-patrol-boat-program/, Australian Government, Department of Defence, *2016 Defence White Paper*, 126

[260] Nobuhiro Kubo, Randy Fabi, "Japan to expand SE Asia security ties with Indonesia pact," Reuters, March 19, 2015, http://www.reuters.com/article/us-japan-indonesia-defence-idUSKBN0MF0UP20150319

the South China Sea's many stakeholders. Security in the South China Sea will not be decided by alliances or alignments between two great powers; rather, the future will call for a more robust network of interlinking and interdependent stakeholders building the regional community they desire.

Indeed, recent scholarship suggests that as the world becomes more complex and interconnected, metrics of state power have become more nuanced. The combined military and economic might of a state and its ally is no longer as informative as the web of actors inside which any one state is connected. In the modern economy, scarce information and resources travel along these networks, and the more densely connected a state is to these networks, the more network-derived power it can be said to have.[261] These connections can also constrain, however; while networks can endow influence through scarce information, they can also draw actors into conflicts they would not otherwise prefer if they were not so well connected.

China, for all its recent aggressive tendencies, is a densely connected country. It benefits tremendously from the economic, cultural, and political ties it shares with countries throughout the region. It benefits from and is empowered by these dense networks. China is also changed by them, as was evident by its decision to open up to the global economy in the 1980s and 90s. North Korea, in contrast, is sparsely connected to any global networks, and indeed, is perhaps only connected in any meaningful way to China.[262] As a result, China is constantly pulled into tensions and conflicts that its tiny neighbor provokes. North Korea, in contrast, eschews connections to networks that could change it, fearing that the changes that such global engagement brought to China would in turn loosen the Kim dynasty's grip on power.

The diversity and scale of the Asia-Pacific community suggests that ensuring regional security will require a networked architecture rather than a traditional bilateral alliance system. Numerous interlocking and overlapping relationships and institutions have developed to organize the region, argue scholars like Victor Cha, and as long as actors are not pressured to "pick a side" between the United States and China, those

---

[261] Emilie M. Hafner-Burton, Miles Kahler, Alexander H. Montgomery, "Network Analysis for International Relations," *International Organization*, 68 no. 3 (July 2009), 570

[262] Ibid, 572

structures could provide both the security and flexibility needed to suit a region with diverse and variegated interests.[263] Indeed, U.S. policy should actively seek to avoid pressures for regional actors to "pick a side," instead fostering, as Anne-Marie Slaughter calls it, an agenda focusing on "network centrality," connecting states and stakeholders within those states around common international interests.[264]

Even while fostering such a distributed, networked security architecture, the United States will still necessarily need to be one of its central nodes – just not *the* central node. Establishing a common operational picture will likely require U.S. political and technological leadership.[265] The Maritime Security Initiative holds great promise to improve the capabilities of regional actors to establish credible defense, patrol their waters, and share information, but also holds political risks in being seen as too closely aligned with U.S. strategic interests opposed to Chinese interests. Nonetheless, if handled properly – with patience, nuance, and an eye toward building regional networks and interconnectedness – the future of Asian-Pacific security could yet be bright.

---

[263] Victor D. Cha, "Complex Patchworks: U.S. Alliances as Part of Asia's Regional Architecture," *Asia Policy*, no. 11 (January 2011)

[264] Anne-Marie Slaughter, "A Grand Strategy of Network Centrality," in Robert J. Art, Richard K. Betts, Peter Feaver, Richard Fontaine, Kristin M. Lord and Anne-Marie Slaughter, "America's Path, Grand Strategy for the Next Administration," (Center for a New American Security, May 2012), 43-56

[265] Van Jackson, Mira Rapp-Hooper, Paul Scharre, Harry Krejsa, and Jeff Chism, "Networked Transparency: Constructing a Common Operational Picture of the South China Sea," Center for a New American Security, March 2016.

The Impacts of PCA Ruling on Regional Strategic Environment in the South China Sea

Siswo Pramono

Personal Opinion

It should be noted in advance that my paper represents my personal opinion.

The limits of law and political means

We have learned about the limits of law for the resolution of issues in the South China Sea (SCS). I would like to underline, nevertheless, that international law, including UNCLOS, provides a good basis for political solutions panels.

In my view, the political solution should be in line with existing international law, since the later represents the convergent norms and values of the international community.

---

[266] Development Agency, Ministry of Foreign Affairs, Indonesia. This draft is prepared for later publication.

On the limits of law, we can observe the following:

1. The nature of the dispute in the SCS is very complex. The issues are clustered into: territorial ownership (or issues of sovereignty); freedom of navigation; and, an Exclusive Economic Zone (EEZ), which includes matters relating to fisheries, oil exploration, etc. Not all of the issues in contention, in particular the one relating to territorial ownership (sovereignty), can be resolved solely by employing UNCLOS.
2. The limits of UNCLOS aside, we have also learned that states can seek remedies through other relevant international laws and relevant legal mechanisms.
3. In the long term, settlement of the complex issues of overlapping jurisdiction in the SCS would encompass both legal and political measures.

The growing legal culture

If we learn from history, there is evidence that more and more Asian countries rely on international law for conflict resolution. As shown in the following table, Asia's legal culture has grown. The data comes from the International Court of Justice (ICJ) website, and it shows that from 1947 to 2016, the number of Asian countries that benefited from the judgment, advisory opinion, and orders of ICJ has been growing.

Asia's Legal Culture (1947-2016):
Judgment, Advisory Opinion, and Orders by ICJ

- 2015: Order of 19 May 2015 - Obligations concerning Negotiations relating to Cessation of the Nuclear Arms Race and to Nuclear Disarmament (Marshall Islands v. India)
- 2013: Request for Interpretation of the Judgment of 15 June 1962 in the Case concerning the Temple of Preah Vihear (Cambodia v. Thailand) (Cambodia v. Thailand)
- 2010: Order of 13 July 2010 - Whaling in the Antarctic (Australia v. Japan: New Zealand intervening)
- 2008: Sovereignty over Pedra Branca/Pulau Batu Puteh, Middle Rocks and South Ledge (Malaysia v. Singapore)
- 2002: Sovereignty over Pulau Ligitan and Pulau Sipadan (Indonesia v. Malaysia)
- 2000: Judgment of 21 June 2000 - Aerial Incident of 10 August 1999 (Pakistan v. India)
- 1973: Order of 15 December 1973 - Trial of Pakistani Prisoners of War (Pakistan v. India)
- 1972: Judgment of 18 August 1972 - Appeal Relating to the Jurisdiction of the ICAO Council (India v. Pakistan)
- 1960: Judgment of 12 April 1960 - Right of Passage over Indian Territory (Portugal v. India)
- 1997-2010: Cambodia Tribunal
- 1946-1948: Tokyo Tribunal

From 1947 to 1999 (about 52 years), there were only 3 episodes of dispute among Asian countries settled by ICJ. From 2000 to 2015 (15 years) legal settlements increased to 6 episodes. This means more legal settlements in a shorter amount of time. Among Asian countries having experience settling disputes according to international law through the ICJ mechanism, were India, Pakistan, Cambodia, Thailand, Indonesia, Malaysia, and Singapore. Thus, Asia's legal culture has been strengthened. And this is a good thing.

As Asia's legal culture strengthened, at the same time, we also learn from history about the waning of war in Asia, and particularly in South East Asia, with the inception of ASEAN in 1967. ASEAN, as an international legal personality, has committed itself to promoting legal culture in South East Asia and beyond.

In other words, South East Asia has relied more on political and legal solutions as a means of conflict resolution.

It is hoped that the long-term resolution of South China Sea issues will follow this general trend. Legal adjudication is by no means a necessity, but it does underline the importance of international law as a guiding principle for peaceful resolution. It is also in this context that the PCA ruling has a legal and political implication to the strategic environment of the region.

At present, the real politics of East Asia (and also the Asia Pacific) is fluid and dynamic. On the matter of legal and political implications to the region, we need to observe not only the real capacity of major powers to maintain regional stability (if not *status quo*), but also their respective limitations. My point is that, we should not "overvalue" or "undervalue " the key players of the region.

Partnership, not conflict, should be the order of the day

The following table indicates the limits on China in controlling the outcome of her diplomacy.

Limitation of Parties (1)

China:
- Slowing down of economic growth, over capacity of production/ miss planning of the economy
- Bridging the gap among and within provinces
- The growing of middle class and associated political implication
- The peaceful rise of China (RCEP, OBOR, etc.) and the dynamics of the region (challenge and support)

Interdependence is the norm of the region. It is not only that East Asia depends on China but China also depends on East Asia. China's economy is still growing but the growth is slowing down. Despite all of the good reports on China's fundamental economy, the era of China's two digit growth has long gone, and China is now facing the reality of about 6-7 per cent growth; similar to other developing economies in South East Asia.

The slowing down of the China's economy means the slowing down of, for instance, China's military expenditure. At the same time, China is struggling to overcome the burdens of her economic mismanagement and over capacity. For instance, 50 per cent of global steel is produced in China. And China depends on North America and East Asia markets to absorb this overcapacity.

The statistics indicate that among the ten largest trade partners of China, in terms of total trade, are the US (about US$550 billion), ASEAN (about US$480 billion), Japan (about US$ 300 billion), Taiwan (about US$200 billion), and Australia (about US$40 billion). So, about US$2 trillion of real money is at stake in China's relations with its aforementioned trade partners. The logic that follows from these statistics is that it is in the best interest of China, and its trading partners, to maintain the best relations it can instead of embarking on a political adventure that might risk mutually beneficial ties.

Trading and investment interests aside, one needs to also look at the sensitive issues relating to how China should cope with the growing middle class and associated political implication, as well as China's ability to bridge the socio-economic gap among and within provinces. For example, narrowing the gap between Guangdong where GDP amounted to US$1.1 trillion, and Qinghai with about only US$37 billion. Indonesia understands the complex nature of this issue, because it too is struggling to cope with the uneven development between provinces in the Western and Eastern parts of that country. The logic that follows the statistic is that it is in the best interests of China and its neighbors to maintain good neighborly relations, so that every country can concentrate more on addressing domestic issues.

Last but not least, the peaceful rise of China is the best expectation of everyone in China and in the region. China's mega projects, such as One Belt One Road (OBOR), can only materialize with the support of the region. And regional support can only be assured if good relations are maintained and improved.

All of the limitations that I previously mentioned are not only a challenge, but also an opportunity for China and its partners to work together. China aside, the US also has limitations that need to be addressed, as indicated in the following table.

Limitation of Parties (2)

The US :

- End result of presidential election (Trump vs Clinton), composition of congress (Republican vs Democrat)
- The future of US pivot to Asia
  - US alliances (Korea, Japan, the Philippines, Australia)
  - US naval presence in Indo-Pacific region
  - The future of TPP, broadening options of market architecture for East Asia economies

The world is now carefully reading the best outcome of the US presidential election. There is a kind of wariness in East Asia since future relations between the US and East Asia has been missing in the substance of the recent US presidential debates. Most of the candidates presented their view on the future of US relations with Europe (including Russia), and the Middle East. The debate on security was somehow tided up with the issue of religious extremism, which we fully understand since the US security nightmare was triggered by the September 11 terrorist attacks. The South China Sea is important for US interests on freedom of navigation, but it is not part of US psychological anxiety derived from a traumatic experience (such as September 11).

Not everyone has the same view and expectation on "US rebalance toward Asia" in terms of policy and technicalities. In South Korea, the introduction of the United States' Terminal High Altitude Area Defense (THAAD) has triggered controversy, as much as the introduction of China's Air Defense Identification Zone (ADIZ). A Japanese plan to amend the constitution to enable Japan to be more active militarily in the region (as was the case of the German constitutional change), has raised objections in some countries. The point is that it is important to find a formula in which the need for security will not complicate the feeling of insecurity. For Indonesia, it is important for the region to assure that these dynamics don't result in the delicate issues of power projection and security dilemma.

Many US allies, and other countries in East Asia, are wondering about the future of the "US pivot to Asia." Even in the context of US soft power diplomacy, the future of Obama's foreign economic policy of Trans Pacific Partnership (TPP) is called into question. After all, during the US presidential campaigns, most of the candidates made negative remarks about TPP. Adding to this complexity is the uncertainty on the congressional approval of America's involvement in the TPP.

For some South East Asia nations, free trade agreements, with all of the criticisms directed against them, offer the opportunity for developing economies to improve the quality of their trade in Asia Pacific markets. This applies to the competing Regional Comprehensive Economic Partnership (RCEP) – a Pacific FTA without the US, and the TPP, a Pacific FTA without China. Some countries in the region lean toward RCEP, others lean toward TPP, many lean toward the two, and some haven't decided.

Vietnam is a good example, where domestic economic reform has been driven by the urgency to join TPP. And the economic reform has, in fact, been able to improve the economic performance of Vietnam. Indonesia is likely to follow the Vietnamese path. At present, Indonesia is in the midst of preparation, as President Joko Widodo has announced Indonesia's intention to join TPP. We know that such preparation is a very tough but necessary process, involving the review of about 500 laws, 8000 ministerial regulations, etc.

But if, as a result of such reform, Indonesia can improve its competitiveness, ease of doing business, innovation, standardization, and other qualifications, then, Indonesia would be able to better compete in the regional and global market. We expect that the nature of Indonesia's trade can shift from traditional commodities and extractive industries, such as our main export to India and China, into manufacturing high value added products. Only then, can Indonesia have a solid basis for market diversification, thus reducing our dependency on specific markets.

For Indonesia, market diversification, would support the realization of a "free and active" foreign policy. At present, Indonesia's five main trading partners include, in term of total trade: ASEAN (about US$72 billion); China (about US$44 billion); Japan (about US$31 billion); US (about US$24 billion); Korea (about US$16 billion). More competitive Indonesian products would give Indonesia greater freedom to enter new markets in the Pacific region and beyond.

The US aside, it is also important to look at the possible ASEAN limitation. Some have argued that ASEAN is not meant to be a hegemonic power of South East Asia, and analysis meets the reality of the real politics of the region. For me, ASEAN power relies on the commitment of its members. And for non-member countries, ASEAN power is more in the realm of soft power. In other words, ASEAN leadership is an intellectual leadership.

Despite its significant achievement on the maintenance of political stability and improvement of regional welfare, ASEAN is struggling to maintain unity and centrality. The following table summarizes some of ASEAN's limitations.

Limitation of Parties (3)

ASEAN:

- The question of unity and centrality, amid the formal establishment of ASEAN Community
- The question relating to the capacity of ASEAN-based architecture (EAS, ARF, ADMM Plus)
- Interregional linkage (ASEAN-EU, ASEAN-IORA, etc.)

Nevertheless, ASEAN is becoming more open and outward looking. An ASEAN dialogue partner is growing in number. And ASEAN-based regional architecture is also developing (i.e. Asian Regional Forum – ARF, ASEAN Defense Ministerial Meeting Plus – ADMM Plus, and East Asian Summit – EAS, ASEAN Plus Three – APT, etc.). At the same time, ASEAN has outreached other strategic regionalisms (i.e. ASEAN-EU, ASEAN-IORA, etc.). And yet, ASEAN needs to respond to high expectations from the global community.

Recent developments in the SCS have again put ASEAN to the test, and they are even more complicated than the situation in 2012. However, the ASEAN Ministerial Meeting (AMM) in the mid-July 2016 in Vientiane, Laos, proved that ASEAN as a community is able to address this kind of geopolitical challenge.

The international expectation is that ASEAN should be able to come up with a statement on the PCA ruling. It should be noted, however, that the case of the Philippines vs. China adjudicated by the PCA, a dispute settlement mechanism under UNCLOS, is essentially a bilateral matter between the Philippines and China. It is equally true, however, that the PCA ruling provides legal precedent for similar cases in the future. Thus, the ruling is part of jurisprudence development. Most ASEAN countries, however, as indicated in the following table, would see the PCA ruling more as a general principle of promoting rule-based order and the respect for international law.

Prior to the issuance of the PCA ruling on 12 July 2016, the position of ASEAN member countries, as indicated in their respective national statements, were as follows:

Country	Adherence to UNCLOS	Adherence to rule-based order/ international law	Maintenance of peace and security: peaceful dispute settlement	Supporting the PCA ruling
Cambodia			x	
Indonesia	x		x	
Malaysia	x	x	x	
Myanmar		x	x	
Philippine			x	
Singapore		x	x	
Thailand			x	
Vietnam	x	x	x	
Brunei	n/a	n/a	n/a	
Lao	n/a	n/a	n/a	

Note: x = the matter is indicated in the national statement

Learning from the respective national statements, one can infer that ASEAN members overwhelmingly underline the importance of maintaining peace and security as well as peaceful dispute settlement. Many members also underline the importance of adherence to rule-based order or international law. Owing to this political denominator, in the July 2016 AMM in Vientiane, Indonesia initiated a Stand-Alone Statement on the Maintenance of Peace, Security, and Stability in the Region.

In Vientiane, ASEAN also managed to conclude the 49th AMM Join Communiqué, one section of which is devoted to addressing the situation in the SCS. The Communiqué was able to pinpoint not only the political general denominator (i.e. peace, security, stability, safety and freedom of navigation) but also the call for self-restraint, peaceful resolution of disputes, adherence to international law, the inclusion of UNCLOS, non-militarization, and the issue of land reclamation. The communiqué also urged the implementation of DOC and early adoption of COC as well as the establishment of hotline and code for unplanned encounters at sea.

Last but not least, the 2016 AMM in Vientiane also managed to issue another important document relating to full and effective implementation of DOC. As such, despite the challenges and its limitations, it shows that ASEAN is still able to work in unison.

ASEAN Stand-Alone Statement on the Maintenance of Peace, Security, and Stability in the Region (Indonesian Initiative)	49th AMM Joint Communiqué: South China Sea Section – Key Words
• South East Asia → peaceful, stable, secure region; • South East Asia → prosperity in the region and beyond • ASEAN → To uphold UN Charter, ASEAN Charter, TAC, ZOPFAN, Declaration of the East Asia Summit on the Principles for Mutually Beneficial Relations ...... • ASEAN → 49th AMM Joint Communiqué • ASEAN → self-restraint • Other states → Respect ASEAN's norms and principles	• Reaffirms: peace, security, stability, safety and freedom of navigation in and over-flight • Reaffirms: self-restraint, pursue peaceful resolution of disputes, international law, UNCLOS • Emphasis: self-restraint, non-militarization, land reclamation • Implementation: DOC, early adoption of COC • Establishment: MFA to MFA hotline, code for unplanned encounters at sea (CUES)

Convergence of interest and value

In conclusion, despite of the aforementioned embedded limitations, on the part of China, US, and ASEAN, we can see the convergence of interests and values for those involved in the security of East Asia and South East Asia. The following table indicates such convergence of interest and value.

Convergence of Interest and Value

- China-US-ASEAN common interest on economic interdependence
- China-US-ASEAN common values on stability and prosperity (TAC, UN Charter)

China – US – ASEAN share a common interest on economic interdependence. The liberal theorists would agree that the shared interest in trade (with a value of US$2 trillion per year), in which the vital issues of food security and energy security are embedded in it, would guarantee strong ties amid the dynamics of the *realpolitik* in SCS.

China – US – ASEAN also share common values on stability and prosperity. After all, both the US and China are parties to the ASEAN's Treaty of Amity and Cooperation (TAC). They also abide by the universal values enshrined in the UN Charter.

I would like to add one more note in here, namely, that it is important for the US to ratify UNCLOS as the common values on regime of the sea.

The Strategic Importance of Strengthening Vietnamese-U.S. Cooperation: Critical Timing, Prospects and Challenges

Anders Corr

Abstract

Co-operation between Vietnam and the U.S. will be crucial to Vietnam's ability to defend its independence, international market access, and exclusive economic zone (EEZ) over the next 10 years. As China continues to build its naval power relative to the U.S., a window of opportunity exists for Vietnam, the U.S., and other allies to set and enforce international legal limits on China's maritime and commercial dominance. The sooner those limits are set and defended the better will be the outcome for Vietnam. Time is on China's side. With time, China's People's Liberation Army Navy (PLAN) gets stronger, and China's strategy of "take and talk" progresses. China's strategy entails the incremental capture of territory while distracting adversaries with diplomatic negotiations. The U.S. Navy (USN) is the only Navy capable of defeating the PLAN today. Therefore, the U.S. is the linchpin bilateral alliance partner for claimant states in Asia that plan to defend their maritime rights. A strong multilateral defense alliance of other states could successfully resist China, and such an alliance should be pursued. However, coordination is challenging.

Bilateral alliances between states facing Chinese territorial aggrandizement, and the U.S., should be pursued in tandem with broader multilateral alliances. These bilateral alliances are in the interests of not only claimant states, but of the U.S. If China captures Vietnam's maritime resources, for example, China will be economically strengthened and militarily emboldened to capture more. While the prospects and benefits of strengthened cooperation abound, serious challenges persist. First, China uses international business ties to influence both Vietnamese and U.S. politics, and to discourage U.S. involvement in Asian politics, especially in the South China Sea. Second, Vietnam and the U.S. lack trust given their different political values (on issues such as democracy and freedom of speech) and a history of warfare. These challenges can be overcome through:

- Political decisions to reorient business ties away from China, and towards each other, e.g. through the Trans Pacific Partnership;
- Increased development aid;
- Increasing militarytomilitary agreements, training, aid, and cooperation;
- Increased diplomatic track-2, and citizen diplomacy;
- Striving to find areas of commonality and agreement, rather than difference.

Above all, military cooperation should be pursued in order to further the potentiality of a VietnameseU.S. defence alliance.

Since World War II, The U.S.Vietnamese relationship has undergone remarkable, and often tragic, transitions.[267] After World War II, Ho Chi Minh sought to extend his alliance with the U.S., Ho Chi Minh wanted

---

[267] Manyin, Mark E. "U.S.-Vietnam Relations In 2010: Current Issues And Implications For U.S. Policy." Washington, DC: Congressional Research Service, August 6, 2010.

U.S. support for decolonization, including against France. But at that time France wanted to regain the colony it lost to Japan. The U.S., trying to keep France in NATO against what it saw as the primary threat of the Soviet Union and concerned about Ho Chi Minh's communist leanings, decided to side with France against all threats it faced in Vietnam including Ho Chi Minh's nationalists. While the U.S. officially supported decolonization, and generally oversaw decolonization globally (and to its own benefit as U.S. influence increased substantially through the U.N. and international financial institutions), the U.S. sacrificed decolonization in Vietnam to try and keep France as a strong NATO member.[268]

This tragic decision on the part of the U.S. led Ho Chi Minh to ally closely with first China, and then Russia, against the U.S. The U.S. consequently lost a bloody war in which nobody was clearly in the right. The U.S. was pro colonial and not sufficiently supportive of democratic principles in Vietnam through support of an authoritarian government in the South. The U.S. committed the My Lai Massacre. The Viet Minh had their own excesses, including overzealous imposition of communism in the south, killing of South sympathizers, and land reform that may have gone too far.[269]

A U.S. Apology To Pave The Way For A Defensive Alliance With Vietnam

It is time for the U.S. to apologize for its very large part in the tragedy that was the Vietnam War. It is also time for the Vietnamese government to apologize for any mistakes it made during its struggle for independence. None of that is politically easy, and it may never happen.

Regardless, it will be a more important exercise for academics, who can come to a better level of understanding on these sensitive topics than can politicians and diplomats. If the latter groups can find an opportunity for apologies that are politically realistic and don't compromise other important longterm goals, they should and will make such apologies. If not, the academics can pave the diplomatic way by writing frank histories of the time in lieu of official apology. This work of apologizing is important for

---

[268] U.S. Department of State. "Dien Bien Phu & the Fall of French Indochina, 1954." https://history.state.gov/milestones/19531960/dienbienphu, accessed 8/16/2016.

[269] Thayer, Carlyle A. "SinoVietnamese Relations: The Interplay of Ideology and National Interest." Asian Survey, Vol. 34, No. 6. June 1994, pp. 513528

reconciliation. As the Vietnamese have in the past asked for development aid as part of the normalization process,[270] including requests as far back as the 1979 normalization negotiations, it would be a simple and effective matter for the U.S. to supply such aid.[271]

Apologies should not be demanded from one side or the other. This only polarizes the debate. China uses repeated demands for an apology from Japan as a way to drive apart South Korea and Japan, and to appease or keep the Chinese population angry long after normal public anger subsides. While Chinese foreign ministry officials and the media have at times been less antiJapanese than the general public,[272] this is not necessarily the case with military cadre and the standing committee. These anti-Japanese actions could be seen as a form of authoritarian demagoguery or authoritarian populism that problematize the notion that nationalism and domestic opinion drives Chinese misbehavior. Rather, China deliberately stokes nationalism to enable its misbehavior. Vietnamese public opinion is friendly to the U.S. because state media makes an effort in this direction.[273]

During World War II, U.S. anger at Japan was virulent and allowed the government to drop two nuclear weapons on two cities, plus firebomb Tokyo. Now that animosity is almost entirely gone. This is not the case in China and South Korea, perhaps because those countries were occupied by Japan, but also because China has kept the animosity alive by frequent presidentiallevel mentions, commemorations of Japanese excess, and anti-Japanese media. AntiJapanese television dramas increased from 15 in 2004, to greater than 175 in 2011.[274] Purely state media focuses on sensitive topics

---

[270] Weinstein, Franklin B. "U.S.-Vietnam Relations and the Security of Southeast Asia." Foreign Affairs Vol. 56, No. 4, July 1978, pp. 842856.

[271] Blatz, Craig W., Karina Schumann and Michael Ross. "Government Apologies for Historical Injustices," Political Psychology, Vol. 30, No. 2, April 2009, pp. 219241.

[272] Stockmann, Daniela. "Who Believes Propaganda? Media Effects during the AntiJapanese Protests in Beijing." The China Quarterly, No. 202, June 2010, pp. 269289.

[273] Dix, Robert H. "Populism: Authoritarian and Democratic." Latin American Research Review, Vol. 20, No. 2, 1985, pp. 2952.

[274] Ng, Grace. "Beijing's strong drive to instill nationalism fires up young." Asia News Network, February 24, 2014, http://www.nationmultimedia. com/opinion/Beijingsstrongdrivetoinstillnationalismfires30227557.html, accessed 8/16/2016.

such as Japan and the South China Sea, while more commercialized media sources cover less sensitive topics.[275] All sources are increasingly subject to censorship and state direction, so to the extent that the Chinese population maintains its anger at Japan, the state media shares blame.

Over the last decade, the U.S.Vietnamese relationship has undergone a remarkable thaw. In the 1960s and early 1970s, The U.S. dropped explosives, napalm, and Agent Orange on Vietnam from the air and had covered the south with ground troops. China and Russia were strong supporters of Vietnam during those difficult times, and helped Vietnam win its independence struggle. Then as part of President Nixon's thaw with China to gain it as an ally against Russia, the U.S. withdrew from Vietnam and started supporting China with diplomatic and trade relations.

Remarkably, in 1979, China attacked Vietnam in part to prove to the U.S. that China was a worthy ally against Russia.[276] This raises the question as to whether the U.S. had a hand in encouraging China to attack in 1979. This seems unlikely, as the fairly pacifistic President Carter was President at the time. He attempted to further reconciliation, but the House of Representatives chilled that venture.[277] As part of a reconciliation process, why Deng Xiaoping thought his war against Vietnam would improve relations with the U.S. should be researched and clarified.

These are all highly sensitive topics and will or have created much controversy among scholars, but more so, among politicians and diplomats. I have confidence, however, that addressing these mistakes with full transparency is the right step to take at this juncture in the history of U.S. Vietnamese relations. The threat from China and I use those words while being keenly aware of their certain negative reception in China now puts U.S. and Vietnamese national interests in much closer accord. Genuine apologies at all levels, from citizen diplomacy to heads of state, will go far in reconciling the U.S. and Vietnam, and pave the way for a potential defensive alliance.

---

[275]　Stockmann, Daniela. "Who Believes Propaganda? Media Effects during the AntiJapanese Protests in Beijing." The China Quarterly, No. 202, June 2010, pp. 269289.

[276]　Zhang, Xiaoming. Deng Xiaoping's Long War: The Military Conflict Between China And Vietnam, 1979-1991. Chapel Hill: University of North Carolina Press, 2015.

[277]　Weinstein, Franklin B. "U.S.-Vietnam Relations and the Security of Southeast Asia." Foreign Affairs Vol. 56, No. 4, July 1978, pp. 842856.

Vietnamese U.S. Alliance Building To Support The Territorial Status Quo

Since 1988, when China violently occupied features in the South China Sea, and 1989, when it suppressed protesters in Tiananmen Square, the U.S. is not only worried about Russia, but also about China's military and domestic intentions. China is expanding into other countries' territory both maritime and in the Arunachal Pradesh region of India. By economic expansion is generally welcomed by all, as it entails cheaper goods on international markets and more international demand for exports from domestic markets, territorial expansion calls for containment. Such containment of territorial expansionism should not be conflated with a generally nonexistent containment of economic expansion. I use the term "containment", fully knowing that it is practically a swear word in China. But against territorial expansion, it is the right word, and action, to use. It that context, containment is simply the preservation of the territorial status quo, and is purely defensive in nature.

To that end, U.S. troops are cooperating with Vietnam on goodwill projects like building schools, the TransPacific Partnership trade deal (TPP) that includes Vietnam but not China, Fulbright University, and a U.S.funded university in Ho Chi Minh City established in 2014. There is now talk of a defense alliance between the two countries, aimed at containing, or at least balancing against, China. Analysts are belittling such a prospect, and justifiably point to Vietnam's fence sitting and hedging between the two superpowers. But the international dynamics are highly conducive to a U.S.Vietnamese alliance.

China is not the only country that should contain itself territorially. While the U.S. does not have territorial designs on foreign territories, and this is a critical difference with China that lends countries to trust U.S. bases abroad, the U.S. can be overzealous in promoting its values through military force. This has led to disaster. Historical hindsight is perfect, but we now know that the U.S. overstepped when it militarily supported France and the South, leading to a horribly devastating war with a worse outcome than had it not fought the war. The U.S. is now fighting in Afghanistan, Iraq, Syria, Pakistan, and Yemen. Islamic fundamentalism, especially when it supports terrorism, is indeed repulsive. But is it worth tearing apart the fabric of the countries in which we fight most notably Afghanistan, Syria, Iraq, and Libya? In these countries, the cure of counterinsurgency is surely worse than the disease of Islamic fundamentalism. It is far preferable to fight terrorists with targeted strikes, rather than trying to change governments. Since successfully rebuilding Germany and Japan, and installing pro U.S. market democracies in those countries, the U.S. has tried to repeat the process elsewhere, with much less success.

The U.S. war against Islamic terrorism, with the exception of Al Qaeda and their supporters, the Taliban, is not really about Islamic terrorism. It is, like the Vietnam War, about superpower rivalry. These are, somewhat unfairly, known as brushfire wars. They used to be called wars on the periphery of empires. The tacit agreement, in these wars, is to use proxies to fight each other in "buffer" states, far from the financial and political capitals of the great powers. Remember that in the 1980s the U.S. funded and armed Islamic fundamentalists against the Soviets. Now we are again funding and arming Islamic fundamentalists against the Russians in Syria. The real fight here is about not letting the other great power win. Unfortunately, when the elephants fight, the grass suffers. Yet in most brushfire wars in the media age, the elephants, perversely, claim to be fighting to help the grass. It couldn't be farther from the truth.

It is critical for the U.S. to have perspective on the failure of its counterinsurgency wars in Vietnam and the Middle East, so as to avoid that mire in the future. As China's power grows, the U.S. will need to conserve its force to balance with countries against this rising threat. To do so, the U.S. should refrain from counterinsurgencies and most Islamic terrorism, and focus its military force on protection of the territorial status quo, and deterring major powers such as China and Russia from incremental territorial expansion. The U.S. military is optimally configured for this mission, and is ill suited for counterinsurgency. Promotion of American values such as democracy, equality, freedom of speech, human rights, and market economics can be more effectively promoted through peaceful dialogue.

U.S., Chinese, And Russian Influence In Vietnam

Competition between values and ideas is the realm of soft power, ideas, and influence. As China grows its economy and builds its military, it gains more influence in neighboring countries.[278] Indeed, it feels entitled to such

---

[278] Shie, Tamara Renee. "Rising Chinese Influence in the South Pacific: Beijing's 'Island Fever,'" Asian Survey, Vol. 47, No. 2, March/April 2007.

influence. I occasionally puzzle over whether this sense of entitlement is what Kissinger is advising China on his many visits there. It certainly accords with his realist philosophy.

While influence does follow economic and military growth, it is the use of that influence that determines good will. China seems to be attempting to use its influence to further and expand its core interests, from historical claims to Tibet, Xinjiang and Taiwan to more contemporary claims of core interests in the South China Sea.[279] China's use of its newfound influence in a narrow pursuit of its national interests has progressively destroyed what good will it built in the 1990s and early 2000s. A lack of good will towards China has destroyed its soft power, and now China relies on economic carrots, and military sticks, to gain its ends. This is an expensive and inherently unsustainable grand strategy.

The improvement in U.S.Vietnamese relations is the product of "push and pull" factors of a changing geopolitical landscape. Chinese attacks on Vietnamese maritime and other territory in the 1970s, including a land invasion in 1979, pushed Vietnam away from its alliance with China. Vietnam's strongest ally since 1979, Russia, has lost economic and military steam. The collapse of Russia's economy after privatization, followed by sanctions and most importantly the drop in oil price, is pushing Vietnam to seek new defense and trading partners. As China still seeks to claim Vietnam's exclusive economic zone, and wants Vietnam to join a Chinese defense alliance as a junior partner, Vietnamese public opinion has a very dim view of China. This constrains Vietnamese politicians in their dealings with China, and pushes China towards other partnerships.

At this historical juncture, the U.S. and E.U. are strong proponents of development aid, free trade, and international law, including maritime law. The U.S. and E.U. are closely allied, and would make excellent allies, if Vietnam can woo them. An alliance also makes sense from a U.S. and E.U. perspective. It would help contain China's territorial expansion, and thus divert China to more productive pursuits of domestic economic growth, and cooperative international trade.

---

[279] Wong, Edward. "Security Law Suggests A Broadening Of China's 'Core Interests.'" New York Times, July 22, 2015, http://www.nytimes.com/2015/07/03/world/asia/securitylawsuggestsabroadeningofchinascore-interests. html, accessed 8/16/2016.

National Interest And Principle In Asian Politics

Every country has a choice to make when its influence grows. When U.S. influence increased following World War II, it chose to combat authoritarian politics including the Soviets, Chinese Communists, Cubans, and tragically, the Vietnamese Communists. The U.S. conflated socialism with authoritarianism, in part because the two most powerful authoritarian governments were also socialist. So the U.S. supported authoritarian governments that were market oriented. This was an ethical shortcoming, perhaps a mistake, and made the U.S. look hypocritical.

I spend a lot of time at the United Nations. Most diplomats I know claim that all politics is based on "national interest." I disagree, and would call such a politics of national interest a base cover for selfishness. The worst of politics is based on national interest. The best of politics the real international statesmen of history are those who transcended national interests on the basis of principal, and succeeded.

I believe there are some enduring principles that underlay the statesmen of history. These principles include self-determination, equality, democracy, human rights, and freedom of speech. I grant that all of these principles must be qualified to some extent. Self-determination by the elite using government power to benefit only themselves is not self-determination for the average citizen. Equality, when overdone, stifles individual incentive. Democracy, when untempered by deliberation and representation, can be demagogic. On human rights, some cultures do not have the government and financial capacity to provide the due process to which I in the U.S. am accustomed. We see in the Philippines and Afghanistan, for example, that many average citizens support summary justice because they believe that otherwise no justice at all will be done. Many of those same citizens suffer from that same summary justice unfairly levied against them.

On the subject of human rights, I am the first to admit that the U.S. has a long way to go. African Americans are discriminated against on every level in the U.S., including in the execution chamber. We elected our first African American president 8 years ago, and again 4 years ago, so I like to think we are making progress. All we should ask of each other, as countries, is that we not trespass on the territories of each other, and that we all gently support improvement in each other's systems. I welcome well meaning international suggestions on how the U.S. might improve its human rights and equality. I hope others welcome U.S. suggestions as well. It is only through dialogue criticism and self-criticism, as Marxists would say that we can as a globe improve.

China, Russia, and even ASEAN speak much about a principle of "noninterference in internal affairs." Once again I must respectfully disagree. All three entities espouse noninterference hypocritically, since their histories are full of interference.[280]

While the U.S. has certainly overdone its interference Vietnam, Afghanistan, Iraq, Syria, and Libya are the tragic examples to which China rightfully points an accusatory finger we have also done much to support the principles above in countries around the world, with gentler nonmilitary means. Here is the key. When supporting change through ideas, not military force, countries can hold the moral high ground. As soon as countries try to force their ideas on unwilling populations, they very quickly run into disaster and moral hypocrisy. The U.S. and other countries, including China and Russia, have wasted economies and hundreds of thousands of lives trying to promote ideas through the use of force. This was counterproductive.

But where force is needed, so is the protection of the territorial status quo. This protection is where the U.S. is currently lagging in pursuit of not only claimant states, but in its own self interest. This is because if claimant states lose territory to China, as mentioned previously, China will strengthen economically and become emboldened militarily.

Chinese Military And Economic Advances Relative To The U.S.

According to RAND Corporation (a U.S. Government think tank), China's military power is growing to the point where a war between the U.S. and China would be prohibitively costly for the U.S. starting in 2025. This is only 9 years away. China's "anti access" and "area denial" (A2AD) capabilities are improving to the point where a limited war in the Pacific would not necessarily go according to the U.S. plan. China would still lose a war in 2025, but a war at that point could disable the U.S. fleet in Asia for years to come. Such a war would also likely bring China's strongest allies Russia in particular to take concurrent military operations, perhaps in Ukraine and Georgia.

---

[280] Ramcharan, Robin. "ASEAN and Noninterference: A Principle Maintained." Contemporary Southeast Asia, Vol. 22, No. 1, April 2000, pp. 6088.

So the next 9 years are critical for the U.S. and the world. Will the U.S. fight a preemptive war against China? This seems unlikely, but it could happen if China makes a mistake and allows a small military incident to spark a larger war. Will China democratize? This also seems unlikely, but appears to be the best strategy for both avoiding war, and creating a status quo power out of China.

If neither of the above happens, we can expect China to assert much greater dominance in Asia than it already has. This has huge implications for Vietnam. First would be a greater likelihood of Chinese oil exploration and development in Vietnam's EEZ. Second would be greater Chinese influence on Vietnam's foreign policy. Third would be a greater likelihood of a Chinese attempt to subjugate Vietnam's economy to a subordinate position through bilateral trade and investment treaties. This could look like a new form of Chinese mercantilism.[281]

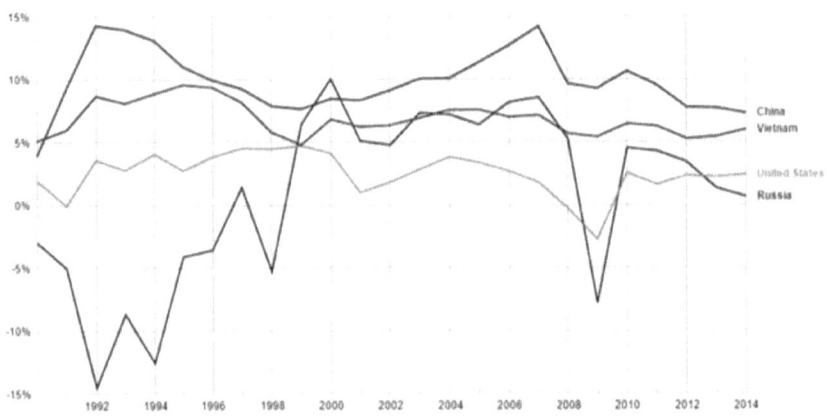

Figure 1: Comparison of GDP growth rates in China, Vietnam, the U.S., and Russia. Source: World Bank.[282]

[281] Mearsheimer, John J. "China's Unpeaceful Rise," Current History, April 2006, pp. 160162.

[282] World Bank. Google Public Information. https://www.google.com.vn/ publicdata/explore?ds=d5bncppjof8f9_&ctype=l&strail=false&bcs=d& nselm=h& met_y=ny_gdp_mktp_kd_zg&scale_y=lin&ind_y=false& rdim=region&idim=country:USA:RUS:CHN:VNM&ifdi m=region &tstart= 650739600000&tend=1408122000000&hl=en&dl=en&ind= false, accessed 8/16/2016.

As mentioned earlier, Vietnam's strongest traditional ally has been Russia. But Vietnam cannot expect Russia to support it against China over the next decade. Russia's economy imploded during privatization in the 1990s, and suffered reversals after the oil price was halved and sanctions related to Ukraine contracted Russia's stocks, currency and economy.

Russia's military spending suffered, and its military degraded. Its failure to show real progress in Syria, a former stronghold and ally, is telling. What military power and assets remaining with Russia has been concentrated on nuclear sabre rattling, plus the Ukraine and Georgia struggles, where it hopes to expand territorially in the future. But these strategies are self defeating, like those pursued by China, as they involve the destruction of goodwill towards Russia, and of its soft power.

Russia is already subordinate to China as a lesser partner in defense and economic relations. China's GDP of 10.9 trillion[283] is multiples of Russia's GDP of 1.3 trillion.[284] As shown in Figure 1, Russia's growth rate has been on a lengthy downward trend since 2000, when Putin won his first national election. Compare this to China's consistently higher growth rates since that period.

Russia is currently seeking China as a primary export market, including for oil and defense related technology. There is no chance that Russia would risk its relationship with China to help Vietnam in any manner other than to sell weapons, such as the kilo class submarines that Vietnam purchased in 2009. Purchasing high technology weapons from Russia is a strategy fraught with risk. Had China seen these submarines as a real threat to its aspirations in the South China Sea, China would have been able to convince Russia not to make the sale. China likely prefers a compliant Russia as the seller of the submarines, compared to Japanese, French, or U.S. submarines. Russia is more likely to put pressure on Vietnam through withholding spare parts or expertise, than Western manufacturers would.

Also, unless Vietnam can substantially improve its relationship with the U.S., it cannot hope to gain U.S. protection in case of war with China. Vietnam, in that case, might be the perfect target for a China itching for a war, but unable to attack U.S. allies such as the Philippines or Japan. Vietnam's purchases of a few weapons on a small defense budget could

---

[283] World Bank. http://www.tradingeconomics.com/china/gdp, accessed 8/16/2016.

[284] World Bank. http://www.tradingeconomics.com/russia/gdp, accessed 8/16/2016

simply make it a target for China. Bringing a knife to a gunfight, as the saying goes, is a risky strategy.

Conclusion

Over the next decade, China's military growth, if left unchecked by military action or internal democratization, will be increasingly felt as a coercive force by its neighbors, including Vietnam. This has strategic considerations not only for Vietnam, but also for the rest of the world. We are at a tipping point in world history, and Vietnam has a front row seat.

Vietnam has a sophisticated knowledge of Chinese intentions and the U.S.China conflict, that is borne out of necessity, and which most other countries lack. Vietnam's diplomacy with the U.S., China, and in ASEAN, is subtly in support of the U.S. and maintenance of the territorial status quo. But it is hedging this bet by remaining officially neutral.

In U.S. politics we say, where goes Iowa, goes the nation. This is because Iowa is a centrist state and has historically almost always voted for the winner in a presidential election. Vietnam is in the same position internationally. Its leaders are watching international developments closely. Given China's proximity and aggressiveness, Vietnam has every reason to side with the U.S., international law, and a balancing alliance of countries against China.[285] However, if Vietnam perceives a lack of will on the part of the U.S. to resist China's expansion of territory and influence, Vietnam will side with China against the U.S.

At this historical juncture, the U.S. must make another ethical decision with respect to Vietnam. It will either support Vietnam and its valid claims to its EEZ in the South China Sea, or it will give China its tacit approval by doing nothing substantive to defend the EEZs of not only Vietnam, but of the Philippines, Indonesia, Malaysia, and Brunei. As with the U.S. decision to support the French in the First Indochina War, the decision that the U.S. makes on this issue will have global historical repercussions.

If the U.S. decides to let China to gradually increase its territory at the expense of Vietnam and other claimants, China will become both economically stronger and militarily more confident. This will likely lead

---

[285] Scott, David. "Conflict Irresolution In The South China Sea." Asian Survey, Vol. 52, No. 6 November/December 2012, pp. 10191042.

to small wars led by China throughout Asia as it attempts to suppress any resistance to expansionist policies.

If, instead, the U.S. decides to draw the line today in support of international law, especially the EEZs of claimant countries, China is too militarily weak to enforce its 9dash line. By holding fast to this principled position even after China improves its military, the costs of military action on the part of China will be too great and China will more likely divert its attentions to internal economic development and positive international trade.

Now is the time for the U.S. to draw a line against China's territorial expansion. The whole world is watching, and in 10 years, it could be too late.

Vietnam's Possible Action Plan on the Land Features in South China Sea (Biên Đông Sea) After the Arbitral Award in the Philippines v. China Case

Ta Van Tai

The unanimous Arbitral Award of the Permanent Court of Arbitration on July 12, 2016, being declaratory and unenforceable but not appealable and binding on the parties with its compulsory jurisdiction, is a resounding victory for the Philippines and a humiliating legal defeat for China in its overambitious assertion of power and authority over vast expanses of the maritime area of the South China Sea. In discussing issues under the light of the UN Convention on the Law of the Sea (UNCLOS), this landmark decision does not deal with claims of territorial sovereignty over land features, i.e. rocks and islands, of Paracels and Spratleys, which are the purview of Traditional or Customary International Law, but it does have indirect effects on the characterization of the land features.

In this short paper, we will point out the implications of this Award for Vietnam's interests in the South China Sea, especially in the land features of Paracels (Hoang Sa) and Spratleys (Truong Sa).

I. SUMMARY OF THE CONTENTS OF THE AWARD OF THE PERMANENT COURT OF ARBITRATION

The July 12, 2016 Award was an overwhelming legal victory for the Philippines on the basis of the law on maritime zones in UNCLOS: China cannot legally use the U-shaped line to claim historical rights on almost 80% of the South China Sea, and must respect and not interfere with, as it did, the sovereign rights on fishery and oil, mineral resources of the Philippines in its EEZ and continental shelf, and cannot do 'irreparable harm", as it did, to the integrity of the marine environment. These legal victory scores of the Philippines also benefit other coastal states, such as Vietnam, without their having to file a courageous lawsuit.

The August 17, 2016 workshop in Nha Trang City was the continuance of two previous 2013 and 2014 workshops in Quang Ngai City and Da Nang, we would like to reproduce some paragraphs of our previous papers to say that we are happy that the Court, with the holdings in the Philippine case of 2016, indicates our Vietnam's position we presented some years ago in Quang Ngai and Da Nang:

> *"China cannot show any international law basis for this ridiculous claim [U-Line] and has been self-contradictory at international conferences when providing various vague rationales for this claim: "historical circumference" or "adjacent waters". But such sweeping and unfounded claims are clearly in violation of the other Southeast Asian coastal states' claims on their own territorial seas of 12 miles, their exclusive economic zones and their continental shelves of 200 miles width measuring from the base line. In these maritime zones, the coastal states are protected in the exercise of their exclusive sovereign rights under the 1982 UN Convention on the Law of the Sea (UNCLOS), articles 56, 57, 76, and 77. These sovereign rights over natural resources are exclusive to the coastal states, which they can enjoy without being required to proclaim a claim to them, and they may construct artificial*

structures on rocks, whether submerged or not, into artificial islands, and carry out sea research, regulate protection of environment, provided that they respect the rights of other states to freedom of navigation or to laying of oil pipelines or cables. Other states than the coastal states cannot exploit natural resources in the EEZ and Continental Shelf of the coastal states without their explicit consent. UNCLOS has reserved these exclusive rights to coastal states as firmly as 'nail hit into a wooden pole' (as we say in the Vietnamese proverb: "chắc như đinh đóng cột"). The U-shaped line, which claims vast ocean areas for China, is unsupported by UNCLOS (article 89 says "No State may validly purport to subject any part of the high sea to its sovereignty")".

After the protests against the compulsory jurisdiction of the Court since the filing of the case in 2013 and then, after the early belligerent words, in July-August 2016, of not recognizing the final award on substantive issues, issued at various levels of the Chinese government, from President Xi to Foreign Minister and spokesman, China has been actually low key and calm in its reaction against the award (some scholars even suggested it is time for some recognition of some aspects of the award), and seems not to be ready to carry out implied threats of actions such as building more on Scarborough shoal or on submerged reefs, and establishing Air Defense Identification Zone (ADIZ) in South China Sea. China even seems to veer toward negotiation, as Chinese ambassador to the US said, and toward also the legal struggle: with China no longer hinting at withdrawing from UNCLOS, China's Supreme Court issued its own anti-Hague ruling, i.e. China is thinking that the better warfare is "law fare".

That is why we should also concentrate on legal arguments in the following program of action for Vietnam, although we know that big powers with strong navy, like the United States, can reinforce the legal warfare with some credible threat of some coercive force, by steaming aircraft carrier through the South China Sea and near the disputed land features.

II. IMPACT ON THE LEGAL STATUS OF LAND FEATURES IN SPRATLEYS AND POSSIBLY IN PARACELS TOO

Holding of the July 12 2016 Award on the characteristics of the land features in Spratleys: all land features are either rocks (above water at high tide but not an island as defined by UNCLOS) or submerged or low tide features. Only 12-mile territorial sea for rocks but no such territorial sea for submerged features or low-tide elevations (The principle of land dominates the sea). We think that these conclusions of law of the Arbitration Court on Spratleys land features also can be applied to defining the characteristics and legal status of Paracels land features. We wonder about the advisability of a lawsuit at the Arbitral Tribunal, similar to the Philippines case for Spratleys, to confirm this legal status of land features in Paracels.

The Court ruled that no feature in the Spratly Island is a habitable feature in its natural state, and therefore, no feature is an island as defined in UNCLOS, that would be entitled to a 200- nautical-mile exclusive economic zone (EEZ).

This greatly reduces the allegedly legal ground China has been using for fomenting conflict: the unfounded claim of 200-mile Continental Shelf or EEZ emanating from the baseline of some small rocks, which are interpreted by China as islands.

During the two previous workshops in Quang Ngai and Da Nang we have made suggestions similar to the holdings of the PCA's 2016 Award, to move in the direction of a solution based on limiting controversy growing out of excessive claim beyond territorial sea around land features:

> *"[For Paracels] We can ask the Arbitral Tribunal of the Law of the Sea to use the compulsory procedure to interpret and apply UNCLOS (articles 186, 288) and to issue a declaratory judgment to the effect that all land features in Paracels, such as Tri Ton, or even Woody, do not satisfy the conditions for qualification as islands in accordance with article 121 of UNCLOS. Islands must, in their original state of nature, have adequate conditions for human habitation and self-sustaining economy (such as soft water, food raised or planted locally—if only coca-cola is available for drinking, as a Malaysian scholar joked, then it is not island). If not island, then a land feature can only be a reef or rock (article 121, section 3). If only a rock,*

it has no exclusive economic zone or continental shelf, but only the 12-mile territorial sea (article 121, section 3). If island, the land feature would then have territorial sea, contiguous zone, exclusive economic zone, and continental shelf. In front of the Arbitral Tribunal of the Law of the Sea, Vietnam can sue under the compulsory procedure to drag China into the tribunal which would interpret and apply UNCLOS (articles 286, 288) and hear Vietnam's presentation of historical evidence of many centuries on the necessity of Hoang Sa flotilla to bring soft water and food on its expeditions to Hoang Sa, and then to withdraw back to the mainland for not being able to live there all year round, in a self-sustaining economy. Therefor, at the present moment, China cannot ask for the status of island for any land feature in Paracels, despite its construction of artificial structures thereon, or for any recognition of exclusive economic zone and continental shelf emanating from any land feature in Paracels. Even The Chinese who worked in recent years in Paracels have admitted that Paracels do not have enough soft water from rain to live by (well water is polluted by bird excrement and is not potable) and do not have enough vegetables to eat and must rely on canned food, and finally there is no arable land. Supplies of foodstuffs and water must come every month.
(http://www.shtong.gov.cn/.../node839.../ userobject1ai121797.html. (http://baike.baidu.com/view/28617.htm),

Applying this line of argument to the rocks in Spratleys, we can prove that all land features there have been only rocks/ reefs in the original state of nature before artificial construction thereon [The PCA, for its 2016 Award, has hired experts to ascertain this reality]. And therefore, there would be a great reduction of conflict potentiality arising out of the competition of land feature grab (which would not create anything more than 12-mile territorial sea) or out of occupation of submerged rocks and artificial construction thereon (which would not create an island and in any case, only coastal states can build on submerged rocks, article 60 UNCLOS). States would feel less the need to grab a land feature to create exclusive economic zone or continental shelf. Also the nine-dashed line will not be able to rely on any large island in the sea that has only rocks."

III. IMPACT ON VIETNAM'S TERRITORIAL SOVEREIGNTY OVER THE LAND FEATURES IN BOTH ARCHIPELAGOS

Once the physical characteristics of rocks, submerged rocks or reefs and low-tide elevations are clarified and define the legal status of the land features in Spratleys and Paracels, we still have to resolve the issue of which country has territorial sovereignty over them. Vietnam's territorial sovereignty over land in the two archipelagoes is regulated by Traditional Customary International Law.

We have discussed this issue of territorial sovereignty over Paracels and Spratleys as follows in the two previous workshops in 2013 and 2014:

"Claims of sovereignty over each land feature in the Paracels and Spratleys must be based on the customary/traditional/ classical rule of international law of the last 4 centuries on acquisition of territorial sovereignty over land: a government wishing to establish a sovereignty claim over a land area has to assert, after discovery or occupation, its intention to make such claim, and to continue administering such area in peace, and if such land area is taken over by another government through the use of force, it has to protest in order to prevent the new authority to acquire sovereignty by prescription, i.e. continuous and undisputed exercise of sovereignty.

The historical facts about Vietnam's discovery and occupation of Paracels, and also an unspecified number of land features in Spratleys, dated back to centuries-old Vietnamese historical records, such as Phu Bien Tap Luc (Fronties Chronicles), while Chinese historical records did not mention Paracels or Spratleys but stopped at Hainan as the southernmost boundary of China; among these Chinese records is the detailed Kiangsi emperor map of 1717 compiled by the French Jesuits, a copy of which, drawn by J.B. Bourguignon, was recently donated by German Chancellor Merkel to Chinese President Xi Jin-ping. The

Vietnamese historical records under the emperors and under the French colonial rule show Vietnam's repeated assertions of sovereignty over and administration of both Paracels and Spratleys (which were named Hoang Sa and Truong Sa). Western travelers' and Christian missionaries' writings also confirmed them.

During the existence of the two Vietnams from 1954 to 1975, the role of asserting sovereignty over Paracels and Spratleys fell on the Republic of Vietnam --RVN-- which was entrusted with the administration of Paracels and Spratleys, situated south of the partition line of 17th parallel, by the 1954 Geneva Accords, which was signed by a number of big powers, including by China, and by the Democratic Republic of Vietnam represented by Prime Minister Pham Van Dong himself.

But the most resounding assertion of Vietnam's sovereignty over the Paracels was the valiant sea battle the RVN navy fought on January 19, 1974 with China's navy which was sent to occupy Hoang Sa—for a long time occupied and administered by Vietnam-- after China's announcing sovereignty over Hoang Sa and Truong Sa on January 12 and the RVN protested on January 16 with a request for the United Nations Security Council to take action, which request was repeated on January 20, for UN Security Council to hold an emergency meeting. At the June 28, 1974 UN Conference on the Law of the Sea in Caracas, the RVN repeated its claim of sovereignty over the archipelagos and its protest against illegal occupation by China. On September 24, 1975, at talks with a Vietnamese delegation on visit to China, Vice-Premier Deng Xiao-ping admitted there was dispute between China and Vietnam on the archipelagos and suggested discussion to settle the problem.

Ever since the unification of the two Vietnams into one, many times the successor state of Socialist Republic of Vietnam has protested whenever there was an encroachment by China, by presenting historical evidence on the sovereignty of Vietnam over Paracels and many territories in Spratleys, in declarations or white papers, in the years of 1978, 1979, 1980, 1981, 1982, 1984, 1988 (protesting China's declared incorporation of the archipelagos into Hainan), 1990, 1991, 1994 (protesting--- not China's territorial claim-- rather China's signing agreement with Crestone permitting the latter to survey in Vietnam's continental shelf and exclusive economic zone), 2012 (protesting China's overall plan for management of islands). There was also action in defense of Vietnam's sovereignty in 1988 when, in supplying the Vietnamese navy men standing in defense of Vietnam-occupied Gac Ma in the Spratleys, Vietnam suffered 64 casualties. All these words and acts claiming and defending sovereignty make it impossible for China to erode Vietnam's sovereignty by prescription.

During the crisis of the oil rig HYSY-981, from May to July 2014, Vietnam brought to the area surrounding the rig many fishery inspection vessels, the maritime police or coast guard, to demand withdrawal of the oil rig, so as to preserve sovereignty and sovereign rights. Vietnamese fishermen continued to fish in the proximity, despite the harassment of the Chinese vessels, keeping a safe distance to avoid armed clash, with the purposes of earning their livelihood and asserting national sovereignty in a self-controlled manner.

This maneuver to preserve Vietnamese sovereignty by words and deeds has kept intact the claim of Vietnam over Paracels and Spratleys and avoided its erosion."

On the high-tide rocks in Spratleys that Vietnam has occupied and administered for a long time since 1975-76, before the 1982 UNCLOS and under Traditional International Law, even if some rocks are within the continental shelf or EEZ of the Philippines, Vietnam can build and expand on those rocks which are naturally formed area of land (and not submerged elevation or reef) and the legal status of such land or rock remain the same, and therefore, Vietnam would have territorial sovereignty over those rocks, under Traditional/Customary International Law - as the Philippines only has, under UNCLOS, sovereign rights, and not sovereignty, in its continental shelf and EEZ.

But the legal situation is different for submerged features or low tide elevations: Vietnam, or China, could not build installations and structures on submerged features or low tide elevation in the Philippines' 200-mile Continental shelf and hope to create territorial sovereignty, because submerged features or low-tide elevations are part of the seabed in the continental shelf on which the Philippines has sovereign rights as to resources (but no territorial sovereignty either). But could there be an exception of acquired rights to this conclusion on submerged features or low-tide elevations not giving rise to territorial sovereignty? Those submerged features or low-tide elevations in Spratleys that Vietnam occupied before the year of UNCLOS, 1982, and then, up until the effective date of UNCLOS in 1982, continued administering them, building artificial structures on them to make them always above high tide, i.e. no longer submerged, should they be considered territory belonging to the jurisdiction of Vietnam, under Traditional/Customary International Law, with no retroactive application of UNCLOS provisions to Vietnam's acquired rights? And would these land features be also entitled to 12-mile territorial sea?

And the last issue has to do with Air Defense Identification Zones. Whoever does not have territorial sovereignty in an area of land, whether rocks or submerged features/low-tide elevations, would not have the legal right to establish an ADIZ, under UN law. That should be the main argument of other nations against China's claiming to have the right to set up ADIZ in the Spratleys area.

CONCLUSION

As a practical consequence of the Arbitral Award, probably China and other countries would not make any move, especially withdrawing from what they have already occupied, to change the status quo in South China Sea. China needs time to absorb the loss of face, which is real, and figure out what to do next to recover its prestige; and consequently, other countries should not act too aggressively at this time, to avoid the ultra nationalist overreaction among the belligerent people in China; probably for this reasons, the US had advised the Philippines and other countries in South East Asia to stay calm and not sound confrontational, so that China can sit down to conduct negotiation under the guiding light of the award, for such collaborative measures as joint development of resources at sea, respect of all countries' fishermen, stopping environment-destroying excavation to freeze the status quo, thereby saving China's waning prestige and its prosperity in an international rule of law. Therefore, the above suggestions for lawsuits are only advanced preparation of litigation documents for actual launching in another day, and not right now. Of course, even we advocate restraint at the present time about lawsuits, Vietnam should promptly protest any encroachments and adopt countermeasures, and launch timely lawsuits, if China again blatantly violates Vietnam sovereign's rights in the EEZ (fishery) or continental shelf (oil and mineral in the seabed), or builds on submerged rocks or low-tide elevations in the EEZ and Continental shelf of Vietnam.

List of Contributors

Erik Franckx is President of the Dept. of International and European Law, Faculty of Law and Criminology at Vrije Universiteit Brussel (VUB). He also teaches at Vesalius College (VUB), Université Libre de Bruxelles, the Brussels School of International Studies (University of Kent), the Institute of European Studies (VUB), Université Paris-Sorbonne Abu Dhabi, (U.A.E.), and the University of Akureyri, Iceland. He has been appointed by Belgium as: an expert in maritime boundary delimitation to the IHO (2005 -); a member of the Permanent Court of Arbitration (2006 -); an arbitrator under the UNCLOS (2014 -); an expert on marine scientific research for use in special arbitration under Annex VIII of the UNCLOS (2015 -); and a member of the national Commission for the Reform of Private and Public Maritime Law (2012 -).

Aloysius Llamzon received his A.B., J.D., at the Ateneo de Manila University, his LL.M., J.S.D. at Yale Law School, and is a Senior Associate at King & Spalding LLP, New York City. He is former Senior Legal Counsel at the Permanent Court of Arbitration in The Hague.

Jay L. Batongbacal is an associate professor at the University of the Philippines College of Law and Director of the University's Institute for Maritime Affairs and Law of the Sea. He was a US-ASEAN Fulbright Initiative Visiting Scholar in Washington, DC (2014-2015), assisted the Philippines in pursuing its claim to a continental shelf beyond 200 nautical miles in the Benham Rise Region, and is listed as one of the UNESCO/IOC experts for special arbitration under UNCLOS Annex VIII.

Bertrand Theodor L. Santos is a senior researcher with the designation Law Reform Specialist at the University of the Philippines - Institute of Maritime Affairs and Law of the Sea (IMLOS). He also acts as the Deputy to Director Jay L. Batongbacal. Prior to IMLOS, Mr. Santos spent 10 years in the Department of Foreign Affairs as a Foreign Service Officer where he served in various capacities in the Home and Foreign Office.

Nguyen Quy Binh graduated from Diplomatic Academy of Vietnam in 1970, and did post-graduate work at Budapest University of Technology and Economics in Hungary (1973). He also received an LLB at the International Institute of Social Studies in The Hague, the Netherlands (1981) and an LLM from the School of Law of Harvard University, the US (1991). He has previously served as Director General of the Department of Law and International Treaties, Vice Chairman of the National Boundary Commission under the Ministry of Foreign Affairs of Vietnam, Ambassador and Representative of Vietnam to the UN and other international organizations. He is currently Associate Dean of the Faculty for International Studies of Hanoi University and Arbitrator of the Permanent Court of Arbitration (PCA) in The Hague.

Carlyle A. Thayer is Professor Emeritus at The University of New South Wales at the Australian Defence Force Academy in Canberra. Thayer is a Southeast Asia regional specialist with special expertise on Vietnam. Thayer was educated at Brown University, holds an M.A. in Southeast Asian Studies from Yale and a PhD in International Relations from The Australian National University. Dr Carlyle Thayer is internationally acknowledged for his expertise in Vietnam studies and Southeast Asian politics and regional security.

Shekhar Dutt was appointed Deputy National Security Advisor for a two-year term and governor of the Indian state of Chhattisgarh. He previously served as an IAS officer, Secretary in the Ministry of Defence of the Government of India and later as the Defence Secretary of India in 2005.

Nguyen Dai Trang holds a Bachelor of Commerce, Honours Economics from Concordia University (Montreal), a Masters in Economics, and a PhD (2004) in Interdisciplinary Studies and Asian Research, both from the University of British Columbia (Vancouver). She is the author of two books on Ho Chi Minh, both written in English and Vietnamese (2010 and 2013). She is currently a Professor and Program Coordinator in International Development and International Business at Centennial College in Toronto, Ontario, Canada. She is also the Founder and Director of the Canada - Vietnam Trade Council, a non-profit organization that promotes trade and investment between the two countries.

Dmitry Mosyakov is the Director of the Center for Southeast Asia, Australia, and Oceania and the Institute of Oriental Studies of the Russian Academy of Sciences. He graduated from IAAS MSU, majoring in history, and understands the Khmer language. He is a recognized lead researcher at the Institute of Oriental studies of the Russian Academy of Sciences. In June-July 2015 he served as interim Director of the Institute of Oriental Studies. A specialist in modern problems of Eastern countries, especially in Southeast and East Asia, and the history of Cambodia, he has written almost 200 scientific works, including 10 monographs.

Gerhard Manfred Fasel Johannes Will is a former senior expert at the German Institute for International Politics and Science. He was born in 1948 in Donauworth, Bavaria, and studied political science and modern Chinese and Southeast Asian studies. He has worked at the Institute of Asian Affairs in Hamburg; the Federal Institute of Eastern European and International Studies in Cologne; and from 2001 to 2013 he was a senior research associate at the German Institute for International and Security Affairs.

Kavi Chongkittavorn is a Senior Fellow at the Institute of Strategic and International Studies, Chulalongkorn University in Thailand. He is also assistant group editor of Nation Media Group, publisher of the English-language daily, *The Nation*, and local Thai newspapers, Krungthep Turakij and Kom Chat Luek. He has been a journalist for more than two decades reporting on issues related to human rights, democracy and regionalism. He was named Human Rights Journalist of 1998 to commemorate the 50th Anniversary of The Universal Declaration of Human Rights by Amnesty International, Thailand. From 1999-2003, he served as the president of the Thai Journalists Association. He also serves as jury president of the UNESCO/Guillermo Cano World Press Freedom Prize.

Ngo Vinh Long is a professor of history at the University of Maine, where he has taught for more than twenty-five years. He is also a research associate at Duy Tan University, Da Nang City, Vietnam. He has contributed to the Journal of Contemporary Asia, The American Historical Review, and other publications. He is a frequent commentator on Asian affairs on the Vietnamese-language broadcasts of the BBC, and Radio Free Asia.

Jeong Gab Yong is Director of the Sea Law Research Center of Youngsan University and Vice President of the Korea International Maritime Law Association.

Koichi Sato is a recognized scholar on China at J.F Oberlin University. He graduated from Tokyo Metropolitan University and received his Ph.D. in International Studies from Waseda University. He has served as a Research Fellow at the Japan Institute of International Affairs (JIIA), and a lecturer at the Tokyo University of Foreign Studies. He concurrently served as a lecturer at the Japan Maritime Self-Defense Force (JMSDF) Staff College, as lecturer at the National Institute for Defense Studies (NIDS), and as Policy Adviser to the Japan Coast Guard.

Go Ito from Meiji University is an expert on the Asia Pacific region and China-U.S.-Japan triangular relations; U.S. strategy towards East Asia; China-Chinese Taipei cross-strait relations; Japanese security policy; and theories of international relations. In his dual roles as an Associate Professor of International Relations at Meiji University and a Research Fellow at the Japan Forum on International Relations, he has significantly impacted both research and policy-making in these areas, and he has received numerous domestic and international honors for his work.

Anders Corr is the Principal of Corr Analytics Inc, providing international political risk analysis to governmental and commercial clients. He has been a member of the American Political Science Association (APSA) since 2004, and the Society of Professional Journalists since 2013. He is also a team leader at the Department of the Army, Human Terrain System, ISAF JC Headquarters (Afghanistan), and statistical analyst at State of Hawaii Department of Labour and Industrial Relations (Honolulu). He studied political science at Yale University and received a PhD at Harvard University in 2008.

Dr. Ta Van Tai, Ph.D. (University of Virginia), LL.M. (Harvard Law School), was former professor of law and lawyer in South Vietnam prior to 1975. He is a former research associate and lecturer at Harvard Law School, and is a practicing attorney in Massachusetts, USA.

Nguyen Manh Hung is Professor Emeritus of Government and International Relations at George Mason University and non-resident Senior Associate in the Southeast Asia Program at the Center for Strategic and International Studies. Dr Hung has participated in major policy working groups on Vietnam and Indochina, including the Indochina Policy Forum of the Aspen Institute, the Indochina Study Group of the Council on Foreign Relations, and the Southeast Asia Working Group of the Center for Strategic and International Studies. He is author of several books, and articles in journals such as World Affairs, Asian Survey, Pacific Affairs, Global Asia, Amerasia Journal, Asia Pacific Bulletin and Journal of Asian Thought and Society.

Brig. Vinod Anand (Retd.) Vinod Anand is a Senior Fellow at the Vivekananda International Foundation (VIF), New Delhi, India. He holds a post-graduate degree in Defence and Strategic Studies and is an alumnus of Defence Services and Staff College and College of Defence Management. He was a Senior Fellow at the Institute for Defence Studies and Analyses, New Delhi. Brig. Anand has also been a Senior Fellow at the United Service Institution, New Delhi. His recent publications include monographs on *Pak-Af Equation and Future of Afghanistan*, *MultiVector Politics of Central Asian Republics and India*, and *Strategic Environment in Central Asia and India*. He previously wrote a monograph on *Joint Vision for Indian Armed Forces* and a book titled *Defence Planning in India: Problems and Prospects*. He writes on military and strategic issues, including regional and international security. At the VIF, he coordinates research activity focusing on China and ballistic missile defence.

Nguyen Chu Hoi is Associate Professor, Faculty of Environment, VNU University of Science, Vietnam National University and is a former Deputy Director of the Vietnam Administration of Sea and Islands, Vietnam.

Harry Krejsa is a Research Associate at the Center for a New American Security (CNAS), working in the Asia-Pacific Security Program. Prior to joining CNAS, Mr. Krejsa worked as a policy analyst for the Congressional Joint Economic Committee. He also served as a Researcher with the Center for the Study of Chinese Military Affairs at National Defense University, where he published a report on Chinese investment in the United States and its security implications. He was a Fulbright Fellow in Taiwan. His policy writings have appeared in *War on the Rocks*, *The National Interest*, *The Diplomat*, and *PacNet*, his analysis has been featured in *Politico*, *Bloomberg Radio*, and *Japan Times*, and he has given televised Chinese-language commentary on Voice of America.

Siswo Pramono is the Head of Central Development and Policy Planning in the Indonesian Foreign Ministry. He obtained a post-graduate Diploma at Australia National University (ANU), a Masters Degree from Monash University and a Ph.D. in Political Science from ANU. He also obtained High Commendation - Dialogica Award while pursuing his PhD at ANU. Mr Pramono has served his country as a diplomat for almost 27 years and has become the "researcher diplomat" for his dedicated work in the Research and Development Division.

SOUTH CHINA SEA REFERENCES

Territorial Disputes in the South China Sea: Selective Bibliography
*Compiled by the Peace Palace Library in The
Netherlands and by James Borton

- Almond, R., Clearing the Air above the East China Sea: The Primary Elements of Aircraft Defense Identification Zones, *Harvard National Security Journal*, 7 (2015), No. 1, pp. 126-198.
- Amer, R. and Nguyen Hong Thao, "Conflict Resolution in the South China Sea: an Overview of Progress Made and Remaining Challenges", in Tran Truong Thuy and Le Thuy Trang (eds.), *Power, Law, and Maritime Order in the South China Sea*, Lanham, Lexington Books, 2015, pp. 267-292.
- Anderson, D. and Logchem, Y. van, "Rights and Obligations in Areas of Overlapping Maritime Claims", in Jayakumar, S., T. Koh and R. Beckman (eds.), *The South China Sea Disputes and Law of the Sea*, 2014, pp. 192-228.
- Andreeff, D., "Legal Implications of China's Land Reclamation Projects in the Spratly Islands", *New York University Journal of International Law and Politics*, 47 (2015), No. 4, pp. 855-910.
- Bateman, S., "Maritime Boundary Delimitation, Excessive Claims and Effective Regime Building in the South China", in Yann-huei Song and Keyuan Zou (eds.), *Major Law and Policy Issues in the South China Sea: European and American Perspectives*, 2014, pp. 119-136.

○ Batongbacal, J.L., "Extended Continental Shelves in the South China Sea: Delimitation Prospects and Challenges", in Tran Truong Thuy and Le Thuy Trang (eds.), *Power, Law, and Maritime Order in the South China Sea*, Lanham, Lexington Books, 2015, pp. 167-195.

○ Beckman, R., Townsend-Gault, I., Schofield, C., Davenport, T. and Bernard L. (eds.), *Beyond Territorial Disputes in the South China Sea: Legal Frameworks for the Joint Development of Hydrocarbon Resources*, Cheltenham, Edward Elgar, 2013.

○ Beckman, R., "International Law, UNCLOS and the South China Sea", in Beckman, R., Townsend-Gault, I., Schofield, C., Davenport, T. and Bernard L. (eds.), *Beyond Territorial Disputes in the South China Sea : Legal Frameworks for the Joint Development of Hydrocarbon Resources*, 2013, pp. 47-90.

○ Beckman, R., Townsend-Gault, I., Schofield, C., Davenport, T. and Bernard L., "Factors Conducive to Joint Development in Asia - Lessons Learned for the South China Sea", in Beckman, R., Townsend-Gault, I., Schofield, C., Davenport, T. and Bernard L. (eds.), *Beyond Territorial Disputes in the South China Sea : Legal Frameworks for the Joint Development of Hydrocarbon Resources*, 2013, pp. 291-311.

○ Beckman, R., Townsend-Gault, I., Schofield, C., Davenport, T. and Bernard L.,, "Moving forward on Joint Development in the South China Sea", in Beckman, R., Townsend-Gault, I., Schofield, C., Davenport, T. and Bernard L. (eds.), *Beyond Territorial Disputes in the South China Sea : Legal Frameworks for the Joint Development of Hydrocarbon Resources*, 2013, pp. 312-331.

○ Beckman, R., "UNCLOS Part XV and the South China Sea", in Jayakumar, S., T. Koh and R. Beckman (eds.), *The South China Sea Disputes and Law of the Sea*, 2014, pp. 229-264.

○ Beckman, R., "The 'Philippines v. China' Case and the South China Sea Disputes", in Jing Huang and Andrew Billo (eds.), *Territorial Disputes in the South China Sea: Navigating Rough Waters*, 2015, pp. 54-65.

○ Beckman, R., "Legal Framework for Joint Development in the South China Sea", in Wu, S., Valencia, M. and Hong, N. (eds.), *UN Convention on the Law of the Sea and the South China Sea*, Farnham, Ashgate, 2015, pp. 251-266.

o Beckman, R., "Disputed Areas in the South China Sea", in Tran Truong Thuy and Le Thuy Trang (eds.), *Power, Law, and Maritime Order in the South China Sea*, Lanham, Lexington Books, 2015, pp. 103-117.

o Boon, K.E., StartFragment International Arbitration in Highly Political Situations: The South China Sea Dispute and International Law, StartFragment *Washington University Global Studies Law Review*, 13 (2014), No. 3, pp. 487-514.

o StartFragment Bouchat, C.J., *The Paracel Islands and U.S. interests and approaches in the South China Sea*, StartFragment Carlisle Barracks, PA, Strategic Studies Institute and U.S. Army War College Pres, 2014.

o Burgos Cáceres, S. (ed.), *China's strategic interests in the South China Sea: power and resources*, London : New York, Routledge, Taylor & Francis Group, 2014.

o Buszynski, L. and C.B. Roberts, (eds.), *The South China Sea Maritime Dispute: Political, Legal and Regional Perspectives*, London, New York, Routledge, Taylor & Francis Group, 2015.

o Charlermpalanupap, T., "Review of the ASEAN-China Declaration of the Conduct of Parties in the South China Sea and Prospects of a Code of Conduct in the South China Sea: an ASEAN Perspective", in Tran Truong Thuy and Le Thuy Trang (eds.), *Power, Law, and Maritime Order in the South China Sea*, Lanham, Lexington Books, 2015, pp. 37-48.

o Charney, J.I., "Rocks That Cannot Sustain Human Habitation", *American journal of international law*, 93 (1999), No. 4, pp. 863-878.

o Coito, J.C., "Boundary Conflict: the China-Philippines Confrontation over the Scarborough Reef, and the Viability of UNCLOS Dispute Resolution Procedures", in H.N. Scheiber, J. Kraska and M.-S. Kwon (eds.), *Science, Technology, and New Challenges to Ocean Law*, 2015, pp. 395-431.

o Cronin, P.M., "The United States, China, and Cooperation in the South China Sea", in Jing Huang and Andrew Billo (eds.), *Territorial Disputes in the South China Sea: Navigating Rough Waters*, 2015, pp. 149-163.

o Cruz De Castro, R., "The 2012 Scarborough Shoal Stand-Off: From Stalemate to Escalation of the South China Sea Dispute?" in L. Buszynski and C.B. Roberts (eds.), *The South China Sea*

Maritime Dispute: Political, Legal and Regional Perspectives, 2015, pp. 111-129.

o Do Thanh Hai, "Vietnam's Evolving Claims", in L. Buszynski and C.B. Roberts (eds.), *The South China Sea Maritime Dispute: Political, Legal and Regional Perspectives*, 2015, pp. 83-100.

o Dua, Andre, Esty, Daniel C., 1997. Sustaining the Asia Pacific Miracle: Environmental Protections and Economic Integration. Institute for International Economics, Washington, DC.

o Dutton, P.A., "An Analysis of China's Claim to Historic Rights in the South China Sea", in Yann-huei Song and Keyuan Zou (eds.), *Major Law and Policy Issues in the South China Sea: European and American Perspectives*, 2014, pp. 57-73.

o Emmers, R., "The De-Escalation of the Spratly Dispute in Sino-Southeast Asian Relations", in Bateman, S. (ed.), *Security and international politics in the South China Sea: towards a cooperative management regime*, Abingdon [etc.], Routledge, 2009, pp. 128-139.

o Erickson, A.S., "America's Security Role in the South China Sea", *Naval War College Review*, 69 (2016), No. 1, pp. 7-20.

o Finnemore, Martha, 1993. International organizations as teachers of norms: the United Nations Educational, Scientific, and Cultural Organization and science policy. International Organization 47, 565-597.

o Fravel, StartFragment M.T., *Threading the needle: the South China Sea disputes and U.S.-China relations*, MIT Research paper, 2016.

o Fu, K., "Freedom of Navigation and the Chinese Straight Baselines in the South China Sea", in Nordquist, M.H. (et al.) (eds.), *Freedom of navigation and globalization*, Leiden, Boston, Brill Nijhoff, 2015, pp. 190-195.

o Gaunce, J., StartFragment *The South China Sea Award and the duty of "due regard" under the United Nations Law of the Sea Convention*, Calgary, Calgary Faculty of Law, 2016.

o Gipouloux, F., "Un nouveau "Grand jeu" en mer de Chine du Sud", *Revue défense nationale* (2016), No. 789, pp. 61-67.

o Goa, J., StartFragment "The Obligation to Negotiate in the Philippines v. China Case: a Critique of the Award on Jurisdiction", 47 (2016) *Ocean Development and International Law*, No. 3, pp. 272-288.

o StartFragment Hiebert, M., Nguyen, Ph., and Poling, G.B. (eds.), *Perspectives on the South China Sea : Diplomatic, Legal, and Security Dimensions of the Dispute*, Lanham, MD : Rowman & Littlefield, 2014.

o Hayton, Bill. *The South China Sea The Struggle for Power in Asia.* Yale University Press, 2014.

o Hong, N., *UNCLOS and ocean dispute settlement: law and politics in the South China Sea*, London [etc.], Routledge, 2012.

o Hong, N., "State Practice of UNCLOS in the South China Sea", in Wu, S., Valencia, M. and Hong, N. (eds.), *UN Convention on the Law of the Sea and the South China Sea*, Farnham, Ashgate, 2015, pp. 267-299.

o Hong, N., "China's Evolving Appoach to the South China Sea Issues", in Tran Truong Thuy and Le Thuy Trang (eds.), *Power, Law, and Maritime Order in the South China Sea*, Lanham, Lexington Books, 2015, pp. 49-60.

o Hoog, A. de, *Jurisdictional Qualms about the Philippines v. China Arbitration Awards* (EJIL Talk, 11 August 2016).

o StartFragment Houck, J.W. and Anderson, N.M., The United States, China, and Freedom of Navigation in the South China Sea, *Washington University Global Studies Law Review*, 13 (2014), No. 3, pp. 441-452.

o Huang, J. and Billo, A. (eds.), *Territorial Disputes in the South China Sea: Navigating Rough Waters*, Basingstoke, Palgrave Macmillan, 2016.

o Jayakumar, S., T. Koh and R. Beckman (eds.), *The South China Sea Disputes and Law of the Sea*, Cheltenham, Edward Elgar, 2014.

o StartFragment Jenner, C.J. and Tran Truong Thuy (eds.), *The South China Sea: a Crucible of Regional Cooperation or Conflict-making Sovereignty Claims?* Cambridge, Cambridge University Press, 2016.

o Jia, B.B., "The Principle of the Domination of the Land over the Sea: a Historical Perspective on the Adaptability of the Law of the Sea to New Challenges", *German Yearbook of International Law*, 57 (2015), pp. 63-93.

o Jimenez, A.A., "Philippines' Approaches to the South China Sea Disputes: International Arbitration and the Challenges of a Rule-Based Regime", in Jing Huang and Andrew Billo (eds.), *Territorial*

Disputes in the South China Sea: Navigating Rough Waters, 2015, pp. 99-127.

o Joyner, C.C., "The Spratly Islands dispute: rethinking the interplay of law, diplomacy, and geo-politics in the South China Sea", *The international journal of marine and coastal law*, 13 (1998), No. 2, pp. 193-236.

o Kardon, I.B., "China's Maritime Interest and the Law of the Sea: Domesticating Public International Law", in Garrick, J. and Bennett, Y.C. (eds.), *China's socialist rule of law reforms under Xi Jinping*, London : New York, Routledge, 2016, pp. 179-196.

o Ku, J., Game Changer? Philippines Seeks UNCLOS Arbitration with China Over the South China Sea, Opinio Juris (January 22, 2013).

o Le Duy Tran, "Scenarios of the China's ADIZs above the South China Sea", *Journal of East Asia and International Law*, 9 (2016), No. 1, pp. 278-291.

o Lin, C.-y., "Confidence-building Measures in the South China Sea and Implications for US-Taiwan-China Relations", in Yann-huei Song and Keyuan Zou (eds.), *Major Law and Policy Issues in the South China Sea: European and American Perspectives*, 2014, pp. 257-275.

o Li Jianwei and Amer, R., "Managing Tensions in the South China Sea: Comparing the China-Philippines and the China-Vietnam Approaches", in Tran Truong Thuy and Le Thuy Trang (eds.), *Power, Law, and Maritime Order in the South China Sea*, Lanham, Lexington Books, 2015, pp. 243-266.

o Loja, M., The Spratly Islands as a Single Unit Under International Law: A Commentary on the Final Award in Philippines/China Arbitration, 47 (2016) *Ocean Development and International Law*, No. 4, pp. 309-326.

o McDorman, T.L., "Rights and Jurisdiction over Resources in the South China Sea: UNCLOS and the 'nine-Dash Line'", in Jayakumar, S., T. Koh and R. Beckman (eds.), *The South China Sea Disputes and Law of the Sea*, 2014, pp. 144-163.

o McDorman, T.L., "The International Legal Framework and the State Activities Regarding the Continental Shelf beyond 200-n. Miles in and adjacent to the East and South China Seas", in Van Dyke, J.M. and Park, C. (eds.), *Governing ocean resources: new challenges and emerging regimes: a tribute to Judge Choon-Ho Park*, Leiden : Boston, Martinus Nijhoff Publishers, 2013, pp. 165-193.

o Ming, L., "The Paradox of Economic Integration and Territorial Rivalry in the South China Sea", in Togo, K. and Naidu, G. (eds.), *Building confidence in East Asia: maritime conflicts, interdependence and Asian identity thinking*, New York, Palgrave Macmillan, St. Martin's Press LLC, 2015, pp. 27-43.

o Mitchell, R., "An International Commission of Inquiry for the South China sea?: Defining the Law of Sovereignty to Determine the Chance for Peace", *Vanderbilt journal of transnational law*, 49 (2016), No. 3, pp. 749-817.

o Nguyen, H.T., "Vietnam's Position on the Sovereignty over the Paracels & The Spratlys: Its Maritime Claims", *Journal of East Asia and International Law*, 5 (2012), No. 2, pp. 168-211.

o Nguyen Dang Thang, "Joint Development in the South China Sea: Selected Issues", in Tran Truong Thuy and Le Thuy Trang (eds.), *Power, Law, and Maritime Order in the South China Sea*, Lanham, Lexington Books, 2015, pp. 219-239.

o Ong, D.M., "Implications of Recent Southeast Asian State Practice for the International Law on Offshore Joint Development", in Beckman, R., Townsend-Gault, I., Schofield, C., Davenport, T. and Bernard L. (eds.), *Beyond Territorial Disputes in the South China Sea : Legal Frameworks for the Joint Development of Hydrocarbon Resources*, 2013, pp. 181-217.

o Oude Elferink, A., "Do the Coastal States in the South China Sea have a Continental Shelf beyond 200 Nautical Miles?", in Jayakumar, S., T. Koh and R. Beckman (eds.), *The South China Sea Disputes and Law of the Sea*, 2014, pp. 164-191.

o Oude Elferink, A.G., "Arguing International Law in the South China Sea Disputes: The Haiyang Shiyou 981 and USS Lassen Incidents and the Philippines v. China Arbitration", *The international journal of marine and coastal law*, 31 (2016), No. 2, pp. 205-241.

o Oxman, B.H., "Offshore Features Subject to Claims of Sovereignty", in Jayakumar, S., T. Koh and R. Beckman (eds.), *The South China Sea Disputes and Law of the Sea*, 2014, pp. 8-20.

o Pedrozo, P.(. (ed.), "The Building of China's Great Wall at Sea", *Ocean and coastal law journal*, 17 (2012), No. 2, pp. 253-289.

o   Pernetta,J.C., Brewers, J.M., 2013. Introduction to the special issue of Coastal and Ocean Management entitled the South China Sea Project: a multilateral marine and coastal area management initiative. Ocean and Coastal Management 85, 126-129.

o   Pham Lan Dung and Nguyen Ngoc Lan, "Some Legal Aspects of the Philippines-China Arbitration under Annex VII of the United Nations Convention on the Law of the Sea", in Tran Truong Thuy and Le Thuy Trang (eds.), *Power, Law, and Maritime Order in the South China Sea*, Lanham, Lexington Books, 2015, pp. 331-348.

o   Poling, G.B., *The South China Sea in Focus: Clarifying the Limits of Maritime Dispute CSIS* (last visited July 31, 2015).

o   Poling, G., "US Interests in the South China Sea: International Law and Peaceful Dispute Resolution", in Tran Truong Thuy and Le Thuy Trang (eds.), *Power, Law, and Maritime Order in the South China Sea*, Lanham, Lexington Books, 2015, pp. 61-75.

o   Roach, A.J., "China's Shifting Sands in the Spratlys" (ASIL Insight of July 15, 2015).

o   Rosenberg, D., Beyond the Scarborough Scare: Joint Resource Management in the South China Sea (e-International Relations, May 1, 2012).

o   Rothwell, D.R., "The 1982 Convention on the Law of the Sea and its relevance to maritime disputes in the South China Sea", in L. Buszynski and C.B. Roberts (eds.), *The South China Sea Maritime Dispute: Political, Legal and Regional Perspectives*, 2015, pp. 46-59.

o   Rothwell, D.R., "UNCLOS Navigational Regimes and their Significance for the South China Sea", in Wu, S., Valencia, M. and Hong, N. (eds.), *UN Convention on the Law of the Sea and the South China Sea*, Farnham, Ashgate, 2015, pp. 149-189.

o   Rothwell, D.R., "Maritime Regulation and Enforcement: the Legal Framework for the South China Sea", in Tran Truong Thuy and Le Thuy Trang (eds.), *Power, Law, and Maritime Order in the South China Sea*, Lanham, Lexington Books, 2015, pp. 197-218.

o   Schaeffer, D., "The South China Sea: a Piece in the Global Naval Encirclement Strategy of Taiwan by Mainland China", in Yann-huei Song and Keyuan Zou (eds.), *Major Law and Policy Issues in the South China Sea: European and American Perspectives*, 2014, pp. 245-254.

o Schofield, C., "What's at Stake in the South China Sea? Geographical and Geopolitical Considerations", in Beckman, R., Townsend-Gault, I., Schofield, C., Davenport, T. and Bernard L. (eds.), *Beyond Territorial Disputes in the South China Sea : Legal Frameworks for the Joint Development of Hydrocarbon Resources*, 2013, pp. 11-46.

o Schofield, C., "Defining the 'Boundary' between Land and Sea: Territorial Sea Baselines in the South China Sea", in Jayakumar, S., T. Koh and R. Beckman (eds.), *The South China Sea Disputes and Law of the Sea*, 2014, pp. 21-54.

o Schofield, C., "Adrift on Complex Waters: Geographical, Geopolitical and Legal Dimensions to the South China Sea Disputes", in L. Buszynski and C.B. Roberts (eds.), *The South China Sea Maritime Dispute: Political, Legal and Regional Perspectives*, 2015, pp. 24-45.

o Schofield, C., "Trouble over the Starting Line: State Practice Concerning Baselines in the South China Sea", in Wu, S., Valencia, M. and Hong, N. (eds.), *UN Convention on the Law of the Sea and the South China Sea*, Farnham, Ashgate, 2015, pp. 123-147.

o Sheng-ti Gau, M., "The Prospects for the Sino-Philippine Arbitration on the South China Sea (U-Shaped Line) Dispute", *Chinese yearbook of international law and affairs*, 31 (2015), No. 2013, pp. 195-230.

o Song, Y., "Legal Status of Taiping Island under the United Nations Convention on the Law of the Sea", *Korean Journal of International and Comparative Law*, 3 (2015), No. 2, pp. 115-138.

o Song, Y., "Possibility of US Accession to the LOS Convention and its Potential Impact on State Practices and Maritime Claims in the South China Sea", in Yann-huei Song and Keyuan Zou (eds.), *Major Law and Policy Issues in the South China Sea: European and American Perspectives*, 2014, pp. 75-118.

o Song, Y., "Article 121(3) of the Law of the Sea Convention and the Disputed Offshore Islands in East Asia: a Tribute to Judge Choon-Ho Park", in Van Dyke, J.M. and Park, C. (eds.), *Governing ocean resources: new challenges and emerging regimes: a tribute to Judge Choon-Ho Park*, Leiden : Boston, Martinus Nijhoff Publishers, 2013, pp. 61-98.

- Symmons, C.R., "Maritime Zones from Islands and Rocks", in Jayakumar, S., T. Koh and R. Beckman (eds.), *The South China Sea Disputes and Law of the Sea*, 2014, pp. 55-120.
- Symmons, C.R., "Historic Waters and Historic Rights in the South China Sea: a Critical Appraisal", in Wu, S., Valencia, M. and Hong, N. (eds.), *UN Convention on the Law of the Sea and the South China Sea*, Farnham, Ashgate, 2015, pp. 191-238.
- Symmons, C.R., "Rights and Jurisdiction over Resources and Obligations of Coastal States: Validity of Historic Rights Claims", in Tran Truong Thuy and Le Thuy Trang (eds.), *Power, Law, and Maritime Order in the South China Sea*, Lanham, Lexington Books, 2015, pp. 145-166.
- Tahindro, A., "The Concept of Regional Common Heritage: its Possible Application in the South China Sea", in Wu, S., Valencia, M. and Hong, N. (eds.), *UN Convention on the Law of the Sea and the South China Sea*, Farnham, Ashgate, 2015, pp. 105-120.
- Talmon, S.A.G. (ed.), *The South China Sea arbitration: a Chinese perspective*, Oxford, Portland, Oregon, Hart Publishing, 2014.
- Talmon, S.A.G., "Objections Not Possessing an 'Exclusively Preliminary Character' in the South China Sea Arbitration", *Journal of Territorial and Maritime Studies* 3 (2016,) pp. 2-28.
- Talmon, S.A.G., StartFragment *The South China Sea Arbitration and the finality of "final" awards*, StartFragment Bonn research papers on public international law: paper No 12/2016 (24 November 2016).
- Tanaka, Y., StartFragment "Reflections on the Philippines/China Arbitration: Award on Jurisdiction and Admissibility", StartFragment *The Law and Practice of International Courts and Tribunals* 15 (2016), No. 2, pp. 305-325.
- Thayer, C.A., "China-ASEAN and the South China Sea: Chinese Assertiveness and Southeast Asian Responses", in Yann-huei Song and Keyuan Zou (eds.), *Major Law and Policy Issues in the South China Sea: European and American Perspectives*, 2014, pp. 25-53.
- Thayer, C.A., "South China Sea Tensions: China, the Claimant States, ASEAN and the Major Powers", in Tran Truong Thuy and Le Thuy Trang (eds.), *Power, Law, and Maritime Order in the South China Sea*, Lanham, Lexington Books, 2015, pp. 3-35.

o   Till, G., "Close Encounters of the Maritime Kind: Freedom of Navigation and its Impact on the South China Sea Problem", in Yann-huei Song and Keyuan Zou (eds.), *Major Law and Policy Issues in the South China Sea: European and American Perspectives*, 2014, pp. 177-195.

o   Tønnesson, S., "Could China and Vietnam resolve the Conflicts in the South China Sea?", in Yann-huei Song and Keyuan Zou (eds.), *Major Law and Policy Issues in the South China Sea: European and American Perspectives*, 2014, pp. 207-243.

o   Tønnesson, S., "The 2002 Declaration on the Conduct of Parties in the South China Sea: why has not it Brought More Peace and Cooperation?", in Tran Truong Thuy and Le Thuy Trang (eds.), *Power, Law, and Maritime Order in the South China Sea*, Lanham, Lexington Books, 2015, pp. 91-100.

o   Triggs, G., StartFragment *Maritime Boundary Disputes in the South China Sea: International Legal Issues*, StartFragment Sydney, The University of Sydney, Sydney Law School, 2009.

o   Truong, T.-D. and Knio, K., "The United Nations Convention on the Law of the Sea (UNCLOS III) and China's Assertion of the U-shaped Line", in Thanh-Dam Truong, Karim Knio (eds.) *The South China Sea and Asian Regionalism: a critical Realist perspective*, 2016, pp. 61-83.

o   Tran Truong Thuy, "Code of Conduct and the Prevention and Management of Incidents in the South China Sea", in Tran Truong Thuy and Le Thuy Trang (eds.), *Power, Law, and Maritime Order in the South China Sea*, Lanham, Lexington Books, 2015, pp. 317-330.

o   Truong Thuy, T. and Trang, T. le (eds.), *Power, Law, and Maritime Order in the South China Sea*, Lanham : Boulder : New York : London, Lexington Books, 2015.

o   StartFragment Tzanakopoulos, A., StartFragment *Resolving disputes over the South China Sea under the compulsory dispute settlement system of the UN Convention on the Law of the Sea*, 2016.

o   Valencia, M.J., Van Dyke, J.M. and Ludwig, N.A., *Sharing the Resources of the South China Sea*, The Hague, Nijhoff, 1997.

o   Vu Hai Dang, "Establishing a Marine Peace Park in The Spratlys: an Option for Implementing the Declaration on the Conduct of Parties in the South China Sea", in Tran Truong Thuy and Le

Thuy Trang (eds.), *Power, Law, and Maritime Order in the South China Sea*, Lanham, Lexington Books, 2015, pp. 293-315.

○ Wagner, B.K., "Lessons from Lassen: Plotting a Proper Course for Freedom of Navigation Operations in the South China Sea", *Journal of East Asia and international law*, 9 (2016), No. 1, pp. 137-166.

○ Wang, K.-H., *Peaceful settlement of disputes in the South China Sea through fisheries resources cooperation and management*, Baltimore, Maryland, Carey School of Law, University of Maryland, 2015.

○ Wu, S., (ed.), *Recent developments in the South China Sea dispute: the prospect of a joint development regime*, London, New York, Routledge, Taylor & Francis Group, 2014.

○ Wu, S., Valencia, M. and Hong, N. (eds.), *UN Convention on the Law of the Sea and the South China Sea*, Farnham, Ashgate, 2015.

○ Yee, S., "The South China Sea Arbitration: the Clinical Isolation and/or One-sided Tendencies in the Philippines' Oral Arguments", *Chinese Journal of International Law*, 14 (2015), No.3, pp. 423-435.

○ Zhang, J., "China's South China Sea Policy: Evolution, Claims and Challenges", in L. Buszynski and C.B. Roberts (eds.), *The South China Sea Maritime Dispute: Political, Legal and Regional Perspectives*, 2015, pp. 60-82.

○ Zhang, X., "The Latest Developments of the US Freedom of Navigation Programs in the South China Sea: Deregulation or Re-balance?", *Journal of East Asia and international law*, 9 (2016), No. 1, pp. 167-182.

○ Zhao, Jimin, Ortolano, Leonard, 2003. The Chinese government's role in implementing multilateral environmental agreements: the case of the Montreal Protocol. The China Quartery, 708-725.

○ Zou, K., "Historic Rights in the South China Sea", in Wu, S., Valencia, M. and Hong, N. (eds.), *UN Convention on the Law of the Sea and the South China Sea*, Farnham, Ashgate, 2015, pp. 239-250.

www.ingramcontent.com/pod-product-compliance
Lightning Source LLC
Chambersburg PA
CBHW030426290526
45786CB00001B/165